War & Peat

The remarkable impacts of conflicts on peatlands and of peatlands on conflicts - a military heritage of moors, heaths, bogs and fens.

Edited by Ian D. Rotherham and Christine Handley

Landscape Archaeology and Ecology, **Volume 10, 2013.**

Edited by Ian D. Rotherham and Christine Handley

ISSN 1354-0262
ISBN 978-1-904098-55-3

Published by:
Wildtrack Publishing, Venture House,
103 Arundel Street, Sheffield S1 2NT

Typeset and processed by Christine Handley

Supported by:
Biodiversity and Landscape History Research Institute.
Sheffield Hallam University.
HEC Associates.
South Yorkshire Biodiversity Research Group.
Landscape Conservation Forum.

Sponsored by:
British Ecology Society.
International Peat Society.

Front cover picture: 1807 Napoleonic battlefield *Sur le Nemen*

German and Russian troops at the Battle of Tannenburg in 1914

Contents

The Impacts of Conflict and War

War & Peat in the Peak District

Non-military Campaigns

An Introduction to War & Peat

Ian D. Rotherham
Sheffield Hallam University

A short introduction

As we approach the centenary of the commencement of World War One, matters of landscape, terrain, resources and strategies become increasingly topical and relevant. The themes of this book were addressed at a major international conference in 2013, and the expanded papers are presented here as chapters. The conference and book are mostly focused on temperate environments, but the interactions of peatlands and conflicts are more global. From the Second World War in for example the Philippines, to the British in Burma, and later the Americans in Vietnam, wetlands have been hugely influential in tropical conflicts too.

The relationships of people and landscapes, of economies and conflicts, and ecology and history, are complex and multi-faceted. For peatlands, including bogs, fens, moors, and heaths, the interactions of people and nature in relation to history and conflicts, are both significant and surprising. The idea of '*War & Peat*' in fact emerged from long-term studies of peatlands, their histories of utilisation, and the impacts on ecologies. In particular, it became clear that conflicts and strife such as war, political and economic unrest, or extreme weather for example, had had great impacts of peatlands. Furthermore, peat landscapes of various sorts had not only affected regional economics, but

had been hugely influential in the theatre of war. It was these wide-ranging and varied issues, which we set out to address under the banner of '*War & Peat*'.

However, the theme of this research is not restricted to the conflicts described above. Throughout history, peatlands have been contested landscapes and resources. These 'battles', such as the '*Peat Campaign*' of the 1980s and 1990s, to save the last remaining lowland raised mires in England, are one such example. Without the campaign, sites like Thorne Moors and the Humberhead Levels would now be landfill, mineral extraction landscapes, or perhaps intensive farming. From the 1920s and 1930s, the access campaigns grew in cities like Sheffield and Manchester, to claim back access rights to moors and bogs lost under enclosures in the 1700s and 1800s. By the early millennium, access to the wider countryside in England was finally given back as a legal right; another battle won.

These peat-based landscapes have been radically affected by human history and human utilisation. Important to realise too, is that the major effect of historic usage has been a reduction in extent of peatlands which is almost beyond imagination. To understand more fully the roles of peatlands in times of conflicts and stresses, you must firstly appreciate just how widespread they were. Additionally, the nature and condition of pre-industrial sites were dramatically different from the sites that remain today. Bogs for example, were wetter and deeper, and more abundant and widespread in the landscape, and so their influence on people was much greater.

An approach to the subject

The approach we have developed to the subject is to consider both the integrated whole in terms of peatlands and people, but also the component elements separately. This allows us to separate out the individual stories but then to bring together the overall context and description of the relationships between war & peat.

1. Peatlands influence war and conflict through topography and nature, often being of critical significance to strategy and outcome.

2. Heaths and moors were often used as military training grounds, from early times up to the present day.

3. Peatlands were used as wartime bases especially during World War 2 when they were brought into usage as airfields and similar facilities.

4. Bogs and moors especially, had unplanned and passive roles in warfare such being the last resting places for stricken or lost bombers of both sides during World War 2.

5. Peatlands, especially bogs and fens, provided materials of immense value to wartime efforts such as supplying horse litter, sphagnum moss, alder buckthorn or peat fuel.

6. Conflicts, socio-economic stresses or extreme weather all influenced fuel use and competition and therefore peat exploitation.

7. Fens and bogs as places of sanctuary, of non-conformism, and independence.

Some final points

Most of the uses noted above had impacts on the peatlands and these vary from complete removal, to drainage, to modification and perhaps recovery. Some, such as the strategic significance in battlefields left relatively little evidence of a perhaps pivotal role.

However, many wartime or conflict uses have left a visible heritage such as the pockmarked boulders of the Peak District moors, scarred by wartime bullets and mortar blasts. Other activities such as *Sphagnum* moss harvesting left little visible record and indeed, only a tenuous documentation or oral history; so much more remains to be found out and recorded.

Many of the uses, through alteration to sites, drainage and even topography itself, had far-reaching consequences for the resource. This is perhaps the story of this conference.

With the 2014 anniversary of the start of the First World War, the major conference at Sheffield Hallam

Figure 1. Durham Light Infantry

Figure 2. Control Stirling Castle and with the River Forth and Flanders Moss, then you control Scotland

Figure 3. WW1 Belgium battlefield

Figure 4. WW2 USA Army in the Philippines

University, and now this book are called fittingly, '*War & Peat*'. Involving not only researchers and academics, but ordinary local people too, this addresses impacts of conflicts on peatlands and their usage and products. The subjects range from battlefields and strategic impacts of peatlands and wetlands in conflicts, harvesting *Sphagnum* moss, peat as horse litter, and as fuel, use for military training, and the battles for access, for conservation and more. Along with recollections, we also have photographs of people involved and this formed the basis of an exhibition at the September 2013 Conference.

The research continues and people across Yorkshire or beyond, may still remember the *Sphagnum* harvests or maybe their parents or grandparents were involved. If so, then we need to hear from you to record and celebrate this remarkable tale of the healing harvest of the peat bogs. Photographs or other memorabilia would be hugely interesting too. Additionally, other memories or information on uses of heaths, moors, bogs, fens, *Sphagnum* moss, or related matters, from the Home Guard to the RAF, would be very useful to our studies. The event was organised with Sheffield Hallam University by the South Yorkshire Biodiversity Research Group, the Biodiversity & Landscape History Research Institute, The Landscape Conservation Forum, the British Ecological Society, and the International Peat Society, and we are grateful for their support. Wildtrack Publishing published the book on their behalf.

Bibliography & References

Rotherham, I.D. (1999) Peat cutters and their Landscapes: fundamental change in a fragile environment.In: Peatland Ecology and Archaeology: management of a cultural landscape. *Landscape Archaeology and Ecology*, **4**, 28-51.

Rotherham, I.D. (2005) Fuel and Landscape – Exploitation, Environment, Crisis and Continuum. *Landscape Archaeology and Ecology*, **5**, 65-81.

Rotherham, I.D. (2008) *The importance of cultural severance in landscape ecology research*. Abstract paper in: *Governing Shared Resources: Connecting Local Experience to Global Challenges*. Proceedings of 12th Biennial Conference of the International Association for the Study of Commons (IASC), Cheltenham, July 14-18, 2008. 189.

Rotherham, I.D. (2009) *Peat and Peat Cutting*. Shire Publications, Oxford.

Rotherham, I.D. (2010) *Yorkshire's Forgotten Fenlands*. Pen & Sword Books Limited, Barnsley. 181pp.

Rotherham, I.D. (2013) *The Lost Fens: England's Greatest Ecological Disaster*. The History Press, Stroud.

Rotherham, I.D., Egan, D. and Ardron, P. A. (2004) Fuel economy and the uplands: the effects of peat and turf utilisation on upland landscapes. *Society for Landscape Studies Supplementary Series*, **2**, 99-109.

Rotherham, I.D. & Handley, C. (2012) *Moor Memories from across the Peak District.* Wildtrack Publishing, Sheffield, 44pp.

Rotherham, I.D. & Handley, C. (2012) *Mosses and Cloughs. Moor Memories in the Holme Valley area.* Wildtrack Publishing, Sheffield, 32pp.

Rotherham, I.D. & Handley, C. (2012) *Hills, Dykes and Dams. Moor Memories in the Bradfield, Midhope and Langsett areas.* Wildtrack Publishing, Sheffield, 32pp.

Rotherham, I.D. & McCallam, D. (2008) *Peat Bogs, Marshes and Fen as disputed Landscapes in Late eighteenth-Century France and England.* Lyle, L. &McCallam, D. (eds) *Histoires de la Terre: Earth Sciences and French Culture 1740-1940.* Rodopi B.V., Amsterdam & New York, 75-90.

Figure 5. Tolstoy and our aplogies to the great man

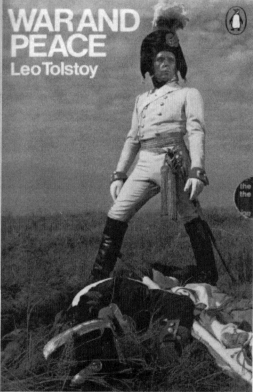

Figure 6. *War & Peace* **as published by Penguin and based on the colossal BBC dramatization**

War & Peat: exploring interactions between people, human conflict, peatlands, and ecology

Ian D. Rotherham
Sheffield Hallam University

Summary

This chapter addresses the issues of people, peatlands, conflict and ecology. It does so by considering seven main interactions and presents pertinent examples to illustrate these.

1. Peatlands influence war and conflict through topography and nature, often being of critical significance to strategy and outcome.

2. Heaths and moors were often used as military training grounds, from early times up to the present day.

3. Peatlands were used as wartime bases especially during World War 2 when they were brought into usage as airfields and similar facilities.

4. Bogs and moors especially, had unplanned and passive roles in warfare such being the last resting places for stricken or lost bombers of both sides during World War 2.

5. Peatlands, especially bogs and fens, provided materials of immense value to wartime efforts such as supplying horse litter, *Sphagnum* moss, alder buckthorn or peat fuel.

6. Conflicts, socio-economic stresses or extreme weather all influenced fuel use and competition and therefore peat exploitation.

7. Fens & Bogs as places of sanctuary, of non-conformism, and independence.

The central argument is that peatlands of varying sorts have been hugely important to people in times of conflict or stress, and that the resulting interactions have had major impacts on the ecology and landscapes we see today. In addition, it is suggested, that most of these complex phenomena have been largely overlooked or at least forgotten.

Introduction

Peatlands such as heaths, moors, bogs and fens have all been of importance and significance in the landscape and to people in many parts of the world and throughout many centuries. In terms of the land areas covered, *sphagnum* moss itself must rate as one of the most abundant plants on Earth. This scale of significance and the nature of these landscapes have led to a remarkable relationship throughout the history of human conflicts and stresses and peatlands, especially in times of war.

Some of the issues and observations are discussed in my three books, *Peat & Peat Cutting* (Rotherham, 2009), *Yorkshire's Forgotten Fenlands* (Rotherham, 2010), and the *Lost Fens* (Rotherham, 2013). However, whilst issues of landscapes and conflict, and especially '*landscapes of conflict*' have received attention in recent years (e.g. Pearson, 2008, 2012; Cole, Coates, & Pearson, 2010), the roles of wetlands generally, and peatlands specifically, have for the most part, been ignored. Academic authors have begun to address these issues for example in relation to broader matters of terrain and warfare (e.g. Doyle & Bennett, 2002), and in relation to environmental factors (e.g. Tucker & Russell, 2004).

For moors, bogs, heaths and fens, conflict does not just mean battlefields for conventional warfare, but for contested spaces. From the battles for Kinder Scout and access to the moors, to saving Thorne Moors and Hatfield Chase, peat bogs and moors have been evocative places for the region's people. Not only this, but they played a major role in the war effort of two World Wars too. Forgotten wartime aspects of peat bog and fen were things like the supply of vital horse-litter (cut peat turf) from sites such as Thorne Moors in South Yorkshire. Conflicts over the proposed drainage of the Fenlands were even a key factor in triggering the English Civil War in the 1600s. It is clear that people and peatlands interact in many complex and complicated ways. Furthermore, human conflicts affect and are influenced by these once vast landscapes.

I suggest there are perhaps seven main ways in which people and peatlands have interacted in times of conflict or other stresses, and I present examples below. Some of the uses and interactions are developed further later in the paper.

Impacts, utilisation and examples

1. Peatlands influence war and conflict through topography and nature, often being of critical significance to strategy and outcome

Examples: The military significance and use of moors, heaths, fens and bogs, extends over millennia. The moors and bogs around the western edge of Sheffield with their Iron Age hillforts can trace a military presence across millennia. In modern times, they were not only used as military training grounds, but also during WW2 as a decoy area to protect the vital steel industry to the east of Sheffield. Moors and heaths also provided the sites for airfields for the Battle of Britain and the strikes against Nazi Germany.

However, there is more. Wetlands, especially peat bogs, fens and moors were of huge significance to military campaigns. In the landscape, these treacherous areas of neither firm ground nor navigable water were a serious problem for soldiers or warriors, most of who could not swim anyway. Furthermore, slip into a fen or bog when wearing armour and you sink slowly to a very unpleasant death. The

Saxon troops of Hereward the Wake, holding out on the Isle of Ely in Cambridgeshire, drove the Norman invaders off the fragile causeways by firing the reeds. The Normans in their chainmail sank deep into the quagmire. The battle of Stamford Bridge had earlier been settled in a vast wetland landscape in which the one river crossing was vital strategic key. This aspect of wetlands in the landscape was used to great effect by the Scots against the English at the battles of Stirling Bridge and of Bannockburn. Battles

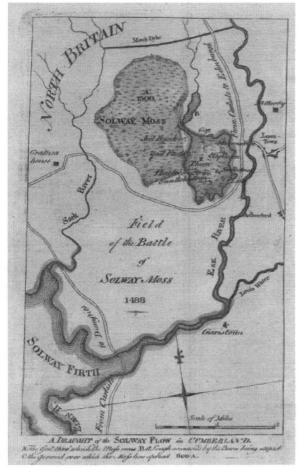

Figure 1. Battle of Solway Moss November 1542 15,000-18,000 Scots routed by 3,000 English

such as Solway Moss, Culloden, and Flodden all turned on the impact of a bog or wet moor, in these cases with catastrophic consequences for the Scots.

Flanders Moss and the River Forth were of huge strategic significance in Scotland, and it was said that he who controlled Stirling Castle, the gateway to the Highlands, controlled Scotland. In England, many of the battles of the civil wars such as the Wars of the Roses, and of the English Civil War, were acted out on heath, moor, and bog. The Battle of Sedgemoor itself was a tragedy played out in a foggy, dank marshland, and earlier, Alfred the Great had sought refuge in the nearby wetlands of Athelney.

In the European arena of the two World Wars, peat bogs and fens played a major strategic role, with the Dutch for example, flooding the former peat cuttings to halt the German advance as they retreated. The Somme and other catastrophic campaigns were fought in vast wetlands and peat bogs.

2. Heaths and moors were often used as military training grounds, from early times up to the present day

Examples: Around Sherwood, the famous heaths of old Sherwood Forest became military training grounds, and in WW2, Clumber Park was a transit and camouflaged storage site for tanks. Dartmoor, Cannock Chase and other heath and bog sites were used for military manoeuvres probably as far back as the Crimean War.

Figure 2. Cannock Chase 1873

Figure 3. Dartmoor 1870

Figure 4. Hampstead Heath August 1860

3. Peatlands were used as wartime bases especially during World War 2 when they were brought into usage as airfields and similar facilities

Examples: In Nottinghamshire and Lincolnshire, commons, heaths, and fens were turned to use as airfields; some still surviving today. Moors and heaths provided the sites for airfields for the Battle of Britain and the strikes against Nazi Germany.

4. Bogs and moors especially, had unplanned and passive roles in warfare such being the last resting places for stricken or lost bombers of both sides during WW2

Examples: In Roman times, the fens and bogs were brought under varying degrees of control through ambitious drainage schemes, but the primary function of these waterways was probably military in moving men, animals and supplies speedily through otherwise difficult terrain.

These landscapes also became the last resting places of aircraft and crews that crashed on Kinder Scout and Bleaklow in the uplands, and Thorne Moors in the lowlands. This is a tragic history, which should not be forgotten.

5. Peatlands, especially bogs and fens, provided materials of immense value to wartime efforts such as supplying horse litter, *Sphagnum* moss, alder buckthorn or peat fuel

Examples: Early twentieth century wartime aspects of peat bog and fen such as the supply of vital horse-litter (cut peat turf) from sites like Thorne Moors in South Yorkshire, or the harvesting of *sphagnum* for wound dressings,are now almost forgotten.

One of the main uses of peat in the late 1800s and early 1900s was litter for animal bedding. With huge numbers of animals powering farms, towns and cities, there was a big demand for material to keep things clean, and peat was ideal. Once soiled, its nutritive qualities enhanced, it went on the land as fertiliser. At Thorne Moors in South Yorkshire, the English Moss Litter company extracted peat moss up to the 1960s, and from 1923 to 1962, the Midland Litter Company took moss from Fenn's Moss near Wrexham. Although raw peat was widely used as litter by farmers and peasants, wider usage took off in the early 1900s. Processed and packaged as a commercial product, during the First World War with its absorbent and fibrous combined with antiseptic properties it was used extensively as horse bedding for the military.

It was also used as animal feed, mixed with green fodder and perhaps molasses. Again its antibacterial properties may have a therapeutic effect and it was used either coarse or as a powder mixed into a cattle cake.

To give some indication of the emerging demands for peat moss litter, there was now nationally an increase of around 98,353 working horses between 1901 and 1906. These were employed by railways, tramways, omnibus companies, various local authority undertakings and of course many other businesses. Peat moss litter (dried peat) made an ideal bedding material for them. By the late 1890s, at Thorne Moors, the British Moss Litter Company was formed and took over a number of established peat works across the region between the Rivers Don and Trent. Alongside the system of canals and boats there developed a network of narrow gauge railways and connections beyond to the wide rail network. A new *'pressing mill'* still known as the *'Paraffin Mill'* or the *'Paraffin Works'* was being built in 1895. This was to produce gas for fuel, ammonia water, paraffin, creosote, methyl alcohol, tar and even alcohol for motorcars. Peat dust was used to pack fruit and peat was even fed to cattle. However, these diversifications did not last long and the mill closed in 1922. With declining use of horses for industry and transport, the moss litter business also collapsed.

Established as a major centre for moss litter production, and employing at its peak around 350 men, Thorne Moors in South Yorkshire produced vast quantities of peat litter for the horses sent to the World War 1 front line. In the First World War, many horses were despatched to war zones and they had to be catered for. Horticultural use of peat was a much later afterthought that brought catastrophe to the region's peat moors and bogs, triggering the battles by *'Bunting's Beavers'* and others to save the last remnants of the once vast South Yorkshire moors. The region's moors and bogs were also used to harvest *sphagnum* moss for wartime medical uses. (See Griffiths, Rotherham & Handley, this volume).

6. Conflicts, socio-economic stresses or extreme weather all influenced fuel use and competition and therefore peat exploitation

Examples: Often forgotten, are the effects of post-conflict scenarios such as after WW2 in Britain and the resulting energy crisis for domestic and industrial fuels. At Holme Moss, in the south Pennines, one of England's last community turbaries (legal peat cuts for domestic fuel), two discharged soldiers arrived after the Second World War to set up business. Recently discharged from the army, they used their money to set up a peat fuel business and for several years, in the post-war energy crisis, they supplied peat fuel to factories as far away as Sheffield and Leeds. Similar exploitation affected the post-WW2 blanket peats of the south-west Pennines as large areas were cut for peat fuel to supply Pilkington Glass.

War also meant on the one hand intensification of land use and WW2 brought about the final demise of the remaining Southern Fens of eastern England. On the other hand, conflict could lead to the abandonment of for example, drainage schemes. At Walberswick in Suffolk, marshland drainage was unmaintained and this allowed reversion to fen and marsh. Around Leighton Moss, the long-standing peat cuttings were abandoned as the site re-wetted due to neglect of drainage. The ultimate result in both cases has been the development of major nature conservation sites by the twenty-first century.

7. Fens & Bogs as places of sanctuary, of non-conformism, and independence

Throughout history, peat bog and fen have provided sanctuary for people in times of conflict or oppression, and for non-conformists and others seeking to distance themselves from the law or the church. Rich in natural resources for those who knew and understood their ways, but difficult to enter or transverse if you did not, these were ideal hideaways from the time of Alfred the Great to Hereward the Wake, and from the nineteenth-century French forces in the Franco-German war, to the Marsh Arabs of Iraq seeking protection from Saddam Hussein. One consequence of the sanctuary that wetlands gave from those in authority was that those in power sought to remove them from the landscape and to control both the environment and the people.

Results: The case studies in more detail

The particular case of the *Sphagnum* harvest

The once widespread peat bogs and moors of Yorkshire also helped a remarkable national and international effort to save the wounded in two world wars. As a part of the research building up to this conference, we made a remarkable discovery. Something found by me and Thelma Griffiths of the National Trust at Longshaw in the Peak District resonated with an interview with locals at Holme Moss who had spoken of people collecting *Sphagnum* or bog moss for the war effort in 1940s. We were told of a hitherto forgotten way in which people across Yorkshire went out to collect a healing harvest from peat bogs and mires across the county. *Sphagnum* moss, today associated with hanging baskets, has remarkable properties to hold liquid and to cure or stop infection. In a medical world pre-antibiotics the combination of the power to mop up copious quantities of blood and staunch open wounds, and its healing powers, made *sphagnum* invaluable for helping the terrible injuries of war. (The *sphagnum* story is presented in more detail in other papers).

The story relates to landscape change across the county, since at the time, peat bogs and wetlands were more widespread across England, and especially prevalent and important in Yorkshire. Therefore, the call went out to communities and people across the county to go to the bogs and harvest the *sphagnum*. This was then carefully processed and shipped out to the front or to hospitals where the injured were being treated. Our research has found that some people still remember how this was done, if not themselves directly, then from parents or even grandparents. At Longshaw in the Peak District, we have found a family whose relative, a nurse, helped gather moss for

SPHAGNUM FOR THE HOSPITALS.
[TO THE EDITOR OF "COUNTRY LIFE."]
SIR,—In your issue of December 11th you had an extremely interesting article on sphagnum collecting. As the writer remarked, it is a harvest

WRINGING OUT THE SPHAGNUM.

which can be reaped in winter as well as in summer, but, of course, it takes a good deal of drying. The picture I enclose depicts a preliminary wring in a coarse cloth before spreading the moss to dry. By this means, what is otherwise a lengthy process, owing to the absorbent nature of the sphagnum, is considerably shortened.—M. A.

Figure 5. Sphagnum for the hospitals, *Country Life*, **XXXIX, Saturday January 1st 1916**

the sick. Thelma met the family at a National Trust event and the story unfurled about their grandmother. Doris Emma Elliott was born in Stannington in 1898, and worked at Longshaw as a VAD (Volunteer) nurse in 1918. This was when she was 20 years old. Her granddaughter, Beverley Hardy, came to one of Thelma's World War 1 talks a couple of years ago. Beverley recounted how, when she used to go for walks with her grandmother, who would tell of collecting *sphagnum* moss at Longshaw for use in dressings. This is exactly the kind of information for which we are now searching. Amazingly, the family even had a photograph of Doris as a serving nurse. Interestingly too, until Beverley

attended the National Trust talk by Thelma, they had only half-believed grandma's tales of roaming the moors in search of moss. However, further north in the Pennines, at Holme Moss, we have older people that still recall the collection of *sphagnum* during the Second World War. A pattern is emerging, and it is now clear that this was no cottage industry but a major undertaking and in places an industrial operation. Huge efforts went into collecting, sorting, processing and packaging the healing harvest, and this was across Britain, from North America, and in Europe itself.

Magazines and newspapers carried stories and calls for action from volunteers. The Northern Rambler, June 1942, for example stated '*FOR MOORLAND WALKERS. Sphagnum moss is wanted for surgical dressings. There is an urgent demand for this. It is only necessary to squeeze out the surplus moisture before packing. Supplies should be sent to EV Benett-Stanford, Pythouse Hospital Supplies and Comforts Depot, Tisbury. Postage will be refunded.*'

Nevertheless, there were still contentious issues of access to moors '*preserved*' for game shooting. These included ones in both Yorkshire and Lancashire. On the Burnley moors for example, there were notices stating '*These moors are strictly reserved for game. You are, therefore, requested not to trespass and to help that which is sport for some, work for others and in some measure food for all.*' Another note by the editor observed that '*Under*

THE GRAPHIC, SEPTEMBER 2, 1916

THE WOUNDS OF WAR
Healed by the magic of ·· SPHAGNUM MOSS ··
from the peaceful moor

Sphagnum Moss is one of Nature's oldest elixirs for wounds, and wherever the moss exists, especially in Scotland, people of all ages and social conditions are on their knees, as it were, collecting it for the soldiers wounded in the Great War. This article, describing what Sphagnum is, has been specially written by one of the most enthusiastic helpers at a big Sphagnum Moss organisation in the North of Scotland.

ECONOMY, from being an uninteresting necessity, has become a patriotic virtue, and much ingenuity has been expended on the problem of "how to save" during the great war. Various new industries have sprung up, which have for their main objects the saving of money, time or labour, and not the least interesting and useful of these is the voluntary Sphagnum Moss industry, now being so rapidly developed that it already engages the services of thousands of workers, whose numbers are being enormously increased from day to day.

THERE are very few parts of Scotland to-day where the Sphagnum Moss gatherer is not to be found, and the work is being extended all over Ireland, England and Wales. It is many years since Sphagnum Moss was first suggested as a practical and economical substitute for cotton wool, and rumour has it that it was first used as a surgical dressing in Germany, though in Joyce's "Child's History of Ireland" we are told that it was similarly employed in Ireland as early as 1014. But it was little used, and comparatively little known, until a short time after the outbreak of the war, when a tremendous impetus was given to the subject by the experiments and writings of Mr. Charles Cathcart, of the Edinburgh Royal Infirmary. Since this time the collecting, drying, cleaning and making into dressings of Sphagnum Moss has become a national industry.

THE moss grows so abundantly in nearly every part of the United Kingdom that it is almost inexhaustible. It is always found in wet or damp places, growing very closely packed together, so that it often forms large cushions or clumps. There are various kinds of the moss, some large, some small, and a wide range of colours, from very light green, which is the most common, through all shades of pink, to deep red and brown. It is very easily recognised by those who have no botanical knowledge, by the little branching "flower" always found at the top, as well as by the way in which it grows.

SPHAGNUM Moss has three great advantages over cotton wool—its cheapness, its absorbency, and the fact that its preparation is so simple that it can be carried out entirely by quite unskilled workers. Since it is so abundant it is very easily obtained, and, owing to the ready assistance granted by all proprietors of large estates, headed by the King and the Princess Royal, collectors have hitherto found no difficulties in their way. The only expenditure involved is the cost of transport from the moors to the Central Depots established by the Director-General of Voluntary Organisations, where the moss is prepared and made into dressings; but in many cases the central depots are prepared to pay carriage, and in Scotland, at least, various centres have been arranged from which free transport is granted by the Director-General of Voluntary Organisations.

WHAT SPHAGNUM MOSS LOOKS LIKE
The fragments shown are half their natural size.

THE moss is very much more absorbent than cotton wool, and will take up about twelve times its own weight in water. It has the further advantage that it absorbs moisture very quickly and evenly, distributing it over the whole surface of the dressing, whereas cotton wool will absorb at one point, leading the moisture through at that point, while the rest of the wool may remain dry. The even absorption of the moss is one of its principal virtues, for this means, as several doctors have pointed out, that the patient is saved a good deal of disturbance and manipulation, since the dressing does not require to be changed so frequently.

ONE can fully appreciate the value of this only after reading the comments of many over-worked doctors and nurses at the front, who are profoundly thankful for a dressing which lasts a little longer than cotton wool, and thus saves time and suffering as well as expense.

THE preparation of the moss is very simple. It should be gathered with a reasonable amount of care, as cleanly as possible, and in order to dry it a very common method is to spread it out on the heather or grass near the spot where it grows, and to leave it to dry in the open air and wind. Another plan is to hang it out on a clothes-line in open bags made of a very coarse open muslin or sacking, or to spread it out on sheets in gardens or on lawns, so that it is easily carried indoors at night, or during rain. Experiments have been tried of drying the moss artificially, in an oven, or in the drying-room of a laundry, but neither plan was very successful, as when it is rapidly dried it becomes very dusty and brittle, and the workers who make it into dressings find it both wasteful and unpleasant to handle. It must be dried slowly, either in the open air, which is by far the best method, or by spreading it out indoors, on racks, or on the floor of an empty room.

THE cleaning is equally simple, and this is best done while slightly damp. All other substances, such as grasses, twigs, bits of heather, etc., must be picked out, and this part of the work must be carefully and conscientiously done, and should be well supervised, for one of the most insidious things in the world is the pine needle, which has a trick of disappearing among the moss and reappearing later on to push its sharp point through the dressing; and a very desirable thing to bandage on to a wound! The moss should be used whole, not broken up into short pieces.

THE final stage is the putting of the moss into bags, of sizes varying from as small as five inches square to a very large dressing, both oblong and square, according to hospital requirements. The bags are made of a fairly close but very thin muslin, not fine enough to limit the absorbency of the moss, but close enough to prevent dust filtering through into the wound. (Continued on page 288.)

THE SPHAGNUM MOSS ARRIVING   MAKING THE SPHAGNUM INTO DRESSINGS   CLEANING THE SPHAGNUM
These pictures were taken at the Aberdeen War Dressings Depot, where excellent work is being done.

Figure 6. Sphagnum in war

the Access Act, Sect 6 (h), anyone picking Sphagnum moss would be liable to a fine not exceeding forty shillings. That Act makes it an offence to wilfully injure, remove, or destroy any plant, shrub, tree, or root or any part thereof.'

On Dartmoor too, local people set out to the moors and bogs to gather and process *Sphagnum* moss for the wartime efforts. As told to us by Tom Greeves of the Dartmoor Society, this contribution is commemorated by an inscribed shell outside Church House in Widecombe-in-the-Moor.

Conflict and energy supplies

Sometimes, war or extreme weather might trigger a move from the utilisation of say coal, back to peat, a resource either not used or used historically but then abandoned. This was described for farmers in the south Lancashire Pennines, apparently as a response to bad winters and coal not being available. They reverted to using the local peat turbaries. However, on reflection this seems unlikely since the peat fuel needs careful harvest and drying in order to be useful. In a bad winter, the peat would not solve the immediate problem since you have to plan 6-9 months ahead. It seems more reasonable that the farmers reverted to peat use during the wartime period or the 1920s Depression as a response to economic pressures and energy shortages. Economic problems or matters of fuel price and fuel competition could be disastrous. Richardson (1874) discusses in detail how in Scotland the price of coal had risen so much that it '...*has become*

quite a luxury, and almost beyond the reach of any but the wealthier classes'. The crisis was not of availability but of price and the impacts of competition to export coal abroad, which inflated domestic prices beyond the reach of ordinary people. The total exports of coal from the United Kingdom were increasing at around one million tons per year and the resulting price inflation meant a colossal increase in the domestic expenditure on coal fuel, estimated in 1873 to be about £44 million rise in two years. This threatened to cripple industry and to cause serious problems for the ordinary household consumer. The response was to advocate the widespread exploitation of peat from bogs. Richardson described the state of the potential resource and its state at the time:

'It is evident, therefore, that there is no lack of peat in the United Kingdom, indeed, in so far as it is mere unprofitable and waste land. There is a very great deal too much. Slowly, it is true, but only very slowly, the vast tracts of peat bog are decreasing. Civilisation and agriculture are nibbling at their borders, and many a fine green sward was but a few years ago a dark and filthy moss.' This description gives an insight into the state of the United Kingdom's peatlands at the time, and a dramatic comparison with their condition a little over a hundred years later when most were destroyed. At this time, in the 1870s however, it was suggested that Scotland in particular, possessed a rich untapped wealth of fuel to be used in times of coal crisis.

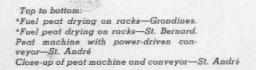

Top to bottom:—
Fuel peat drying on racks—Grondines.
Fuel peat drying on racks—St. Bernard.
Peat machine with power-driven conveyor—St. André
Close-up of peat machine and conveyor—St. André

Above: Building drying racks—St. Jean.

mittee at Alfred, Ontario, between 1919 and 1923, when, during the investigation, between 16,000 and 17,000 tons of peat were made. Since that time small quantities have been made intermittently in Ontario and Quebec for local use.

In 1943, owing to an expected shortage of wood fuel in the Province of Quebec, there was a renewed interest in peat fuel, and, with the co-operation of the Emergency Coal Production Board, a start was made in the manufacture of machine peat on a small scale. The Quebec Department of Mines had developed a portable macerating machine which called for the minimum of equipment and only ordinary labour for operation, and a number of these machines were made available to a selected number of operators. Ten operations were in progress during the summer at different localities in the province and about 1,500 tons of peat were made.

Description of Peat Machine and Method of Operation: The peat macerating machine developed by the Quebec Department of Mines is derived from the Dolberg machine, which was largely used in Europe. Briefly, it consists of two intermeshing worms—one right-handed and the other left-handed—about eight inches in diameter and 30 inches long, enclosed in a cast iron casing provided with a feed hopper at one end and a delivery

Figure 7. *Canadian Geographical Journal* 1945 with move to peat fuel because of wood shortage

PEAT AS FUEL FOR THE FRENCH ARMY: WORK IN PROGRESS ON A PEAT-FIELD IN ALSACE.
Photograph by Schreiner.

Figure 8. Peat as fuel in Alsace 1918

This phenomenon can be seen operating around the world, especially for example, in North America. Peckham (1874) considered the potential of peat and turf for domestic fuel supply in Minnesota. A key point that he makes is the importance of competition with, and of scarcity of, more sought after fuels. Peat fuel might be viable if an area was remote from forests, and away from coal transportation routes. Shaler in 1895 examined the origin, distribution and commercial value of peat deposits for the USA. He noted the relationship between peat use and the lack of available fuel wood. In northern Europe he suggests that the greatest use of peat fuel was during the eighteenth century when forests had been cleared but mineral coal was not in widespread use since transport to rural areas was difficult. The bulk of the rural population of Northern Germany, Scandinavia, Russia, France, and the British Isles, except in the case of the wealthier classes depended on peat and turf for household fuel. He describes the descendants of Native Americans in the town of Gay Head being amongst the last to use peat fuel in that part of the USA. By the late 1800s, the availability of cheap anthracite coal led a move away from peat. The decline in peat use – which was free except for the cost of collecting, was the availability and low price of coal. The first commercial extraction and processing of peat fuel in the USA was in 1902, when a strike of the Pennsylvania miners caused a fuel crisis (Soper & Osbon, 1922). However, in the USA for example, during the First World War, there was considerable interest in a move from coal and wood to peat or turf as domestic fuel. Turp (1916) reported that little machine–

STRETCH OF PEAT-BOG BROKEN UP FOR MACHINE PEAT.
In the manufacture of the best briquette fuel, the surface of a bog is not now broken up in this way, but is cut in thin layers of loose soil and spread out to dry.

Figure 9. Hurrying up the coal mines USA & Canada Nov 1906 - the impacts

processed peat fuel would be extracted in the USA in 1915, but by 1917, there would be a resumption of operations. In 1918, Haanel noted the difficulty in obtaining an adequate and cheap fuel supply in Canada. The reasons related to war were complex and included a labour shortage in the USA that restricted coal imports to Canadian provinces. The situation was considered very grave in that fuel could be reduced or even cut off completely. The report argued for urgent attention to developing peat fuel as '*an excellent substitute for coal*'. He finishes the paper with a plea '....... *to the establishment of a peat industry on a sound basis in Canada, and thus insure the people against a possible shortage of fuel and the suffering it would entail*'. Blizard (1917) reported on the value of peat fuel for industrial steam generation, and considered that the key issue was price competition with coal. As coal

prices rose, so peat would become competitive. According to Soper & Osbon (1922), the wartime coal shortages in the USA in 1917 and 1918 showed that peat fuel could be extracted and be competitive if coal was scarce and expensive. This observation is evidenced by subsequent activities and by numerous governmental and scientific reports. Whilst there is an extensive literature on the possible exploitation of peat for fuel and for other purposes that stretched back to the mid-1800s (e.g. Peckham, 1874), it is clear that in both the USA and in Canada, war and other crises triggered new interest. Following the fuel shortages in the early 1900s, there are numerous reports on resources in the USA and then in Canada(e.g. Nyström & Anrep, 1909), and then more during the war period (Turp, 1916; Anrep, 1914, 1915, 1918; Blizard, 1917; Haanel, 1912, 1918). Fullerton in 1906 asks whether in the event of another coal strike, '*Is there no fuel but coal?*' He then turns his interest to the possible exploitation of peat fuel to alleviate the risk of coal-dependence. Further interest is obvious during the Depression years (e.g. Auer, 1930; New York Times, 1918), and then again during and after the Second World War (Trefethen & Bradford, 1944; Leverin, 1943).

During the Second World War, fuel shortages became critical and Leverin (1943) noted that '*Prior to the war, the Canadian production of peat moss was small and Canada and the United States obtained their supplies chiefly from Europe. When these were cut off, the industry in Canada began to expand and since the commencement of the war many plants have been brought into production. The output is fairly large and is mostly exported to the United States.*' In this case, the main uses of the peat were other than for fuel, and included stock feed, building insulation, peat pads for asparagus growing, metallurgy, preserving food in the home, packing foods and other materials, and as a deodorant and disinfectant for cess pools and earth closets. Leverin also notes the use of peat moss for surgical dressings, but he is considering peat rather than *sphagnum* moss itself. He states that the '*Peat moss and particularly fibrous peat* from *Eriophorum* (cotton grass) specially treated, makes very good surgical dressing, and was used during the war of 1914-1918 by the armies of the Allies and the Central Powers. The United States army used 600,000 pads made of moss obtained from the bogs in

that country. It was found to be an excellent substitute for absorbent cotton. A similar material made in France , known as peat batting or peat wool, was used widely during the war for bandaging. It was also employed as filler for mattresses, pillows, and for upholstery in the military hospitals.' Some of these materials to which Leverin refers, are clearly peat products but the US army pads were almost certainly processed *sphagnum* moss.

Leverin goes on to note other potential war uses as a substitute for materials that were in short supply. Examples that he quotes included cork for the insulation of aeroplanes, as linoleum filler, and as peat yarn for making coarse blankets for both horses and cattle. Peat fibres were mixed with wool to make underwear, which, due to the insulating properties of the peat, was apparently warmer than pure wool. Additionally, peat was used to manufacture paper, cardboard, building bricks, sweeping compounds, and various chemical compounds such as waxes, dyes, alcohol, and dyestuffs. Wartime manufacture of paraffin could be added to Leverin's list. Swinnerton (1945) provided a detailed account of the peat industry in Canada by the latter stages of World War Two.

The Irish Question

The Irish Department of the Environment has a useful website with background information on the peat industry and its history. Traditional peat cutting has been of huge importance to the Irish people and cutting for domestic fuel has caused the greatest decline in

Figure 10. Clothes from peat fabric

Northern Ireland peatlands. With the demise of native woodlands, peat became the major source of fuel in Ireland during the seventeenth and eighteenth centuries. Rights to cut peat on small plots of land, known as turbary rights, were allocated to landowners. Traditionally peat was cut by hand using a special turf-spade known as a sleán or slane. Interestingly, hand-cut turf production in Ireland reached its peak in 1926 when over six million tonnes of turf was cut. This follows the First World War, the Irish Troubles, and is during the Great Depression.

Over the years, the amount of turf cut declined steadily until World War II, when peat again became a vital domestic fuel source again as the supplies of coal from Great Britain almost ceased. The deep peat in raised bogs and the extensive areas of blanket bogs were cut extensively.

The use of fen peat as a source of fuel, known as mud turf, was less common because the peat is very shallow and cannot be cut with a spade. Instead, mud turf is gathered by digging a hole and mixing water with the peat, then tramping or '*puddling*' it with bare feet, shovelling it onto the bank and finally moulding it into blocks by hand. This was a very labour intensive process and was only practised in a few areas, such as Brackagh Moss in County Armagh. After the War, the low price of coal and oil kept peat cutting to a minimum, and by the 1970s, the annual production of peat was down to about a million tonnes, mostly from the blanket bogs in the west. However, the

introduction of tractor-drawn auger machines during the 1980s increased the amount of peat cut again. Since then mechanised peat extraction has become the norm in Northern Ireland and the tradition of hand-cutting turf has almost disappeared.

In Northern Ireland 77.5% of raised bogs have been cut for fuel. The majority of peat cutting was for domestic purposes, but the relatively limited commercial extraction for fuel has had important local effects. Commercial extraction needs planning consent, but the complexity of land ownership and turbary rights sometimes makes the distinction between commercial and domestic cutting difficult to determine. This brief description of the situation in Ireland demonstrates the impacts of utilisation, the variety of approaches, and the potential effects of war and other socio-economic stresses.

Landscapes destroyed: war and the English Fens

With the outbreak of WW2, there was an upturn in British central government interest in farming improvement and drainage. In the Fenlands, as I describe in '*The Lost Fens*' (Rotherham, 2013), the land around Wicken Fen in Cambridgeshire was acquired by the pioneering horticulturalist, Alan Bloom. By the spring of 1940, Alan Bloom was considering ambitious plans. '*There were other more or less waterlogged and inaccessible parts of the Fens, and why should I not try to get a few people together with money to invest, and make a big thing of this reclamation job?*' His scheme did not get much support but it was a hint of things to come, and by June 1940, he was investing in a caterpillar tractor to allow access onto wet and difficult land. Bloom goes on to describe how in his view Priory Farm had become a battlefield on which the forces of dereliction had paused in their encroachment on the farmed land. In fact for years, the advantage had been with '*wilderness*' and nobody could farm against water, but now the tables were turned. The plough was going on the offensive and on the one side '*swamp*', was deliberately encouraged because it gave sanctuary to wildlife. On the other side, there was farmland, its aim, food production. The level of water in the dykes, which divided the two, determined which would prevail, and with flat land on both sides of the drain, there was no possibility of compromise. This very personal account begins to give us an insight into the processes and drivers at work in this bitterly contested landscape. Bloom felt that he had got to '*fight the National Trust, or rather, I supposed, the local governing Committee……., men with mainly academic interests. They could not see things in the same light as those whose interests were agricultural.*' The final stage seemed to be set over the potential to bring into cultivation around fifteen acres of the flooded lands at the request of the War Agricultural Committee. However, this scenario quickly changed when it was decided at a higher level that Adventurers' Fen would actually be used as bombing target; both Bloom for Priory Farm, and

the National Trust for the nature reserve, received the appropriate requisition notices. Then the situation changed abruptly again and the requisitions were cancelled. In August 1941, the Biology War Committee presented a Memorandum on '*R. frangula as a source of charcoal for munitions*', to the Joint Committee of government research organisations. This plant was *Rhamnus frangula* or *R. catharticus*, the Alder Buckthorn, and long known to provide fine grade charcoal needed for explosives. Unfortunately, it is uncommon in Britain and with maritime blockades overseas supplies had been halted and so this was an urgent matter of national security. Because of the report a survey of the distribution of the species was commissioned (November 1941), and it had been found on Adventurers' Fen. This brought a temporary stop to the reclamation work as Bloom and other farmers were commissioned to clear scrub and selectively harvest the Alder Buckthorn, and for this the National Trust got paid. Essentially the work involved cutting or coppicing the Buckthorn and it was anticipated that it would take at least three years for any significant re-growth. However, within a few months, the Buckthorn was all cut out and the War Agricultural Committee was fretting over the state of the Fen, anxious to bring it into cultivation. The proposal was now for the entire two hundred and eighty-six acres of Adventurers' Fen; the rules of engagement had changed: '*.....the Catchment Board engineers and officials, the overseers and their men –*

were of the opinion that Adventurers' Fen could be and would be drained.' Apparently, some of the local farmers were still against the scheme saying that it would be a colossal waste of money and would not work. However, the battlefield was soon to receive a visit from the chairman of the War Agricultural Executive Committee, and then not many months after, by the King and Queen and their entourage. The War Agricultural Committee had already begun work on reclaiming the southern part of the Adventurers' Fen prior to March 1941, and the hope was to be cropping the whole site by summer that year. Apparently, the Catchment Board men had already deepened the drain to the immediate north of Rothschild's Thirty Acres, and the impact in lowering the water-table was considerable for some distance inside the reserve; for Bloom this was a good sign. Apparently, across the Fen the National Trust had done a thorough job of making a swamp with not a drop of water allowed to run into the drainage system. The water could only drain away very slowly and the consequent impact was to render the site exceedingly wet. This was good for the purposes of conservation but was regarded as a major hindrance to those wishing to shed superfluous water from the Burwell Fen and surrounding lands. The first job was therefore to dig out and clear all the dyke outfalls into the '*interline*' and the old main drain, and then to drain off the surface waters to allow ploughing on land adjacent. Major new drains, '*new dykes – in long straight gashes*' were cut across the

ancient landscape to release the pent up waters. As Bloom wrote '*It was sheer delight to watch that water running full pelt from seven or eight points along the boundary of the Fen out of those grips we had been digging*'. After a drying breeze for a few days, they could begin the process of burning off the surface vegetation, and the end of an era was finally closing in on the Adventurers' Fen. Lighting just a small pile of Sedge litter, the flames burst up as if the area had been doused in paraffin.

'*The flames crackled and licked the lower growth, and ran up the bare, hard reed stems to consume first what plumes remained over winter, leaving them twisted and burnt like spent match sticks. All beyond became hidden in smoke, mounting, swirling higher and higher, black at first but turning a rusty-white against the background of blue sky. Out of the smoke bushes came into view, blistered and gaunt as the flames swept on. ..... the smoke ..... seemed to be hundreds of feet up in a billowing cloud.*'

The result was clear within less than thirty minutes, with the Fen changed completely in appearance with the dull buff-grey turned to black, and except for occasional reeds persisting in damp turf pits, the charred bushes and smouldering sedge hassocks were all that remained. Bloom and his companions grinned through their blackened, sweaty faces as they surveyed their victory over ancient nature. The cultivation costs were grant aided at £2 an acre plus the cost of ploughing. Half of the grant was to cover costs and half went to the landowner or farmer. The tenancy on this land was to run for three years after the end of the war, the same as the power of the War Agricultural Committee. However, as Bloom admitted, it was clear by later in 1942 that the costs of the work had been significantly under-estimated. But as he said '……*there was nothing I could do about it. We had our work cut out to get the two hundred and eighty-six acres cropped by 1943, let alone 1942*', and this despite a colossal investment of public money and a huge effort by Bloom and his colleagues. It was shortly after this time, that King George and Queen Elizabeth, the Minister of Agriculture, the Duke of Norfolk, and Mr Tom Williams MP, plus a huge number of pressmen visited the area to inspect the efforts to feed the landlocked country. They were no doubt impressed. This was just the sort of stirring stuff that the country needed.

By February, the area was losing a massive amount of the topsoil and the losses got progressively worse through March. Nevertheless, the land was soon sown with oats and barley, plus beet and potatoes. With dry weather, there was the ironic spectre of a drought. The solution was to get permission from the Catchment Board to abstract from Wicken Lode; action that would certainly have drawn down the water-table on the remaining nature reserve fen even further. In May, there was an even worse gale which swirled up great black clouds of dust from Swaffham, Waterbeach, Soham, and Isleham, giving the sky '*a queer, dark tinge for*

hours'. This was apparently the worst '*blow*' for years, a certain result of the War Agricultural Committee's efforts. Dust settled across a wide area and was reported from homes in Bury St Edmunds over twenty miles away. The ancient fenland, robbed of its water, was now just blowing away. A further complication of the wind-blow was the infilling of dykes that needed to be re-dug, and the replanting by some farmers of the same crops two to three times. Nevertheless, that summer they were harvesting wheat and barley and plenty of sugar beet. The best crops of all seemed to be off Rothschild's Thirty Acres nature reserve. By the end of 1943, Alan Bloom's initial work was done and the land was moving towards intensive, industrial agriculture. As he says: '*Adventurers' Fen and Priory Farm had proved that crops equal to any other black fens – and better than some –could be grown. Those ideas and hopes, that for so long I'd been pushing back into the pigeon-holes of my mind, could now begin to emerge. More complete fertility, extended mechanization, more and better buildings, a thorough livestock policy, alternative leys to give some of the much-cropped land a rest in turn.*'

He goes on to consider how the improvement of these three hundred acres had cost the nation so dear, but it was the country's fault for neglecting the land in the first place. It was, he felt, the fault of the previous generation and the intensive two years was simply making up for time lost twenty or thirty years before. But he was looking towards what he felt was the permanent recovery of agriculture in Britain and an end to the neglect. He saw signs that '......*the welfare of the land must in future run parallel with that of the nation*', and the main thought of millions of people '.....*was that cheap food, abundant in quantity and variety, is the only thing that matters*'.

Therefore, this was the vision that oversaw the final demise of the ancient fenland in the southern area. Little did he realise how rapid mechanisation and agri-industrial development, spurred on by the post-war zeal to be self-sufficient in food, subsidised by the public purse and petrochemicals would totally transform the landscape and the communities. These factors would make all of Alan Bloom's vision come true only a hundred times bigger. However, perhaps too, he did not foresee or approve of the loss from the land and the villages of the families and communities that for generations had been there. His vision was of vibrant communities living and working around the farms and learning to love the land and the landscape. If only he had known......Alan Bloom, MBE, plantsman, was born on November 19th, 1906, and died on March 31st, 2005, aged 98 years. He was one of the great pioneers of British horticulture in the middle to late twentieth century. His vision and passion drove the move to reclaim what he saw as the derelict and wasted fens for the good of the nation. I would have loved the chance to ask him what he felt about them looking back from the following millennium.

The last of the old fen

Not long after Bloom's wartime account, that most prolific of countryside writers James Wentworth-Day wrote his '*History of the Fens*'. As with much of his work, Wentworth-Day writes from the gut, full of incisive observation and passion. He was raised in a thatched farmhouse close by the Fens that Bloom came to '*improve*', and his ancestors had lived there for generations before. Here he experienced:'.... *in the witch-hours before dawn, the smell of the fen. A strange indefinable smell, scent of reeds and peaty waters, of sallows, and meadowsweet, of rotten lily pads – and of fish. That smell of freshwater fish which is penetrating, ineluctable, indefinable. An old, strange, blended smell, a smell as old as Time, compounded of scents that belonged to an untamed, undrained England, the England of the Saxons*'.

He goes on to describe the whimper of wild ducks' wings at night, with the thin whistle of the teal, and the pig-like squeal of water rails. There was the *kerk-keek* and *ker-erkk* of moorhens moving from lode to lode at night, and then the *br-ooomp-oomp*, hollow and ghostly of the bittern in May and June. These were the quiet chorus of secret voices of the fens during the '*manless*' hours and carried on the soft fenland breeze. This was the fen of Wentworth-Day's childhood, and by the end of his life reduced to just the rump of Wicken Sedge Fen; all else was gone. However, whilst Wicken remained undrained, it was, as Wentworth-Day observed, not unchanged. '*Still a place of dense reed-beds, of sedge jungles, of forests of sallow bushes and creamy oceans of meadowsweet. But the old village proprietors, the fen owners, who each had their few acres of the wild fen, where they cut their reeds, mowed their sedge, and speared their eels, have sold out.*'

He noted that the National Trust now owned the Fen, almost to the last acre; cutting neat grass rides and placing signs on neat white posts to tell you where to go. Nevertheless, the villages had changed too; the mud and thatch cottages tumbled down back into the earth from which they came. They were replaced by '*hideous villas of staring white Cambridge brick, with their grim, unsmiling roofs of alien slate, under which no swallows nest, on whose rooftrees no starlings whistle*'. It was the same in all the villages around in Wicken and in Burwell, they were '...... *divorced from their brown and smiling mistress, the fen. And the villages are the poorer*'.

In 1935, Wentworth–Day bought a part of the old Fen '....*a half-drowned, stinking swamp of disused peat diggings, red-beds, and interlacing dykes*'. He stopped up the drains to hold back the winter flood-waters on the land and the meres were instantaneously re-created. This miniature oasis close to the remnant Wicken Fen, in a very short time, drew in huge numbers of wildfowl and an amazing diversity of water-birds both common and rare. Wentworth-Day recorded pintails and goldeneye, common and arctic terns, six cattle

egrets and a great white egret, mallard, teal, garganey, gadwall, shoveller, curlew, curlew-sandpiper, green sandpiper, common sandpiper, greenshank, a yellowlegs, bar-tailed godwits, ruffs and reeves, little grebes, common snipe and great snipe, and much more. He had starlings coming to roost in flocks half a mile long and a hundred yards deep. There were even nesting black-necked grebes. Hen harriers and marsh harriers swept over the reed-beds and Montagu's harriers bred there. '*A wild and lovely place, which dwells in the memory as a very perfect picture of the older England, the England of Hereward the Wake and St Guthlac, the Saxon hermit.*' On Wentworth-Day's little fen '*Coots clanked, ducks splattered, snipe drummed, pewits wailed, and the redshanks sprang on flickering wings, ringing their carillon of a thousand bells*', and up to 50,000 sand martins swirled in massive migration roosting flocks. It was, in just this few hundred acres of Adventurers' Fen, '....*the old spirit of the Great Fen that once covered half Lincolnshire and Cambridgeshire*', but destined not to last long. The war came along and then:

'*They drained the fen with a great clamour of bureaucratic self-praise. The waters went away and the fish died by the cartload. The reeds stood rustling and dry above the black mud. Then they set fire to the reeds, and for a day or more my secret fen roared and crackled in a tawny yellow, red-hot sea of flame. Great billowing clouds of black smoke rose up and polluted the blue skies and swept away on the wind until dust, ashes, and smoke fell like a grey pall on the roofs and the green heath of Newmarket, away on its windy upland.'* The duck rose up and were away, and the moorhens, rails, bitterns, warblers and others too. When the wind blew the dust, smoke and ashes away, all that was left of the secret fen was '........ *burnt and black and scorched. An insult to the high fen skies. An altar of burned beauty. A sacrifice to man's neglect of pre-war farming, a burnt offering to humanity's failure to live together in harmony. And thus, in a funeral pyre vanished the last and loveliest remnant of what had been a recreation in all its wild glory of the ancient Fens of Eastern England.'* He had bought the fen '... *to preserve it, to save for all time the essential Englishness of it, to love and enjoy the sight of birds and clouds, the wind in the reeds, herons fishing in summer shallows, gulls wheeling against May skies, the sting of winter sleet .....'.* Now however, it was no more and Wentworth-Day questioned the wisdom of it all.

'Is the world any better for this change in my fen, or in the ten thousand acres of other fens which they have drained, burned, grubbed up, and cultivated during the War? Materially, yes. Spiritually, no. Economically, again no. Those are the answers in a nutshell. On my fen they spent thousands of pounds in expensive drainage, in constructing concrete roads which will probably crack, sink, and become derelict in a few years. The bill for our County Agricultural Executive Committees is estimated to be in the neighbourhood of £25,000,000 a year.

Do the Committees grow £25,000,000 worth of food each year? The answer, I think, is no.'

The war had brought a brief reprieve from total destruction for the harvesting of the alder buckthorn, but ultimately the fate of the Fens was sealed. In the wider landscape, the arable production from the old fens rivals the best in the world, though of course it depends on massive inputs of petro-chemical fertilizers and fuels. It is arguable as to whether the wartime '*improvement*' of the relict fens produced much at all from the substantial investment.

Landscapes transformed: fuel allotments and common rights: *Frimley Fuel Allotments, Surrey*

The background to Frimley

The development and roles of fuel allotments were discussed in an unpublished conference paper by Rotherham (2005). A good example and one particularly affected by military use, is that of the Frimley Fuel Allotments Charity, founded in 1801, and has been particularly well documented. The account provides a unique insight into the provision of the upkeep of the poor at the time of enclosure. The Fuel Allotment Charity owns land on which the Pine Ridge Golf Centre is built, along with around 100 acres of open access heath. The Charity was established when Parliament under George III passed the Frimley Enclosure Act in 1801. The common was physically enclosed in 1826 and a portion set aside to provide '*Fuel for Firing*' for the poor of the

Hamlet of Frimley. The history has been documented in detail by Wellard (1995) and provides a very interesting example case study. A perhaps unique aspect of this has been the wealth generated by the arrangement of the golf course on a part of the land holding; generating an income of £65,000 per year in the 1990s.

In 1793 the extensive 'wastes' of Frimley had only a small population (905). Almost all of the modern settlements of Camberley, Frimley, and Frimley Green were built on what was then an expansive tract of open heath, including Frimley Heath, Cow moor, Bisley common, Pirbright Common and Chobham Common. The area was covered by gorse or furze, heather, scrub and sparse grass. It had abundant deer but provided poor grazing for sheep. Commoners held rights to cut turf or wood, and to fish and to pasture cattle. The 1801 Act allowed for the dividing, allotting, and inclosing of the waste grounds and commons and commonable lands within the Manor of Frimley in the Parish of Ash, in the County of Surrey. By 1820 the parish workhouse was established on part of the Fuel Allotments site and this housed nineteen paupers. Throughout the late 1700s and early 1800s, the Frimley overseers dealt with the practicality of helping the poor of the parish, and they were funded by a levy of a Poor Rate on the parishioners. This might be money, clothing, food, or fuel. In some cases the poor might, if not infirm, be employed. According to Wellard (1995), this might include physical labour such as cutting turves for fuel, digging

graves, or extracting stone for building. Turf was cut on the common waste of which much in Frimley was peat moor and not enclosed at that time.

At the time of enclosure the Act stipulated that '....*such part of the waste Lands of Frimley as in the judgement of the Commissioners was adequate to provide a reasonable supply of fuel for those inhabitants of the Hamlet who did not occupy lands or a dwelling of an annual value of more than Five Pounds.*' In effect all agricultural labourers, cottagers, and small tradesmen would qualify for fuel from the '*Firing*' Allotments. Many were poor due to changing urban and rural economics and the demise of small rural crafts and industries, the aftermath of the Napoleonic war, and the rising price of grain. Areas of land were specifically set aside for this purpose. Along with the right, for those qualified under the Act, to take fuel away, the Trustees were empowered to lease the whole or part of the allotments to any person they thought would be suitable as a tenant for a term not exceeding twenty-one years. The rent was to be paid quarterly and on expiration, the tenant would have to leave the land in good condition. The Trustees had to ensure that they spent the money raised on the purchase of '*fuel for firing*' under the £5 qualification.

The cost of providing fuel was not too great when the bulk was wood or peat. However, as these declined and coal became the more commonplace fuel, the costs increased. The situation was becoming acute by the early 1860s when an offer to purchase some of the land from the Trust was made. With permission from the Charity Commissioners, the sale was allowed and the money invested. The Charity Commissioners also provided future guidance on the management of the Trust at various times. This allowed for example a waiver in the interpretation of the original Act to provide fuel, to '*When not required for the purchase of fuel shall be laid out by the Trustees in the purchase of warm clothing and blankets to be distributed by the Trustees at their discretion to the deserving poor resident in the parish of Frimley.*' So fuel was the first priority but warm clothing and blankets could qualify. Those residing in properties valued under £5 already qualified but there was discretion to allow others too. According to Wellard (1995) there followed a series of disputes over the allocation and interpretation of rights allowed under the 1801 Enclosure.

By about 1860, the poor were burning coal along with wood and peat, and money was required. With a total income of around £30 per year from rents and investments, the outlay on coal was about £1 a ton with a quarter of a ton per person per year. For clothing expenditure, a blanket was about 3s (15p), a pair of shoes 12s (60p), a petticoat 5s (25p), and a pair of trousers and a man's coat a £1.

By 1894, the Frimley Urban District Council was formed and after four years, the Fuel Allotment Charity's Trustees passed over responsibility for the Fuel Allotments to it. By the early

1900s, the Council was looking to sell the land and extinguish the rights, and to purchase land for a Recreation Ground elsewhere. The Charity Commission turned down their original proposals as unacceptable. However, combined with a military use of the recently enclosed common now purchased by the army, it did prove acceptable. This also allowed for the maintenance of heath and for the cutting of furze fuel.

The military connection

The British Army was seeking a large area of land for training and close to London. With new developments in warfare and military strategies, a location were large-scale encampments and extensive training trenches could be constructed was essential. In 1902, tentative go-ahead was given for detailed discussions with the War Office. Subsequently, the agreement was approved and signed; bringing an income of around £140 per year. Along with this the Charity Commissioners provided a 'Scheme' of guidance for the Trustees now in the Council in the administration of the Fuel Allotments Charity; and this gave the rules by which the area was managed from then on. In 1904, 112 people or families received the Christmas coal allocation in Camberley and Yorktown (30 tons), and another 120 in Frimley, Frimley Green and Mytchett (19 tons), at a total cost of £50. By 1909, the annual income was around £200, equivalent to around £20,000 at 1990s values. Not everyone received the same allocation of coal with amounts varying from 2

Figure 11. Volunteer camp at Ascot Heath

cwt to 6 cwt. In 1914, there were 327 recipients with 360 paid at 25s per ton. Records over the following period until the 1940s have been lost.

There were serious disputes over the rights to allocations and conflicts between 'rights' to take sand and gravel from the land. This was hard to assess or to police effectively and caused significant nuisance. One of the more interesting observations is that many local residents still assumed a right of common over the area even though the common had long since gone and the remainder was endowed to a charitable trust. This caused confusion and resentment. This applied particularly when the army took over the lease. Restrictions on sand and gravel were clearly displayed but none were stated about any rights to take firewood or to cut trees. Some were allowed to do this

with the agreement of the trustees; for example, Mr Pearce a broom maker could collect brushwood for his trade. Permission could be granted by the caretaker for the occasional taking of trees, with no more than two allowed each year. However, the uncontrolled and indiscriminate cutting of far more than this (up to eighty on one occasion) was causing serious damage.

In 1914, with the outbreak of war, the use of the Allotments for training necessitated the digging of several miles of trenches and the removal of around 1,000 trees to give the impression of a French battlefield. This was combined with the impact of a prisoner of war camp lacking sanitation and generating foul smells across the whole area. At the conclusion of the war, the army compensated the Council for its losses and began a re-planting programme. By

Figure 12. German prisoners marching from the station to the PoW camp at Frimley, 1915.

Figure 13. German prisoners at Frimley PoW camp.

1939, although the price of coal had increased, the income and expenditure of the trust were almost the same as in 1909. The Second World War brought more military training and usage of the Allotments. By the 1960s, with an annual income of £450, there were continuing problems of maintenance of the Allotments and the other assets of the Trust, and in 1967, permission was given to sell part of the site for the building of a County Council school. With increased revenue, the council began to establish partnerships with other local charities to further the aims of the trust and to dispense the awards. Therefore, at this time around £1,255 was given as £5 fuel vouchers, £2,000 for the support of old people, and £750 for other charitable purposes.

Frimley in the modern era

By the early 1970s, with increasing urbanisation, the Fuel Allotments were one of the few remaining open spaces in the Urban District, and they too were under pressure. Alongside pressures to develop was the idea of creating a golf course over the land. At this point, the Charity Commissioners reminded the Council quite forcibly that the Allotments were for the specific charitable benefit of the poor of Frimley Parish and not for the general benefit of all residents. Capital raised from any land sale could not be used for wider recreational or social welfare purposes even if charitable. The debate continued as to whether the Allotments in their entirety should be made Public Open Space, or should some areas be sold off to provide income for the future. At the same time the Local Government Act of 1973 established the new Borough of Surrey Heath from the earlier Councils, the M3 motorway was constructed close to the district and the population rose by 20,000 people in less than fifteen years. With the departure in 1973 of the military presence on the heath, the go-ahead was given for the design and construction of a municipally owned golf course on 210 acres of the Fuel Allotments. However, the whole issue was clouded by suggestions of exchanges of land for housing development and the loss of large areas of currently open heath with public access. There was significant local community objection, the Charity Commissioners were alerted to the concerns of local people, and the scheme was shelved in 1976. However, in 1979, the Council received permission to go ahead with a Local Authority owned golf course on 120 acres with 160 acres left as free public access. There was by now a deep-seated conflict between local people who demanded the unfettered use of the area as '*common land*' which it had not been since the early 1800s, and those who saw the main function as raising funds to dispense to the poor and needy of Frimley Parish. There also those interested in the development opportunities that would inevitably arise should planning consents be granted. In the face of these conflicts, the Council established a new charitable body to oversee the future of the Frimley Fuel Allotments. This came into being in 1983.

By 1985, it was decided that the Council was unlikely to proceed with the golf course proposals. The Trustees therefore decided to move independently and seek a developer interested in taking this forward. The result was that by 1986 there were heated public meetings to discuss the options and the future, with angry exchanges between 'dog walkers' and those interested in the charity income. From these debates, there emerged several developers wishing to pay several millions of pounds for the opportunity to develop the golf course and varying amounts of housing. Delays of at least two years in deciding on the issues by the Charity Commissioners were estimated to lose around £90,000 of charitable income to be distributed to the poor of Frimley.

Figure 14. WW1 Valley of La Tourbe

Eventually, after further debate and protest, permission was granted in 1988, to begin work on the new golf course. The developer funding the scheme would also pay £100 per acre in annual rent plus 8% of the gross income from Green Fees and the Driving Range. This was with a 125-year lease with a break clause after twenty years. The result was the Pine Ridge Golf Course extending over 164 acres of former heath, leaving 98 acres to free public access. Reluctant to employ an officer to manage the remaining area, as '*it would be a drain on their charitable resources*', and with the Council unwilling to pick up the cost, the Trustees cast around for a suitably qualified volunteer. However, on a positive note the Frimley Fuel Allotments Charity was by 1994, dispensing around £60,000 per year to the needy of Frimley Parish, and this still included the elderly needing assistance with fuel bills. This story provides a well-documented example of the military training use of a peatland

site, and the intensive use by the army was a key aspect in the changing landscape and the loss of the common.

Peatlands in the European theatre of war

Peat use was important in many countries of northwest Europe, particularly in Germany, Holland and the other Low Countries, as well as further east into Poland. The French situation was discussed by Rotherham & McCallam (2008), and makes an interesting case study. In 1869, France exported 321,000 tonnes of peat at 10 francs 20 cents per tonne. Comer & Lordier (1903) detail fuel usage and resources in France at the turn of the nineteenth century, but by 1914, the amount was insignificant (Berthelot, 1941). In the early 1940s, there was renewed interest in the industrial exploitation of peat as fuel and for chemical extracts. This focus on peat turf as fuel during times of shortage or of adversity was noted for regions such

Figure 15. Low country defence

Figure 16. WW2 German soldiers crossing a wet field

Figure 17. WW2 German vehicles mired down

Figure 18. Sea floods Holland by Germans

Figure 19. The Stars and Stripes

as Scotland, Canada, and the USA (Rotherham, 2005) and the situation in wartime France was a similar response to crisis. The inventory of French peat resources at the time suggested around 1,200,000 hectares available for exploitation as valley peats, marine peats, lowland plains peats etc. The report in *La Nature* (1941) concluded that in its peat reserves France had a resource to be exploited to help reinvigorate its economy. By 1980, France's annual peat production was 50,000 tons for fuel and 100,000 tons for horticulture, half that in the UK (Bord Na Mona, 1985).

However, a major role of peat bogs and wet landscapes was in the actuality of warfare and the strategic approach to the battlefield. This ranges from the important of a line of massive peat bogs that separated Holland from its potentially aggressive neighbour, Germany, to the strategic flooding of worked peat cuts and polders by the Allies to slow the German advance in WW2. The conquering German forces also broke the dykes in order to flood

and destroy Dutch food production. As noted in *The Stars and Stripes* on Monday October 30th, 1944, bogs and muddy conditions hindered both offence and retreat, as the feeling Nazis were bogged down in the Dutch landscape.

Particularly in WW1, bogs, marshes, fens, mud and peat, were immensely important. The Somme, Flanders and other major battlefields were in generally flat or rolling landscapes dominated by bogs, rivers, marshes and farmland, which quickly degenerated into fields of mud as the conflict developed. This is described in detail by the seminal volume by Johnson in 1921, and is a theme worth exploring further.

One final impact of conflicts on peatlands has been the migration of skilled workers and the application of prisoners of war, to the reclamation of bog and fen. In the 1600's, as I describe in the *Lost Fens* and in *Yorkshire's Forgotten Fenlands*, Huguenots and Walloons, escaping Catholic persecution came to England's fenlands and helped in their drainage. Prisoners of war from

Figure 20. The capture of Breda in 1590

Dutch and Scottish conflicts with the English were put to work on this task, and many of them died in the process, buried in the soft, peaty soils by the drains they had dug.

To end the chapter, there is a further remarkable story of peat and conflict. This is the recapture from the Spanish, of Breda in the Netherlands during the Eighty-Year War, which used a Trojan Horse-type plan. However, in this case a turf barge in which seventy soldiers were concealed replaced the wooden horse and on 25th February 1590, was left for the Spanish to take inside the fortress. The ruse was successful and the vital fortress of Breda fell to Maurice of Nassau, Prince of Orange. The Dutch recall the victory as the '*Turfschip van Breda*'.

Conclusions

This short review of the relationships between peatlands, people, and conflicts of various sorts, establishes the nature of the interactions and the fact that they have been important in various places and at different times throughout history. The research so far, also indicates that much of the knowledge and heritage relating to these uses or interactions has been either lost or forgotten. Most historians and experts on military issues have had little interest in peat or wetlands, and few ecologists are knowledgeable about history or warfare. Furthermore, the evidence presented is that peatlands writ broad, from bog and moor, to heath and fen, were not only landscapes of conflict but were often contested spaces, if not militarily, then socially, politically, and economically. The exploitation of peatlands and their resources were also

Figure 21. Helping an ambulance through the mud WW1 after heavy rains turned the British Front into a quagmire

influenced immensely by conflicts and stresses, from economic issues to poor weather. In times of resource shortages, the versatility and abundance of peat led people to explore a remarkable diversity of uses from chemical extractions to manufacture of fabrics. Yet in a little over a hundred years or so, even the memories of these uses have been forgotten.

The peatlands were seen as both 'waste' lands for which almost any use was an improvement. They were also considered virtually inexhaustible. However, a century or so on, most areas in Western Europe and the Eastern USA for example, have been almost annihilated. It seems that through the interactions described, landscapes have been transformed and ecologies altered, often radically, but the phenomena have yet to be appreciated.

Finally, as a stage for the theatre of war in many conflicts, peatlands were crucially significant. Nevertheless, despite their sometimes-obvious importance such as in World Wars One and Two, historians just don't see it.

Bibliography & References

Adkin, M. (2013) *The Western Front Companion: The Complete Guide to How the Armies Fought for Four Devastating Years, 1914-1918*. Aurum Press Ltd, London.

Anon. (1893) Exploitation de la Tourbe. *La Nature*, **1071**, 17-18.

Anon. (1918) *Summary Report of the Mines Branch of the Department of Mines for the Calendar Year Ending December 31 1917*. Sessional Paper No. 26a, Printed by Order of Parliament, Ottawa.

Anon. (1918) Nos resources locales dans la zone des armées: La Tourbe. *L'Illustration*, **16th February,1918**, 167-168.

Anon. (1918) Find many uses for peat: War-torn Industry Gives Promise of Great development. *The New York Times*, undated and unpaginated extract.

Anon. (1944) Mud bogs Nazis Fleeing Holland: British in Breda. *The Stars and Stripes*, **Volume 1**, **No.101**, Monday October 30th, 1944 p1.

Anon. (1940) Sea Floods Holland. Nazi demolitions and allied Bombs blast dikes that guard lowlands. Unknown magazine extract, p34-36.

Anon. (1940) The Low Countries' Traditional Defence; strategic inundations. *The Illustrated London News*, **May 18th**, **1940**, 647.

Anon. (1940) Holland opens the dykes: floods which confronted the Nazis. *The Illustrated London News*, **May 18th**, **1940**, 648.

Anrep, A. (1918) *Investigation of Peat Bogs*. In: anon. (1918) *Summary Report of the Mines Branch of the Department of Mines for the Calendar Year Ending December 31 1917*. Sessional Paper No. 26a, Printed by Order of Parliament, Ottawa.

Anrep, A.v. (1914) *Investigation of the Peat Bogs and Peat Industry of Canada 1911-12*. Canada Department of Mines, Ottowa.

Anrep, A.v. (1915) *Investigation of the Peat Bogs and Peat Industry of Canada 1913-14*. Canada Department of Mines, Ottowa.

Auer, V. (1930) *Peat Bogs in Southeastern Canada*. Canada Department of Mines, Ottowa.

Bagot, M. (1806) Sur le Charbon de Tourbe exposé en vente par la Compagnie Callias, au Port de la Grève, a Paris. *Annales de L'Agriculture Françoise*, **XXV**, 46-54.

Bairoch, P. (1965) Niveaux de développement économique de 1810 à 1910. *Annales ESC*, **20**.

Bélidor, M. Bernard Forest de (1810) *Architecture Hydraulique, Ou L'art De Conduire, D'élever Et De Menager Les Eaux Pour Les Differents Besoins De La Vie. Avec Des Planches Neuves Dont Les Dessins Ont Eté Revus Ou Refaits En Entier Par M. Martin*. Paris Chez Firmin Didot.

Berthelot, Ch. (1941) La Tourbe. *La Nature*, **3066**, 35-41.

Berthelot, Ch. (1942) Organisation et Avenir de la Tourbière Française. *L'Illustration*, **5187**, 101-103.

Blizard, J. (1917) *The Value of Peat Fuel for the Generation of Steam*. Government Printing Bureau, Ottawa.

Bord Na Mona (1985) Peat fuel in developing countries. *World Bank Technical Paper*, **No.41**, World Bank, Washington DC.

Cole, T., Coates, P. & Pearson, C. (2010) *Militarized Landscapes: From Gettysburg to Salisbury Plain.* Continuum Publishing Corporation, London.

De Vries, J. (1974) *The Dutch Rural Economy in the Golden Age, 1500-1700.* Yale University Press, New Haven and London.

De Zeeuw, J.W. (1978) Peat and the Dutch Golden Age – The historical meaning of energy-attainability. *A.A.G. BIJDRAGEN,* **21**, 3-31.

Doyle, P. & Bennett, M.R. (eds) (2002) *Fields of Battle: Terrain in Military.* Kluwer Academic Publishers, Dortrecht, The Netherlands.

Fullerton, A. (1906) Hurrying Up the Coal-mines. *Technical World,* **November 1906**, 268-274.

Girard, H. (1947) *Peat in Quebec: its origin, distribution, and utilization.* Geological Report 31, Department of Mines, Province of Quebec, Canada.

Haanel, B.F. (1912) *Report on the Utilization of Peat Fuel.* Canada Department of Mines, Ottowa.

Haanel, E. (1918) *Peat as a Source of fuel.* Commission of Conservation, Canada, Ottowa.

Johnson, D.W. (1921) *Battlefields of the World War. Western and Southern Fronts. A Study in Military Geography.* American Geographical Society Research Series No. 3, pp 648.

Kerr, W.A. (1905) *Peat and its Products.* Begg, Kennedy & Elder, Glasgow.

Leverin, H. (1943) *Peat Moss or Sphagnum Moss: Its Uses in Agriculture, in Industry, and in the Home.* Canada Department of Mines and Resources, Ottowa.

M.A. (1916) Sphagnum for the hospitals. Letter to the editor. *Country Life,* **XXXIX**, Saturday January 1st, 1916, p30.

McBryde, G. (1942) *Mossy Medicine.* Country Diary. The Guardian, September 1942.

McIntire, W. (1941) Solway Moss. *Transactions of the Cumberland & Westmorland Antiquarian & Archaeological Society,* **Volume LXI**, 1-13.

Nyström, E. & Anrep, S.A. (1909) *Bulletin No. 1. Investigation of the Peat Bogs and Peat Industry of Canada, During the Season 1908-9.* Canada Department of Mines, Ottowa.

Pearson, C. (2008) *Scarred Landscapes: War and Nature in Vichy France.* Palgrave Macmillan, London.

Pearson, C. (2012) *Mobilizing Nature: The Environmental History of War and Militarization in Modern France (Cultural History of Modern War).* Manchester University Press, Manchester.

Peckham, S.F. (ed.) (1874) *Peat for Domestic Fuel. The Geological and Natural History survey of Minnesota.* Tribune Publishing Company, Minneapolis.

Richardson, R. (1873) *On Peat as a Substitute for Coal.* Adam and Charles Black, Edinburgh.

Rotherham, I.D. (1999) Peat cutters and their Landscapes: fundamental change in a fragile environment. In: Peatland Ecology and Archaeology: management of a cultural landscape. *Landscape Archaeology and Ecology*, **4**, 28-51.

Rotherham, I.D. (2005) Fuel and Landscape – Exploitation, Environment, Crisis and Continuum. *Landscape Archaeology and Ecology*, **5**, 65-81.

Rotherham, I.D. (2008) *The importance of cultural severance in landscape ecology research.* Abstract paper in: *Governing Shared Resources: Connecting Local Experience to Global Challenges.* Proceedings of 12th Biennial Conference of the International Association for the Study of Commons (IASC), Cheltenham, July 14-18, 2008. 189.

Rotherham, I.D. (2009) *Peat and Peat Cutting.* Shire Publications, Oxford.

Rotherham, I.D. (2010) *Yorkshire's Forgotten Fenlands.* Pen & Sword Books Limited, Barnsley. 181pp.

Rotherham, I.D. (2013) *The Lost Fens: England's Greatest Ecological Disaster.* The History Press, Stroud.

Rotherham, I.D., Egan, D. and Ardron, P.A. (2004) Fuel economy and the uplands: the effects of peat and turf utilisation on upland landscapes. *Society for Landscape Studies Supplementary Series*, **2**, 99-109.

Rotherham, I.D. & Handley, C. (2012) *Moor Memories from across the Peak District.* Wildtrack Publishing, Sheffield, 44pp.

Rotherham, I.D. & Handley, C. (2012) *Mosses and Cloughs. Moor Memories in the Holme Valley area.* Wildtrack Publishing, Sheffield, 32pp.

Rotherham, I.D. & Handley, C. (2012) *Hills, Dykes and Dams. Moor Memories in the Bradfield, Midhope and Langsett areas.* Wildtrack Publishing, Sheffield, 32pp.

Rotherham, I.D. & McCallam, D. (2008) *Peat Bogs, Marshes and Fen as disputed Landscapes in Late eighteenth-Century France and England.* Lyle, L. & McCallam, D. (eds.) *Histoires de la Terre: Earth Sciences and French Culture 1740-1940.* Rodopi B.V., Amsterdam & New York, 75-90.

Shaler, N.S. (1895) *Origin, Distribution, and Commercial Value of Peat Deposits.* Government Printing Office, Washington D.C.

Soper, E.K. & Osbon, C.C. (1922) *The occurrence and uses of peat in the United States.* Government Printing Office, Washington D.C.

Swinnerton, A.A. (1945) Peat in Canada. *Canadian Geographical Journal*, **XXX1**, **(1)**, July 1945, 18-29.

TeBrake, W.H. (1985) *Medieval Frontier. Culture and Ecology in Rinjland.* A.&M. University Press, Texas.

Trefethen, J.M. & Bradford, R.B. (1944) *Domestic Fuel Possibilities of Maine Peat.* Bulletin No. 1, Maine Geological Survey, Maine Development Commission, Augusta, Maine.

Tucker, R.P. & Russell, E. (eds) (2004) *Natural Enemy, Natural Ally: Toward an Environmental History of Warfare.* Oregon State University, Corvallis. USA.

Turp, J.S. (1916) *Peat in 1915.* Government Printing Office, Washington D.C.

Wellard, G. (1995) *200 Years of Frimley's History. The Story of the Frimley Fuel Allotments Charity and Pine Ridge Golf Centre.* Pine Ridge Golf Centre and Frimley Fuel Allotments Charity, Camberley, Surrey.

Web sources:

Department of the Environment, Irish Government, Peat/turf cutting. http://www.doeni.gov.uk/niea/biodiversity/habitats-2/peatlands/peatland_conservation/peatland_natural-human_factors/peatland_peat_turf_cutting.htm accessed 2013

Figure 22. Scotch regiment resting in the mud of Flanders WW1 sold in aid of the YMCA Hut Fund to provide shelter and recreation for our soldiers

THE ILLUSTRATED LONDON NEWS, MARCH 2, 1918.—271

A SUBSTITUTE FOR COAL: PEAT FUEL FOR FRENCH FIELD-KITCHENS.

PHOTOGRAPHS BY A. SCHREINER.

GERMAN PRISONERS EMPLOYED IN A FRENCH PEAT-FIELD: WORKING A PUMP TO EXTRACT MOISTURE.

AT A FRENCH PEAT-FIELD IN HAUTE SAÔNE: GERMAN PRISONERS AT WORK CARRYING LOADS OF CUT CLODS.

GERMAN PRISONERS CUTTING PEAT FOR THE FRENCH ARMY: WORK AT A PEAT-FIELD IN HAUTE SAÔNE.

MAKING COAL OUT OF PEAT: A PEAT-STACK IN FRANCE UNDERGOING A CARBONISING PROCESS.

FRENCH WOMEN EMPLOYED IN CUTTING PEAT FOR FUEL: WORKERS OF THE FRENCH LAND ARMY.

THE PREPARATION OF PEAT FOR FUEL: COVERED STANDS FOR DRYING THE CUT CLODS IN FRANCE.

Figure 23. Peat as a substitute for coal

Military pastoral and the military sublime in British army training landscapes

Rachel Woodward
Newcastle University, UK.

Abstract

The British Army's major training areas are, by necessity, mostly remote and under-populated, with non-military uses primarily restricted to basic transport routes, limited housing and non-intensive agriculture. Many training areas, as a consequence of their history and the development of cultural ideas around the rural, have become subject to pressures for civilian access. These demands for greater public access for recreational purposes have over the past decade or so prompted the development (and in places consolidation) of infrastructure to enable such access, primarily in the form of public footpaths. This paper draws on examples from the public paths on the perimeters of Sennybridge Training Area in Powys and the Otterburn Training Area in Northumberland, and considers some ideas about military violence and its appearance in military landscapes that walking on these paths invokes. Environmental management regimes, the organisation and practice of military training, and the methods of facilitating public access all combine to present these landscapes to the civilian visitor as spaces which suggest the possibility of quiet, undisturbed recreation in rural areas of high landscape quality. The primary purpose of these landscapes, which have armed violence at their core, is often obscured. This paper considers the experience of walking on these paths and thinking about ideas of the military pastoral and the military sublime, as part of an attempt to engage with the perplexing question of violence in spaces which so often are only suggestive of peace.

Keywords: military training, British Army, landscape, sublime, pastoral.

Introduction

Underpinning this paper are questions that British army training areas pose about violence. Walking as a civilian visitor around the spaces used for military training is an exercise in engaging with armed violence. However, as many visitors to such places often observe, such engagements are paradoxical. Being in these spaces (particularly on days when there is no live firing) is frequently an encounter with peace, calm and stillness, both despite and because of the central utility of these spaces for military training. This paradox leads in turn to two questions. The first concerns how military violence can be visible and invisible in these spaces. The second concerns our perceptions of military power because of the invisibility of military violence in these spaces. In this paper, I explore these ideas with reference to two army training areas in the UK, the Sennybridge Training Area (SENTA) and the Otterburn Training Area (OTA) in Northumberland, using the experience of walking on both as the starting point. I draw on ideas about the 'military pastoral' and the 'military sublime' as ways of helping think about these two questions along the way.

Although individually distinctive in geomorphological and environmental terms, and in terms of the types of military training which are conducted upon them, like all the major British Army training areas in the UK, the training areas at Sennybridge and Otterburn share certain attributes. They have high environmental quality, officially recognised through various statutory designations in whole or in part. They are both sufficiently far from major urban population centres to feel remote in some way, and although both are sufficiently proximate to such centres to render them accessible (by car) to visitors both are slightly marginal places, distant from centres of power and influence. Both have long histories as military training areas primarily for use by the British Army (Otterburn back to 1911, SENTA back to 1940). Both are predominantly peaty uplands, suited to upland sheep farming and have long histories of agriculture and forestry into the present. Both have a landscape quality, which has prompted civilian demands for public access for recreational purposes such as walking, cycling, horse-riding, and for more general purposes associated with enjoyment of open space, wildlife and landscape. Both have therefore seen an

expansion over the past decade or so in measures to facilitate public access. Both have been subject to criticism and campaigns against the practices of military training carried out there, and in both places those criticisms have been effectively silenced through a combination of downright assertion of the military's priorities for training in these areas and more subtle accommodations (or performances of accommodation) of the complaints. The criticisms and complaints relate to those uneasy for various reasons about the continued military presence there and others wishing for access to these landscapes because of their environmental and geomorphological qualities. In addition, on both of these ranges, to visit on a non-firing day is to wonder, sometimes, what those arguments against the military presence might really be. Both present unusual landscapes in contemporary British terms with their extensive agricultural practices, absence of the usual civilian infrastructure of rural areas and almost total lack of other people. Beyond signs indicating Ministry of Defence ownership and the red flags, which denote live firing, clear signs of the military presence are often absent, and the realisation that things just look, somehow, a bit different comes only gradually. It follows from this that these training areas very often present themselves to the visitor as spaces of quiet, harmony and tranquillity. It is because of this capacity of these training areas to obscure ideas about violence that they become so interesting.

It is through the act of walking in these spaces that these ideas about military violence and its frequent obscurity are most evident. Walking through these spaces brings to mind more abstract, more conceptual questions too, about landscapes and our engagements with them. Walking, using the '*archive of the feet*' (as Simon Schama puts it), is a method shared by the diverse disciplinary approaches to military landscapes. Reflecting broader trends in landscape studies over the past fifty years, studies of military landscapes include analyses of their histories and archaeologies, of their environments and of military environmental impacts, of terrain and tactics, and of the strategic uses of spaces both practically and politically. Studies of military landscapes consider the ways they are represented, deliberately and incidentally, by the state and by military custodians. They consider responses to such landscapes by civilian visitors and interrogators working with both text and image (Woodward, 2004, 2013). Studies are also starting to engage with the affective responses these landscapes invoke in civilian visitors through the experience of walking in such spaces (Davis, 2008; Sidaway, 2009; Harrison & Schofield, 2010). It is this emergent body of work, which provides the conceptual starting point here. Drawing on arguments articulated by Wylie (2007) and others, which in turn look back to a humanist turn in landscape studies within geography from the late 1960s onwards, geographers have become increasingly exercised by landscapes' affectual capacities, by the ways in which personal encounters with landscapes invoke complex individual sensory, perceptual, emotional and haptic responses. My argument here is that the post-phenomenological turn in landscape studies is useful for thinking through the questions posed at the start of this paper, about how military violence becomes obscured in military landscapes, and how we can think about military power because of that invisibility. Although considering affectual responses to such places runs an inherent potential risk of descending into introspection and solipsism. I argue that it is precisely the responses military training areas invoke at a personal level, which raise the most troubling questions about military activities and military violence. How can somewhere that feels so peaceful be so violent? What can we understand about military violence by our engagements with somewhere so peaceful?

Influential to this line of thinking, about absence and concealment, and the centrality we can place on emotional and sensory responses to military landscapes, are ideas raised by non-academic, artistic encounters with such spaces. The work of photographer Simon Norfolk (to which I credit the origins of my thinking on this), particularly his series *The Hebrides: A Slight Disturbance of the Sea*, is a case in point (see also Norfolk, 2006). This body of work explores how military violence can be represented and considered through landscape photography. It has emerged, for Norfolk, as a reaction to what he identifies as an impasse in photojournalistic engagements with war with their capturing of the too-obvious effects and horrors of violence. It is a reaction too to his unease about the seductive capacity of violence working through many photographic representations of war (see www. simonnorfolk.com). In place of this, his work in the UK, and in Iraq and Afghanistan, uses quite conventional ideas of beauty in landscape photography to lull the viewer into a state of calm reflection. This draws the observer in to the image, and after this subtle invitation to suggest a critique of military power and its violent effects precisely because of what is less visible, or unseen, or obscured within the image. Similarly, the work of photographers Ingrid Book and Carina Héden on Norwegian military bases and training areas examines the incidental and subtle effects of military training on landscapes in ways, which seek deliberately to avoid more obvious or usual representations of destruction and its aftermath (Woodward, 2010).

With these two ideas in mind, an awareness of the affectual response to landscape, and an understanding of intangibility as a key feature of military landscapes, in the remainder of this paper I articulate some thoughts about military power and military violence. These relate to ideas invoked by two specific encounters with two different military landscapes, in order to start thinking about violence, its visibility and invisibility, and power.

Sennybridge and the Military Pastoral

The Sennybridge Training Area comprises 12,000 hectares of upland moorland, in essence the Eypynt plateau to the north of Brecon, in the county of Powys, Wales. Historically an area of upland sheep farming, the plateau was requisitioned in 1940 as a training area and its inhabitants relocated to the valleys in the surrounding area (for a comprehensive history, see Dudley, 2012). Its primary use is for infantry training.

In 2003 in response to wider pressures during the 1990s for greater access to military training lands, subject to civilian safety measures, an 80-km long-distance perimeter footpath, the Epynt Way, was established. Following the edge of the plateau escarpment, the Epynt Way used existing rights of way and new pathways. A visitor centre was also opened in a disused farmhouse. The visitor centre provides exhibition space and a wealth of detail about the history, environmental quality and military training practices at SENTA, framed within a standard military environmentalist discourse of easy co-existence between the armed forces and the natural environment. '*Unfarmed*', we are told, '*for 70 years, it has regressed to wilderness. Its high exposed grassy moors are the perfect habitat for hardy troops. It is home to many rare and endangered species of animals, and plants now thrive under MoD care*' (Information board, Epynt Visitor Centre, 2012).

Figure 1. Sennybridge Training Area

Situated on the edge of the training area, and in accordance with contemporary sensibilities about accessibility for all, a path (part of the Epynt Way) suitable for walkers, buggies and wheelchairs departs from the visitor centre for a short distance to the east to reach a picnic spot. Interpretation boards are encountered along the way. Through the provision of this infrastructure, the estate managers for the Ministry of Defence are demonstrably working in accordance with requirements for facilitated visitor access to the training area. A walk from here is not difficult.

At this point on the range, the topography is that of gently undulating enclosed fields incised by streams, with blocks of conifer plantations dotted around on the crests of the low hills. This is resolutely agricultural space. Sheep graze. Birds sing. It is quiet.

Nevertheless, how inviting is this rural, pastoral space? The walker is directed from the visitor centre, the objective pre-given (a set of picnic benches silhouetted on the skyline), the interpretation ready made by the multiple interpretation boards at intervals along the way-marked track. This is access-enabled land, but the growing feeling as we walk the appointed route is that this is access with all the fun taken out. The markers substitute the need to consult the map, and the wide level track indicates a single destination. Interpretations boards bear the logos of a range of public sector bodies – the Ministry of Defence and rural amenity groups – and inform us of the geology and geomorphology and the historic military features visible, such as the line visible on a hill on the opposite side of the valley indicating the traces of a First World War missile training track. The fact of the institutional logos on the interpretation boards emphasises this as managed space. Explanation here, as with the visitor centre, emanates best practice; any mysteries this place holds evaporate as we walk up the track.

However, the mysteries return, of course, and this is a feature of walks on military training areas, the continual switching between that which appears familiar in terms of British agricultural landscapes, that which is explained to the visitor, and that, which appears strange, foreign, different or difficult to place within a landscape otherwise so recognisable. A Dutch army truck, its engine running, sits parked at the point where the access track meets the public road, two occupants in uniforms sitting looking bored in the front seats. The sounds of the sheep and the birds are cut across every so often by the sound of small arms fire way off in the distance, over the hill and up on the plateau. The conifer plantations, such a feature of parts of the British rural landscape in upland areas, are utterly familiar in their rectangular shape, but something in their configuration is different, somehow. Small blocks, spaced at regular intervals, dot across the brow of the hill on one side of the valley. Other blocks, surely of uneconomic size and shape, are angled to one another in relationships at odds with the grain of the rest of the marks of field enclosure. Walking parallel to the edge of one such plantation, we see the familiar planting of spruce at regular intervals, the un-brashed trunks presenting a forbidding inaccessible

gloomy interior, the grey and brown of the dry plantation floor coated in dead pine needles. Nevertheless, we reach the corner of the plantation and see strange litter. A piece of paper showing a table of what we assume to be names (HUNT, KELLY, EKSTEEN, MANN) and numbers and letters (6, 7, 8, T) is gaffer-taped to a tree. A couple of burnt-out glow sticks dangle from a fence. The charcoal remnants of a small fire blacken a patch of ground. Unbranded metallic-effect plastic packaging and a strange canister lie discarded on the path. It is these minor traces, which cause pause for thought. There is something indicative of youthful liminality in the glowsticks and the plastic packaging and the burnt-out fire. Something of escape and fun and camping out, something of the pastoral retreat, is suggested by this litter here.

The idea of the pastoral is less odd than might first appear as a notion to invoke in military space. As Kate McLoughlin (2011) elaborates, drawing on the work of Fussell and others, at first sight the notion of war as somehow anti-pastoral has considerable purchase, as a consequence of the configuration of land as a text of war *recording its prosecution in the script of damaged terrain and denuded vegetation* (p.84). Literary efforts to represent war more commonly suggest the idea of the battlescape as the antithesis of the pastoral, something oppositional to the latter with its values and associations of rurality, retreat and enhanced cognition. Yet, McLoughlin argues, war may be seen as an inverted pastoral, a space proactively entered rather than withdrawn to, and a state demanding and producing special consciousness, productive of insights not disqualified but rather privileged. There is a lingering sense of this idea of the inverted pastoral in the litter and the glow sticks and the gaffer-taped paper and the burnt-out fire. We stand for a while and draw together what we see into a narrative of a rota for guard duty taped to a tree. Glow-sticks are marking out space, canisters for illumination flares or the concealment provided by coloured smoke, the discarded wrappers from military-issue ration packs, a fire for warmth and comfort, but small and sited to be less visible from afar. The sense of retreat, of privileged use, of what McLoughlin terms a distinct *'psycho-physiologico-physical space'* (p.102) is evident in the remains. This says something about violence though not through the deliberate destruction of this small corner of woodland. (Indeed, it would be stretching a point to see the litter as destruction). This is rather through the reach of military power in marking out the most unremarkable, ordinary, uncelebrated corner of a conifer plantation on a shallow Welsh valleyside, as a space for preparations for war. The soldiers (or trainee soldiers) who left the detritus of training behind come to mind, and the inculcation in their bodies and minds of alternative ways of being in the countryside as polar opposites of the leisure camping and festival-going which constitute common contemporary modes of being in rural space. There is something unsettling about the gap between how we read the litter at first

sight, and how we interpret it when we remember where we are. There is a sense of infantry training being domesticated here, made safe.

Driving further round to the north of the training area, along the top of the plateau escarpment and its carpark and viewpoint, we pick up the Epynt Way again. I test it out, walking on the designated footpath parallel to the neat, new freshly Tarmac-ed road, closed for civilian vehicle use, looking out to the north and the views of rural lowland Powys, and to the east and south and the views of the Black Mountain. A pair of red kites rides the thermals overhead. There is nobody else on the path, no vehicles on the road. This is civilian access to military space in all its best-practice glory. However, this is not a place to *enjoy* a walk. Those rambles for enjoyment and pleasure are to be had in the far-off places visible miles away from this point on the escarpment, and from our previous stopping point, in the Brecon Beacons National Park to the south. Beyond the views, there is little alluring or enticing about this path. Walking the Epynt Way at this point brings to mind Nick Mirzoeff's quoting of Jacques Rancière, about the modern anti-spectacle as a phenomenon of contemporary visual practices in the War on Terror: *'The modern anti-spectacle now dictates that there is nothing to see and that instead one must keep moving, keep circulating and keep consuming. The police are above all a certitude about what is there, or rather, about what is not there: 'move along, there's nothing to see'.'* (Mirzoeff, 2005, p.16).

This footpath is anti-spectacle, an anti-footpath. There are no police, of course, insisting that there is nothing to see here, but that idea persists through the walk. There is a gently insistent voice asserting both the generosity of the military land access management regime that permits such access, and asserting a long-standing argument about military priorities for the uses of such spaces and dismissive of civilian interest in this question. There are no interpretation boards up here. Move along, there is nothing to see, beyond the views way off in the distance.

The Sennybridge Training Area and the Epynt Way are strange places to be. The civilian visitor's gaze and movement through this landscape is directed, things are not necessarily as they first appear, and there is, here, a sense of this as a distinctive kind of space. This is not a place of visible and obvious violence, despite its existence as a place for training personnel in the execution of lethal force. The violence lies concealed in the traces that visitors may see, or learn to see, or may not see. It is always there, though; the idea that this is a space purely of civilian agricultural work and rural leisure is not possible to sustain in this space, I think.

Otterburn and the Military Sublime

The Otterburn training area, just over 22,000 hectares of open moorland to the south of the Cheviot, is vast. Occupying one quarter of the Northumberland National Park it encapsulates, depending on your viewpoint, easy

co-existence or uncertain antagonism or practiced accommodation between the demands of environmental and landscape protection, British military capabilities to deploy heavy artillery, and the economies of upland sheep farming. Again, as with SENTA, access is facilitated through pathways and interpretation boards, and carefully managed because of the inherent dangers of live artillery firing. This walk requires not exactly courage and not exactly resilience, but at least a certain assertion of purpose. This is because to proceed to the edge of the range from a small carpark outside the village of Harbottle on the northern edge of the training area requires passing red flags and signs stating quite clearly that the point must not be passed when red flags are flying. Technically, however, the walker passing these flags is still well within the zone of safety, for a public footpath open at all times, live firing or not, takes the walker up and out of the valley of the River Coquet which defines the northern and north-eastern edges of the training area and up to the edge of the plateau. I have taken this walk annually for the past four years with a group of students on my field course on military environments and landscapes.

We walk uphill out of the Coquet valley and stop by a fence and cattle grid on the brow of the hill to look west into the impact area into which live artillery rounds may be fired. There is only really one question to ask at this point. How do you know you are in a military training area? Red flags and warning signs aside, the answers lie in the texture of the terrain. The ground on parts of this military training area, with its hundred-year history of unexploded ordnance, tends not be drained or improved using twentieth century agricultural technologies. Beyond the impact area and outside the boundaries of the wider training area, the slopes of the hills are a bright and specific shade of green reflecting the use of fertilizers and the installation of subsurface systems to drain water from boggier ground. Inside the boundaries, the colours of the grasses are more muted, the bracken and gorse survive because of low intensity grazing, and the land just looks different.

We make a sharp left turn, walking up through a wood, one of many conifer plantations, which, as at Sennybridge, dot the hillsides. We climb gently and steadily uphill, to emerge from the plantation at the top, and the view is waiting. As a frequent visitor, I know what to expect and watch my students

for their reactions. Flat boulders provide seats, Harbottle Lake sits below, and across, looking west, stretching off into the distance, are more impact areas. Through binoculars, and sometimes with the naked eye depending on the light and weather, darker objects are visible strewn across the slopes of the impact area. Thse are tanks, rusting tanks. Their size gives proportion and perspective to the view, a mechanism for the calibration of distance. The views are immense and the tanks are tiny. When the sun shines here, the students do not want to continue. Here, and at an observation point on the other side of the training area, there is something about this view. We stop and consider the military sublime.

The idea of the sublime, with its roots in Romanticism, is a little outmoded in contemporary landscape writing. The notion of suspending reason and rationality in the face of geomorphology and meteorology, sits

Figure 2. The Otterburn Training Area

uneasily with a heritage from natural and social sciences, and humanities, with which to explore and explain our interactions with landscapes and environments. Kathleen Jamie, for example, is apologetic about just this response to the '*surging sea, the wind, the cliffs' bulk against the night sky*' on a December night on Orkney (2005, p.26). John Wylie (2005) has a thoughtful critique of the concept's utility when talking about walking. However, the sublime, the idea of awe and terror as the only possible response to the power of landscape, has a certain utility here. It is there in the response to the view: I notice this in the students as they quieten and gaze. This is more than just being stilled by the visual pleasure of a good vista. The tanks are chilling, unsettling; the observation posts visible on the ridge lines off in the distance are disquietening with their implications of watchfulness. There is something here that brings to mind the words of Simon Norfolk used in commentaries about his photographs of Afghanistan. In these, he attempts to capture something of the awe that these war landscapes invoke, something he identifies as the 'military sublime'. In his articulation of the idea, the military sublime encompasses '*feelings of dread and insignificance in the face not of God but of the power of weaponry', in its distance from democratic control, its distance from the rational and comprehensible. The military sublime is that which is 'inscrutable, uncontrollable, beyond democracy*' (Manaugh, 2006, npn; Finoki, 2006; see also Lee, 2011). There are echoes of this here, a sensation of

unease at the sight of the rusting tanks and pockmarked ground through the binoculars. There is something about this view, which is chilling, which stops many of the students in their tracks. In an upland moorland landscape, particularly on non-firing days when the only sounds are those of the wind in the trees and across the grasses, the sudden realisation about the purpose of this space is disturbing. There is something of the military sublime at work, with the sudden realisation of individual insignificance in the face of power.

Violence and (in)visibility

Above all else, military training areas are spaces for preparation in the use of lethal force. For all the MoD, governmental and statutory managerial regimes and practices that portray these spaces in other terms for other users, as wildlife sanctuaries, as places to ramble, as spaces of quiet and solitude, they exist to facilitate preparations for war. The fact that at first sight this essential function can seem rather obscure or even invisible is significant to the interest these landscapes provoke. The encounters described here, at Sennybridge and at Otterburn, are just two personal responses amongst the multiple possibilities for thinking about military power and space which these landscapes inculcate. In a wider cultural context where military capabilities and activities are overwhelmingly represented through texts and images, which prioritise the visible, the dramatic and the obvious, the landscapes of training areas provide an interesting counterpoint because of the ways in which military power can be seen to work, subtly and quietly. Alluring as they often seem, when I leave these spaces I am always slightly relieved. There is something unsettling about the strange visibility of the marks of preparations for violence in these spaces, and in thinking about what these landscapes are actually for, particularly when they are quiet.

Bibliography

Davis, S. (2008) Military landscapes and secret science: The case of Orford Ness. *Cultural Geographies*, **15**, 143-149.

Dudley, M. (2012) *An Environmental History of the UK Defence Estate, 1945 to the Present*. Continuum, London.

Finoki, B. (2006) A 'Military Sublime'. *Subtopia: A Field Guide to Military Urbanism*. blog posting 12th December 2006.

Harrison, R. & Schofield, J. (2010) *After Modernity: Archaeological Approaches to the Contemporary Past*. Oxford University Press, Oxford.

Jamie, K. (2005) *Findings*. Sort of Books, London.

Lee, H. (2011) The charisma of power and the military sublime in Tiananmen Square. *The Journal of Asian Studies*, **70**, 397-424.

Manaugh, G. (2006) War/Photography: An Interview with Simon Norfolk. *BLDGBLOG*, blog posting, November 2006.

McLoughlin, K. (2011) *Authoring War: The Literary Representation of War from the Iliad to Iraq*, Cambridge University Press, Cambridge.

Mirzoeff, N. (2005) *Watching Babylon: The War in Iraq and Global Visual Culture*. Routledge, London.

Norfolk, S. (2006) Military Landscapes. *Granta*, **96**, 95-132.

Sidaway, J. (2009) Shadows on the path: Negotiating geopolitics on an urban section of Britain's South West Coast Path. *Environment and Planning D: Society and Space*, **27**, 1091-1116.

Woodward, R. (2004) *Military Geographies*. Blackwell, Oxford.

Woodward, R. (2010) *Military landscapes / Militære landskap: The military landscape photography of Ingrid Book and Carina Héden*. In: Pearson, C., Coates, P. & Cole, T. (Eds.) *Militarised Landscapes: Comparative Histories and Geographies*. Continuum, London, 21-38.

Woodward, R. (2013) *Military landscapes: agendas and approaches for future research*. Progress in Human Geography, on-line publication doi:10.1177/0309132513493219 .

Wylie, J. (2007) *Landscape*. Routledge, London.

Wylie, J. (2005) A single day's walking: narrating self and landscape on the South West Coast Path. *Transactions of the Institute of British Geographers*, **30**, 234-247.

A French postcard from World War One.

Beyond the barbed wire: accessing Britain's military training areas

Marianna Dudley
University of Bristol

In December 1943, the villagers of Imber were evicted from their homes, to make way for military training (Dudley, 2010 & 2013). The requisition was perhaps inevitable: the village lies in the heart of Salisbury Plain, an expanse of open grassland that had been used by the military for training since the late-nineteenth century, and the surrounding land had been bought up piece-meal by the military since 1897. By the Second World War, Imber village was an island of civilian life amid a sea of khaki green activity. Requisition during the war meant that villagers were relocated to nearby towns and villages. The road into Imber was closed to the public. Footpaths into and around the village were also closed.

This removal of civilian communities happened numerous times across the Defence Estate during the extensive wartime acquisition of training land. The roll-call of so called 'ghost-villages' is a litany of emptiness and decay: Imber; Tyneham, in Dorset; the community of Mynydd Epynt; the four villages on the Stanford Training Area in Norfolk (Langford, Stanford, Sturston and Tottington). At these places, in order to transform civilian, predominantly agricultural landscapes into militarized zones, access – or, more accurately, the power to prevent and limit it - was actively deployed by the military. It was an immediately effective tool, the restriction of highways and by-ways being written in law, and enforced by the military personnel who had occupied the land. The 'Keep Out!', 'Danger!' and 'Out-of-Bounds' signs that were put up around the boundaries have, to some extent, come to characterize how we see militarized landscapes. This is because, as civilians, we have too often been on the wrong side of the fence, looking in (Woodward, 2004).

But, in recent years, the military approach to civilian access on its estate has changed. It is now possible to go beyond the barbed wire, to walk on permissive routes and rights of way that have been reopened, or newly installed on training areas. I have written two walks that take place in and around training areas for the Royal Geographical Society's Discovering Britain Series of free, publicly available walks (Walk 1: '*Military Environmentalism on Salisbury Plain*' free to download at http://www. discoveringbritain.org/walks/region/ south-west-england/salisbury-plain. html. Walk 2: '*One Place, Two Identities: MynyddEpynt*' free to download at http://www. discoveringbritain.org/walks/region/ wales/mynydd-epynt.html#tabbox). This paper reflects on the relationship between accessing, experiencing and understanding military landscapes. It makes connections between the eviction of civilian communities, and the rise of military-environmentalism as a discourse that informs the MoD's use of its estate, and suggest that now in the twenty-first century, an increasingly pro-access approach from the Defence Infrastructure Organization (who manage and maintain the military training estate) is opening military lands to the public and allowing us to explore their history and wildlife. I suggest that walking is not only an interesting way to explore military lands, which make up one percent of our national territory; but it is an appropriate way to engage with issues of access, public protest, and environmental protection in militarized space (Dudley, forthcoming).

The eviction of Imber, that I've briefly described, was deeply felt by the people whose livelihoods and community were located in the village (Sawyer, 2001). While the move was tempered by a spirit of wartime sacrifice, in the years that followed the peace settlement, resentment turned to anger for some, who lent their voices to a campaign for the *Restoration of Imber* that ran through the 1960s – informed by a perceived injustice by the military, who, villagers swore, had promised to return houses to their inhabitants after the war. Number one on the list of demands by the *Association for the Restoration of Imber* was 'to keep open for public use the rights of way previously closed by Defence Regulations' (Underwood, n.d.).

People had moved to new homes in other villages; but the restriction of access to Imber proved to be particularly upsetting to former residents, and their supporters. Familiar walks were now out of bounds and visits back to the village were made impossible – for example, graves could not be tended. The only place that was not under military control was the Church, which remained consecrated and property of the Church of England. It holds occasional services throughout the year. Cars are escorted to and from it by military vehicles. These remain the only times that people can access the village. Still inaccessible, Imber lies in the Impact Zone just to the north of my walk. The walk takes place in the dry training area to the south, where because no live ammunition is used, it is safe to walk. But by discussing its history, I hope that Imber's presence is felt by walkers, and the restriction of access in one area is contrasted by the freedom to explore in another place nearby.

Sennybridge, the site of my second walk, also saw the eviction of the hill farming community, in 1939. Here, the evictions were met by immediate community action, organized by the National Farmers Union and the Welsh Nationalist group. It was a waste of productive farmland, they argued; and would destroy a cradle of Welsh-speaking culture that had survived on the isolated mountain for generations. Protests were ultimately in vain, as the military moved in. Welsh places names were replaced with military ones; roads were built, and farmhouses were left to ruin. We should remember that at this time other places in Wales were also undergoing extensive change of land use. The valleys of Elan, Tryweryn, and Lake Vyrnwy, had been, or soon would be, put forward for big hydroelectric projects (Gruffudd, 1995; Roberts, 2006). Controversially, these reservoirs were to provide water for English cities. In addition to Mynydd Epynt, the War Office also proposed to use the Llyn Peninsula. In the campaigns against these changes in land use, the presence of English organizations in the Welsh countryside were framed by a language of colonization and oppression. While the restriction of access to Mynydd Epynt – the welsh name for Sennybridge Training Area – was central to the process of militarization, in contrast to the access focus of the Imber campaign, the protests here focused on the cultural and economic damage to local communities and rural Wales. In both places, it was no longer possible to walk on foot within the training areas.

Now, I have purposely presented one side of the story of these military landscapes first. The very human histories of the evictions – complex and emotive – and the protests against the military that they inspired, have proved difficult in the past for the MOD to acknowledge within their training landscapes. Imber remains totally inaccessible to the public, save for a couple of days a year; the only memorialization of the former community *in situ* is a plaque in the church ground, put there by the church. At Sennybridge, however, a pacifist

organization, the Fellowship of Reconciliation in Wales, successfully asked the MoD to place signs bearing the original Welsh names by the former farms in 2007; there is also a Visitor Centre, on the public road that cuts through the training area, that tells the story of the evictions (Cole, 2010).

I wanted first to draw attention to why access has been a historically heated issue on training areas. It shapes not just who lives and works on land, but how the past is remembered. Without access to memorialize a place, its memories and history have to live on in other ways. The protest campaigns did this at both places, while the reintroduction of Welsh names at Sennybridge were another recent success. Installations such as the Visitor Centre at Sennybridge, and the History Barn at Tyneham, are signs that the MoD is beginning to engage with narratives of loss and eviction on their estate.

With the walks, I want people to understand that access has been denied in these places, in the past. The withdrawal of public access, the right to roam free and work the land, was part of the militarization process that changed these places into training areas. And, in the war years at Sennybridge, and in the postwar decades at Imber, the prevention of public access informed, to varying extents, the public protests against a military presence in the countryside. These local protests at times drew nation-wide attention and forced the military to reassess the ways it interacted with local civilian communities. The growing public resentment of the use of extensive areas of the British countryside for military training required a response, which came in the shape of a government committee headed by Lord Nugent that was called in 1973 to determine 'taking account of the long term needs of the Armed Forces and their operational efficiency, and of cost and other relevant considerations… as to what changes should be made in these holdings and in improved access for the public, having regard to recreation, amenity and other uses which might be made of the land' (Defence Land Committee, 1971).

The access issue was driving the protests, and came up repeatedly at the public enquiries that were held at contested sites – Otterburn, Tyneham, Salisbury Plain and Dartmoor, among them. But the Nugent Committee were surprised at the number of representations made by amateur naturalists, birdwatchers and environmentalists who spoke of the abundance of wildlife they could see on military lands, but were not permitted to enter to observe properly.

The committee hearings brought about a realization as to the environmental importance of military lands, alongside an acknowledgement that the British public held a stake in them. The Nugent Committee recommended the creation of the post of Conservation Officer, and the establishment of Conservation Groups, which remain a feature of military environmentalism today. The Nugent

Report effectively signalled the start of conservation, and environmental responsibility, as a day-to-day concern of the Defence Estate and as a structurally-embedded component of its management.

But key to the development of military-environmentalism was the provision of access to training areas to the scientists and environmentalists. Thanks to the reports and wildlife surveys that followed, the military had a wealth of environmental knowledge about their lands that was to help them coordinate training and manage the areas more effectively in the years to come, for example heavily informing the introduction of Integrated Land Management Plans to coordinate training activities and make the training landscapes operate more efficiently. Discursively, knowing the benefits of the military presence has been used by the MoD against complaints of the military presence in the countryside, instead serving to emphasise responsible stewardship. Through press releases, positive news reports that focus on conservation work rather than military activity on home or foreign territories, military environmentalism has been deployed as a discursive tool to secure the military presence at home, on environmental grounds. And, the beneficial effects of allowing access to scientists and environmentalists paved the way for much greater access for the general public, allowing us all to appreciate the military environment, albeit on prescribed footpaths and permissive ways, on the outer edges of the training areas.

Since the 1970s the military-environmental discourse has continued to grow. The MoD's inhouse conservation magazine *Sanctuary* illustrates the increasing sophistication of the military presentation of its home-soil environments. It is one of the most direct ways in which the military promotes itself as an environmentally-responsible landowner. We should, and do, question the extent to which it naturalizes a military presence in the landscape, and remain alert for the way in which the discourse is used to secure a military presence on environmental grounds (Woodward, 2001). For example, the strength of the military environmental record in its British training areas has directed attention away from the more difficult history of the evictions.

On the walks I make the point that it is largely down to the removal of people that habitats and species have thrived on military landscapes; it is an uncomfortable truth that it is too often simply human presence that damages fragile ecosystems. Military training areas are obviously not human-free zones. But the periodic presence of soldiers (and machines) moving through the landscape has not impacted the environment in the same way that long-term habitation, urban sprawl, intensive agriculture, and industrial development has in other places. The grasslands of Salisbury Plain, and the mountain plateau of Sennybridge, are designated Sites of Special Scientific Interest and Special Areas of Conservation. They received funding from the European Union's Habitat Directive to further aid

conservation. The wildlife and landscapes here are important not just on a national, but an international scale, and it is due to the military presence that they have been protected – be it inadvertently, through 'conservation by serendipity' as pre-Nugent military-environmentalism was memorably described in *Sanctuary*; or by active military conservation and land management efforts (Tickell, 1995). This idea is fundamental to the notion of military environmentalism: that the military, by defending our national territory, is also defending our nature (Coates *et al.*, 2011).

I encourage people to look out for the icons of military environmentalism, the charismatic species that feature in *Sanctuary* and in the press releases about the training environment. On SENTA there are the Red Kites, who have been obligingly present every time I've visited, soaring on the thermal updrafts of a particularly steep escarpment. Less easy to find are the Fairy Shrimp, that live in muddy puddles and ditches on Salisbury Plain and are the length of a human fingernail. But I intentionally want to direct people's gaze towards the non-human inhabitants of these spaces, to encourage thought about the military-nature relationship. The Fairy Shrimp is a useful example of the unusual military-wildlife relationship on training areas. The population was seriously threatened thanks to the use of pesticides and decline of grazing on Britain's grasslands. The military presence on the Plain has prevented the use of chemicals on the grass;

furthermore, the shrimps themselves – tiny, delicate creatures – are moved in the mud on the tank tracks, and are deposited to new pools to establish new shrimp communities. This scenario stretches our understandings of how nature and machines can interact and remind us that where we see rusting metal and destructive machines, 'nature' in its different forms can see opportunity, habitat, and resource. This is not to greenwash the vastly destructive environmental impacts of warfare; they remain evident. But I do hope to encourage people to think about how preparations for overseas conflicts take place on home territory; to appreciate that a military presence anywhere will affect the environment; and that the relationship between military and environment here is more nuanced than we may first expect.

My walks introduce these special landscapes, and their unique environments to the public. I aim to reassure them that military landscapes are becoming ever-more accessible, and that the public has a stake in them. By walking on the footpaths provided by the MoD, walkers can play an active role in encouraging more access in the future, helping to normalize the presence of civilian walkers in a landscape of military activity. Richard Brooks and James Nevitt, Access and Environment Officers for the Defence Infrastructure Organisation (DIO), have helped me access the Defence Estate throughout my research, and by supporting my walks, have helped others to do the same. The DIO is working on a scheme that, over the next five years, will see dead-end rights of way and obsolete routes removed and replaced with new paths that enable circular routes and link with other footpaths on military training areas. Access to military lands continues to be an evolving issue, with the success of the Epynt Way (opened in 2004) offering an alternative approach to safe access and recreation provision on training areas, that does not compromise training capacity. The Epynt Way could, I suspect, prove to be a model for future access improvements to military training areas.

Through the walks, I hope to introduce the interesting and complex world of military environments to a wider non-academic audience. Furthermore I want to reassert the value of walking as a tool for historical research, connecting documentary evidence, texts and discourse with real places, people and creatures, and offering a rewarding way of negotiating time, space and place. I think, as historians and geographers of military environments, exploring and experiencing those environments is as valuable a tool in our research toolkit as accessing archives and can certainly ground our documentary research with a strong sense of place. We shouldn't overlook the potential of a walk in a militarized landscape to open up to us the taskscapes and traces of military and non-military use. And by accessing military lands, we become actors in the process of further opening up previously closed sites and insisting on a non-military stake in these landscapes.

Endnote

The Epynt Way is a marked circular permissive bridleway that traces the outer edge of Sennybridge Training Area. It stays mostly within the boundary, though at times it enters surrounding farmland for short stretches. It utilizes the dry training areas (where no live ammunition is used) that act as buffer zones around the dangerous central Impact Zone, and allows access to these areas even when training activities are taking place. It affords walkers, riders and mountain-bikers extensive views of the training area, and experiences of the vast openness of the mountain plateau.

References

Primary Sources

Papers of Austin Underwood, Wiltshire and Swindon History Centre, Chippenham.

Secondary Sources

Coates, P., Cole, T., Dudley, M. and Pearson, C. (2011) Defending Nation, Defending Nature? Military Landscapes and Military Environmentalism in Britain, France and the United States. *Environmental History*, **16**, 456-491.

Cole, T. (2010) *A Picturesque Ruin? Landscapes of Loss at Tyneham and the Epynt*. In Pearson, C., Coates, P. and Cole, T. (eds), *Militarized Landscapes: From Gettysburg to Salisbury Plain*. Continuum, London. 95-110.

Cole, T. (2010) Military Presences, Civilian Absences: Battling Nature at the Sennybridge Training Area, 1940-2008. *Journal of War and Culture Studies*, **3**(2), 215-35.

Dudley, M. (2010) *A (Fairy) Shrimp Tale of Military Environmentalism: The Greening of Salisbury Plain*. In Pearson, C., Coates, P. and Cole, T. (eds), *Militarized Landscapes: From Gettysburg to Salisbury Plain*. Continuum, London. 135-49.

Dudley, M. (2012) *An Environmental History of the UK Defence Estate, 1945-to the present*, Continuum, London.

Dudley, M. (2013) Traces of Conflict: Environment and Eviction in British Military Training Areas, *Journal of War and Culture Special Issue: Traces of Conflict*, **6** (2), 112-26.

Dudley, M. (forthcoming) *Not All Those Who Wander Are Lost: Walking in the Quantock Hills*. In Coates, P., Moon, D. and Warde, P. (eds), *Local Places, Global Processes*, Windgather, Oxford.

Gruffudd, P. (1995) Remaking Wales: Nation Building and the Geographical Imagination, 1925-50. *Political Geography*, **14** (3), 219-39.

Roberts, O. (2006) Developing the Untapped Wealth of Britain's "Celtic Fringe": Water Engineering and the Welsh Landscape 1870-1960. *Landscape Research*, **31** (2), 121-33.

Sawyer, R. (2001) *Little Imber on the Down: Salisbury Plain's Ghost Village*. Hobnob, Salisbury.

Tickell, C. (1995) Conservation by Serendipity. *Sanctuary*, **24**, 3.

Woodward, R. (2001) Khaki Conservation: An Examination of Military Environmentalist Discourses in the British Army. *Journal of Rural Studies*, **17** (2), 201-17.

Woodward, R. (2004) *Military Geographies*. Blackwell, Oxford.

Saint Helena, an island of dry deserts and constant rain: conserving a unique military heritage in a changing climate

Edmund Simons
ATKINS UK

Abstract

"An Island of Dry Deserts and Constant Rain", is how Charles Darwin described this most unusual of British outposts. Sitting at the centre of the South Atlantic almost midway between Namibia and Brazil, the island is the most isolated inhabited island on Earth. The climate varies from semi-desert on the outer fringes of the mountain, to jungles, woodland, cloud forests and semi-moorland.

The strategic importance of the island means that, since the East India Company took possession under the Republic, the island has been fortified and refortified many times. The military remains are extensive and include huge forts, military roads and numerous batteries and barracks.

In this paper, the military heritage and its significance, along with the threats posed by an increasingly wet climate are detailed and explored. Parts of the island, which until recently have been relatively dry, are now being affected by increasing amounts of rainfall and fog. This paper describes how local building materials, particularly mud mortars and plasters, the local stone and roofing materials, are all vulnerable to these changes. The resulting loss of historic assets affects our ability to understand the island's complete military landscapes and to exploit it as an asset for heritage led tourism.

Introduction

Saint Helena is a British Island Dependency located 1300 miles to the west of Namibia and some 800 miles south of Ascension Island. It has been formally occupied by Britain since the mid-seventeenth century, but has been known of since the early sixteenth. The island has been extensively settled and its landscape managed for much of its occupation, though a decline in its political and strategic significance in the twentieth century has lowered the rate of investment and thus the levels of construction and alteration. This low level of modern intervention has left the island blessed with a built heritage of international importance. This heritage includes stunning fortifications, well-preserved houses, townscapes and buildings and remains associated with the island's long history of maritime activity, agriculture and industry.

Before 2006, few heritage professionals had visited the island and those who did were mainly interested in the imprisonment of Napoleon I, from

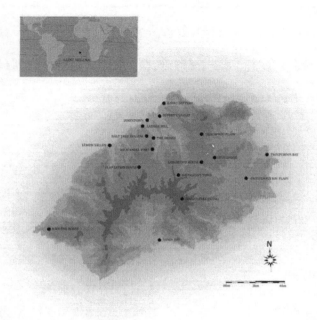

Figure 1. Map of the island showing location and main settlements

1815 to his death in 1821. A notable exception was the architect Hugh P. Crallan in 1973. Crallan created an early form of conservation management plan, with recommendations for listing and repair of historic buildings, particularly in Jamestown (Crallan, 1974). In 2006, the author (Edmund Simons) and Ben Jeffs of Blackfreighter first visited the island and embarked on a programme of work with the Saint Helena National Trust (SHNT). This included, updating Crallan's prescient work, authoring a number of conservation management plans of key sites (see Jeffs and Simons, 2009 and Jeffs, 2011), providing heritage advice and setting up training in historic building repair. In 2011-12 Ben and SHNT produced an innovative, state of the art, immensely detailed digital

Heritage Environment Record (HER) of 968 assets on the island (another 250 are soon to be added), (SHNT, 2011).

The island has an exceptionally unusually broad range of climates in a small area. This is created by the topography of the island, rising as a high volcanic peak from an empty ocean and its exceptionally isolated location at the centre of the South Atlantic Ocean. The island has a number of microclimates, which are created largely by the height above sea level but also by the presence of running water, shelter or man-made intervention such as planting and irrigation. In the broadest terms, the outer parts of the island are arid, seeing little direct rainfall, the valleys have a Mediterranean aspect, with a warm climate and occasional rainfall, whilst the highest points of the interior, are

Figure 2. The rich, wet jungle like cover of the highest peaks

verdant and range from semi-tropical jungle to moorland and, at the top of the mountain, cloud forest.

It was noted during the preparation of the HER and other projects, that the wetter parts of the island were rapidly expanding. It was also noted that this is having an impact on heritage assets, particularly military assets which are now largely disused and whose distinctive materials and locations make them vulnerable to change. This paper details the military history of the island, the significance of military heritage assets and the threats presented to these assets by increased rainfall and the expansion of jungle and moorland.

Military History

The South Atlantic island of Saint Helena was discovered early in 1502 by Joao da Nova. Having found no human inhabitants, the Portuguese introduced fruit trees and goats, and used the island as a source of water and food on return journeys from Asia. Their short visits occasioned the establishment of a temporary settlement and chapel in what became Chapel Valley and is now Jamestown, though the island remained uninhabited aside from occasional wounded or sick crewmen. The valley appears to have had at least two batteries on the shoreline but was otherwise without fortification.

The Dutch claimed the island in 1645 but it remained without permanent inhabitants. It was used by captains of English, Dutch and French origin, as an occasional stop-off point; an uneasy truce punctuated by the occasional capture of a merchant vessel. The original Portuguese owners however found the island increasingly dangerous and avoided it.

Despite claiming the island, the Dutch never settled it and in 1659, the island was claimed and garrisoned by the English Republic and the English East India Company, in the name of "His Majesty Richard Cromwell", under the governorship of John Dutton. After the restoration of the crown, the company renamed Chapel Valley James Valley, for the then Duke of York (soon to be James II) and constructed the first sizeable settlement with a large triangular stone fort and a number of batteries.

The Dutch successfully attacked in 1673 and occupied Saint Helena. A scratch English force of sailors and marines quickly retook it. Another uneasy truce was held with anchorage tariffs charged and dropped according to favour and allegiance, various taxes in kind including gunpowder and slaves. A number of new batteries appear to have been built at strategic locations around the island and a larger garrison was installed. The year 1676 saw the first of many distinguished scientific visitors to the island, the astronomer Edmund Halley (under Royal patronage), who produced much of his work on the southern hemisphere from the island.

The island remained in the ownership of the East India Company and its successor the United East-India Company until 1834, when administration was taken over by the crown. In these years it remained a verdant, highly prosperous stopping off point for merchant shipping. To protect the island a series of defensive lines, batteries and forts were built.

Figure 3. High Knoll Fort, a massive fortress which has recently suffered ill effects caused by increasing rainfall

In 1815, Napoleon Bonaparte was imprisoned on the island, mainly at Longwood, until his death in 1821. This brief phase of the island's history meant increases in the garrison on the island and an increase in military building and fortification. The imprisonment of Napoleon also occasioned the claiming and garrisoning of both Ascension Island and Tristan de Cuhna to deny them use by any French ships attempting to rescue the Emperor.

The island's remoteness led to two further famous imprisonments: firstly, between 1890 and 1897 Dinuzulu kaCetshwayo, son of the Zulu king Cetshwayo was held. A few years later, during the second Boer War, five thousand or more Boer prisoners were held in camps on the island to prevent their release by South African sympathisers. The Boer camp at Longwood was almost a town, complete with a number of two storied timber framed houses.

The island's economy continued to be buoyant until the latter half of the nineteenth century when the opening of the Suez Canal in 1869, the introduction of steam shipping and the screw driven iron ships of the second half of the century, rendered it largely unnecessary as a supply station. It retained some strategic importance however, and new elements were added to the fortifications up until the Second World War. After the war, the island had lost all strategic significance and eventually the garrison was withdrawn and the local defence force disbanded.

What makes the military heritage special?

Number of assets

The sheer number of military sites on Saint Helena is a major contribution to the significance of the island's military history. These include:

11 Barracks

13 Artillery Pieces

20 Defensive Boundaries

6 Defensive Lines

4 Large Forts

5 Guard Huts

58 Gun positions and batteries

36 Magazines

1 Magazine tower

19 Military Ancillary structures

3 Musketry Towers

10 Observation Posts

18 Quarters

2 Searchlights

1 shooting range

The number of fortifications is, in part, due to the changing philosophy of defence over a long period. Early fortifications consisted of detached batteries and a triangular fort at Jamestown. After the Dutch capture and occupation of the island, the deficiencies in defence were remedied throughout the eighteenth century with the construction of large defence lines and batteries across the main valleys as well as an extensive network of military roads. In the early-nineteenth century, fixed defences are still in use but there is an increasing emphasis on defending Jamestown itself rather than the whole island. The presence of Napoleon Bonaparte and a number of other high-profile figures meant an increased garrison and the presence of a small naval flotilla to thwart any attempts at rescuing the Emperor.

By the late-nineteenth century, the fortifications were clearly outdated and many were in a state of advanced decay. The island still has a strategic importance, however and was defended by a more mobile garrison based in the main forts but able to sally out and defend the valleys with accurate fire from magazine rifles. New Armstrong and later breech loading naval guns were installed to defend Jamestown and these still survive to this day. Later military buildings include barrack blocks and the refurbishment of eighteenth and nineteenth century signal stations and lookout posts.

The more vulnerable valleys are the main foci of military activity, particularly at the capital Jamestown which has the most accessible valley and which is set in a deep gorge. Jamestown has the remains of seventeenth century batteries on the coat and the flanking cliffs, the seventeenth and eighteenth century fort of Jamestown Castle is still the seat of government and lies behind the extensive eighteenth century lies with their integral batteries. On the cliffs

above the huge eighteenth-century forts of Munden's and Ladder Hill defend the harbour and Jamestown Roads with their gun batteries with ordnance dating from the eighteenth to twentieth centuries. The vulnerable rear of the town is defended by numerous batteries along the crest and by the giant mountain top fortress at High Knoll, which dominates the centre of the island.

Although the most spectacular fortifications survive in and around Jamestown there are other large-scale groups of fortifications across the island, these include the giant defensive lines at Sandy Bay and Bank's battery, batteries perched in impossible cliffs at Buttermilk Point and Turk's cap and enigmatic isolated musketry towers at Thompson's Valley and Holdfast Tom. Smaller scale fortifications include small gun platforms, isolated look-out posts and barracks. Even the most inaccessible valleys, which are effectively huge gorges where a landing would be difficult to achieve, have some fortification. Perhaps the best example of this is Powell's Valley where a number of small gun platforms held swivel guns (some still present) to shoot down on anyone foolish enough to consider attempting to attack through the valley many hundreds of feet below.

State of Preservation

Saint Helena is the world's most isolated inhabited island; this isolation informed its strategic importance between the sixteenth and nineteenth centuries as a mercantile hub from Europe and America to the Indies. The

Figure 4. Bank's Battery on a nineteenth century photograph, until very recently these survived in almost perfect condition, floods and severe storms have now washed away part of the lines

isolation also however has contributed strongly to the remarkable state of preservation of much of the island's heritage, in particular the military heritage. The isolation of the island meant that there was little impetus to re-use or move materials once a building or structure had become disused or defunct. This is particularly noticeable with ordnance and a number of guns sit in or near the position where they were once mounted and used. The isolation also means that buildings were often left to decay upon disuse and the project even located a number of ruinous magazines still stocked with roundshot, barshot and canister all well preserved and still stacked for use.

The island's unusual climate and topography have also contributed to the state of preservation. In the outer, drier parts of the islands, walls and buildings with their simple mud mortars tend to survive in better condition. Textiles and even papers may also be found which have effectively desiccated in the dry windy desert. Even in the wetter areas and the cloud forest, the state of preservation may be good particularly where buildings retain their roofs and have been maintained.

Completeness of records

The island is blessed with a superb archive, which is currently undergoing a digitisation and restoration programme. Being an island of immense strategic importance to the East India Company and then to the British Crown the records are far more detailed than one would expect elsewhere, particularly in relation to military matters.

The early records from the seventeenth century are fragmentary but a fine collection of bound parchment records details major events in the early colonies (many of these are included in Grosse, 1938). From the early eighteenth century onwards the records are immensely detailed, we know the names, hair and eye colour of the crews of most ships visiting the island. The names of the garrison, labourers and even how many wheelbarrows were required for building individual fortifications is also detailed in the records. The military archive of Saint Helena is of international importance and may be one of the most detailed and complete in existence.

Association with famous people

The island is best known as the final prison for Napoleon Bonaparte, his house, the houses of his staff and military buildings associated with him all survive. The Saint Helena National Trust has recently restored Marshal Bertrand's cottage at Longwood, a cottage graced with a fine regency/ imperial interior installed on the orders of the marshal.

The island also has an association with Edmund Halley, Charles Darwin and even the Duke of Wellington who stayed in the same house in Jamestown, which was later briefly occupied by the Emperor.

Incredibly exciting/ tragic/ heroic stories

The significance of the island's military archaeology is further enhanced by the almost forgotten stories associated with this tiny melting pot of empire. Rebellions of Chinese labourers, attacks by pirates and ghost ships are all important parts of the island's unique history. Perhaps the most important military stories are those associated with the island's pivotal role in the suppression of slavery. A tiny British squadron based on the island and in Sierra Leone took on all-comers to destroy the Atlantic slave trade in the nineteenth century; the port, barracks and a monument relating to the world-changing heroic venture all survive in Jamestown (see Pearson *et al*, 2011).

It is one of the islands biggest assets!

Perhaps the real significance of the island's military heritage is that it is one of the most important assets the island has. The economy of Saint Helena in the future will be largely based on tourism and any visitor cannot fail but to be amazed by the islands rich military heritage. As such, enhancing, exploiting and protecting this unique heritage is key to the island's future.

Threats to the military heritage

The island's remarkable military heritage is not static and it is under threat in a number of ways. This includes lack of awareness by locals, planners and developers about just how significant the heritage is, where it is and how it may be best used. Recent programmes by the Saint Helena National Trust, including the compilation of the HER, a number of conservation plans and training by Ben Jeffs of Blackfreighter in traditional building techniques and restoration have done much to secure the future of these important assets.

At the time of writing, we know what most of the assets are, where they are and have been able to make some analysis of their significance. Together with a new listing and planning system for the island this should do much to help secure the future of the heritage, particularly after the airport (currently under construction) is completed and there is an impetus for change and development.

Historical weather records, historical records, photographs, satellite photography and illustrations all show that the parts of the island have become significantly wetter in recent times. This process has accelerated in recent times meaning that areas, which in living memory were relatively arid, are getting noticeably wetter and are being rapidly colonised by plants and species of animal previously found only at higher altitude on the island. A remarkable example of this is the Heart-Shaped Waterfall, which lies almost at the island's centre. As recently as the 1960s the waterfall spilled over a cliff, which was almost devoid of plants other than hardy aloes and lichens. The waterfall is now surrounded by dense semi tropical forest, which so restricted access to the waterfall that in 2008 a project was undertaken by SHNT to clear the invasive plants.

On an island of such ecological sensitivity as Saint Helena, major changes in environment are worrying as they result in changes to habitats,

particularly for the numerous endemic species of plants and invertebrates found on the island (see Ashmole and Ashmole, 2000). The reasons for the change in climate are obscure, but are probably related to global warming and the rise in sea temperatures. Similar changes are found in the shelf off the island and have caused changes to other sensitive marine habitats.

The increased rainfall has led to a dramatic increase in the incidence of damaging flooding. The very friable volcanic rock is very susceptible to collapsing during episodes of flooding. The island has a history of cataclysmic floods, in part caused by the location of Jamestown in a deep gorge. In recent times however, it appears that floods have occurred in areas, which have been previously untouched. These floods have usually come after prolonged periods of intense downpour, which, naturally run down the mountain. In the more arid areas, without any plant cover, the rain will run down guts or runs (deep stream valleys). Increased rainfall however means that floods are scouring new routes and, in places, causing extensive damage.

In 2006, part of the supporting cliff at High Knoll Fort was washed away during an episode of exceptional flooding. This caused the loss of a large section of nineteenth century loopholed curtain wall of this important fortress, which dominates the centre of the island. The flooding was simply caused by increased rainfall, which washed away the soft volcanic rocks causing a calamitous collapse of the wall above.

Figure 5. Hutts Gate Store a Napoleonic building near Longwood, showing a collapsed wall caused by mortar being washed away

Saint Helena is limited in the range of materials that have been available to it throughout its history. With enormous cost pressures to use local materials, particularly where the imported alternative would be bulky and the size of the island precluded the production of industrial materials the geology limited the quantity of stone and lime usable for carving. The depredations of the introduced goat population and over exploitation have restricted the quantity and quality of local timber. These factors have driven the form and function of much of the island's architecture right up to the 1970s. Even in relatively modern times, into the 1960s and 70s, the vernacular housing was still largely stone with mud mortar.

Pre 1970-island masonry is almost universally rubble laid in a mud-based mortar, sometimes with a lime pointing and very occasionally, on military structures, a lime mortar bedding. Blue surface stone was the predominant building material on Saint Helena up to the 1970s. More than 80% of the island's building stock is constructed from this material. Blue free stone is a similar basaltic rock to the rubble. The huge number of fissures in the rock makes it possible to cut the stone with chisels without it fracturing in undesirable directions. This is the only durable carving stone available on the island. Red Free Stone, from quarries in James Valley and to the north of High Knoll, is a loosely bound consolidated ash based stone capable of being cut with saws and axes. It is easily carved and capable of holding some level of detail, though too soft to be durable in exposed conditions. It is used in many buildings to form openings and corners, where the ease of forming blocks creates a clean edge to rubble masonry. There is also limited use of imported stone and brick particularly limestone

Figure 6. In the drier parts of the island ruins with mud mortar and plaster survive remarkably well but are vulnerable to environmental change

slabs in gun platforms and defensive lines and brick detailing for door and window surrounds, chimneys and magazines.

The local stones (particularly the Red Free Stone) are susceptible to damage from water and none are what may be termed ideal building materials. If exposed to too much damp the Red Free Stone (which is formed of compacted ash) will wear and rapidly disintegrate. As it is frequently used as vouissors for arched openings this presents a problem.

Many of the walls on the island are squared or roughly coursed on the exterior with a rubble core. The outer surfaces of better quality buildings are usually pointed in a mixture of imported lime, mud and beach sands, which makes a tolerably effective mortar. The mud mortar is sometimes with a local pozzelan made of ground red stone. The interiors however are rubble bound in a

mud mortar, using whatever mud is to hand. Lower quality walls may be built and pointed entirely in mud mortar.

Despite the poor quality of material, a great number of mud mortar buildings survive in very good condition. Where roofs have decayed, however and the wall heads are exposed, water has been able to get into the thickness of the wall, dissolving the mud mortar and causing the wall to collapse. In many cases ruins which have been stable for a considerable period of time are now suffering from collapse caused by increased levels of rainfall.

Inappropriate repair or restoration of walls has also caused considerable damage, particularly in areas, which have suffered most from increased rainfall. At High Knoll Fort, a large length of loopholed wall was re-pointed with cement render in the 1990s. The use of this impermeable cementitious mortar meant that water built up in the core of the wall dissolving the mud mortar and causing instability. By 2008, the wall was unstable and a huge section collapsed, this along with flooding undermining the friable stone under another section of the fort severely affected the integrity of this large and important monument.

Increased rainfall and dampness also affects paints (historically lime mixed with seawater), which are required to seal in the mud mortar and need regular replacement. Without maintenance these paints are very susceptible to damp and simply dissolve away. Similarly plasters even if of imported lime are frequently on a mud base coat and very vulnerable to changes caused by increased dampness.

Until the 1840s, the majority of buildings appear to have been roofed in thatch with the more important

structures roofed in imported slate. There appears also to have been a tradition of mortar roofing (although no examples remain). Wrought iron sheet later replaced earlier roofing types and remains the most common roofing material. Where roofing material is lost on abandoned or neglected buildings the roof structure itself become vulnerable, as do the walls beneath.

As well as the physical action of an increasingly wet climate, the increase in the wetter areas of the island also creates a change in local flora, which can, again present a threat to buildings. The change in flora is also, in part caused by the decline of farming and management in many parts of the island. Huge areas of the island are currently covered by New Zealand flax, an imported species which once made up the island's main crop. The flax

Figure 7. Examples of building restoration work

forms dense almost impenetrable swathes of green on even the most vertiginous cliffs and makes access to a number of sites very difficult as well as damaging surface deposits, walls etc. An even greater threat is represented by the many creepers, vines etc which rapidly grow in damp parts of the island. Perhaps the greatest threat though is the ubiquitous wild mango, a South American plant with roots, which will penetrate the hardiest stonework. Wild mango is commonly found on or near ruins and can cause considerable damage.

Conclusion

The change in the climate of Saint Helena represents a real challenge to the integrity of the military heritage of the island. Of the 968 assets identified in the HER, 428 are detraining and 26 detraining rapidly, as most military buildings are no longer in use they make up a high percentage of this figure and increased rainfall has been identified as an important factor in this process.

One thing that makes the island so special is the scale and intactness of the heritage resource. It is not just the large spectacular forts, which make up this military landscape, but a vast network of roads and smaller structures all of which contribute to the significance of the island. Parts of the island have always had high rainfall and lain under cloud (famously Napoleon himself lived in a very damp area which he found very displeasing), but many parts of the island have historically had limited

rainfall or been effectively arid desert. The rapid change means that many sites are visibly decaying in a very short period and enigmatic ruins are in danger of becoming little more than piles of stones. Heroic efforts are being made to assess the scale of loss and come up with possible solutions but if rainfall levels increase, it is clear a number of assets will be lost in the near future.

Acknowledgements
I wish to thank all the present and former staff at the SHNT and Ben Jeffs of Blackfreighter for access to his work.

Bibliography
Ashmole, P. and Ashmole, M. (2000) *St Helena and Ascension: A Natural History*. Nelson, Oswestry.

Barns, J. Capt (1817) *A Tour Through the Island of St Helena*. Richardson, London.

Castell, R. (2008) *St Helena a Photographic Treasury 1856-1947*. Castell, Jamestown, St Helena.

Crallan, H. (2007) *The Crallan Report: the Complete Photographs*. Museum of St Helena, St Helena.

Crallan, H. (1974) *Report on the Buildings and architecture of Saint Helena Island*, St Helena.

Gosse, P. (1990) *St Helena 1502-1938*. ed. T. Hearl. Nelson, Oswestry.

Jeffs, B. and Simons, E. (2009) *Conservation Management Plan High Knoll Fort Saint Helena*, Saint Helena National Trust, Saint Helena.

Jeffs, B. (2011) *Lemon Valley Saint Helena, Conservation Management Plan*, Saint Helena National Trust, Saint Helena.

Pearson, A., Jeffs, B., Witkin, A. and MacQuarrie, H. (2011) *Infernal Traffic Excavation of a Liberated African Graveyard in Rupert's Valley, St Helena*. CBA, York.

Saint Helena National Trust (2011) *Saint Helena Environment Record* (unpublished but soon to be available online)

Cannock Chase: conserving the military heritage

Stephen Dean

Chief Archaeologist, Staffordshire County Council

Introduction

Cannock Chase today represents the largest unenclosed area of land in the West Midlands and lies within several ownerships. Staffordshire County Council manage thirteen hundred hectares of The Chase as a country park which comprises the majority of a European designated Special Area of Conservation (SAC) and a Site of Special scientific Interest (SSSI). The country park is also the core area of the Cannock Chase Area of Outstanding Natural Beauty (AONB).

Cannock Chase hosts a range of significant heritage assets including a pair of Great War camps and their training landscape. While these are not designated, they are recognised by English Heritage as being of national, and in one case, potentially of international importance. This short paper will look to highlight the surviving Great War archaeology of Cannock Chase and the ongoing work of Staffordshire County Council, in partnership with the AONB and Natural England to manage multifarious demands.

A recent survey of visitors to Cannock Chase indicates that around two million people make use of the Chase every year including people from Staffordshire, the West Midlands and from farther afield. It can be argued that this 'amenity' value has been recognised for centuries and indeed for as much as a thousand years and that the landscape of Cannock Chase has been in part been managed for leisure pursuits for much of this period.

The Early History of Cannock Chase

Cannock Chase was formed out of the royal Cannock Forest in 1290 (Greenslade & Kettle, 1967: 343). At this time it was granted to the Bishop of Lichfield by Richard III as a private hunting forest in exchange for the payment of a large fine (to fund a crusade) to legitimise the Bishop's illegal assarting (the act of clearing forested lands for use in agriculture or other purposes). During their tenure, the Bishops maintained the deer park, building a hunting lodge within the Iron Age hill fort at Castle Ring and, in the fourteenth-century, a Bishop's Palace at Beaudesert. At the Dissolution Cannock Chase was granted to William Lord Paget, Lord Treasurer, by King Henry VIII.

Following the Paget family's fall from grace during the sixteenth-century, Cannock Chase was leased to Sir Fulke Greville (a leading Elizabethan courtier) who continued to develop the

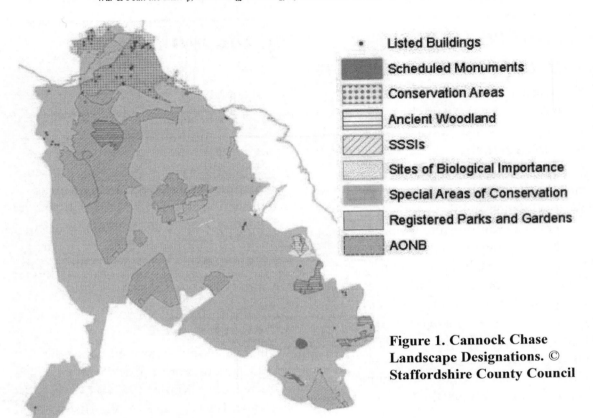

Figure 1. Cannock Chase Landscape Designations. © Staffordshire County Council

Legend:
- Listed Buildings
- Scheduled Monuments
- Conservation Areas
- Ancient Woodland
- SSSIs
- Sites of Biological Importance
- Special Areas of Conservation
- Registered Parks and Gardens
- AONB

burgeoning industrial interests in the area (including glass working, iron making and coal mining), grazing and tree cutting which had started under the Paget family's auspices. The tree felling was to provide the raw materials for charcoal production; Greville was heavily criticised at the time for the severity of his operations on Cannock Chase and was specifically fined for his actions. While, undoubtedly, other activities and landowners were also responsible for deforesting on Cannock Chase, it is Greville who is linked inextricably to this activity; the only trees to survive on Cannock Chase from the sixteenth-century lie today within Brocton Coppice. Enclosed coppices were a feature of management on Cannock Chase up until the eighteenth-

century when they were harvested for the charcoal industry. Commoning was also an important aspect of Chase life with local people maintaining their rights to graze animals and collect firewood throughout the medieval period and into the post-medieval period. By the eighteenth century, the Anson family (later the Earls of Lichfield) controlled much of Cannock Chase and continued to operate it as a private grouse shooting ground grazed by large flocks of sheep. This grazing combined with controlled burning and the promotion of stands of dwarf shrub (heather and bilberry) cover emphasised and maintained the largely open heathland landscape we are familiar with today. Grazing halted in 1914, presumably with the takeover of control by Northern Command and grazing did not return after the end of hostilities. Outside the area of the country park, during the 1920s, over two thirds of Cannock Chase was forested.

This open landscape, lying within the purview of a single landowner, coupled with its central position in the country and in close proximity to good road, rail and canal communications made Cannock Chase perfect for military purposes. During the mid-nineteenth-century, the War Office gave serious consideration to moving the Woolwich Arsenal to Cannock Chase (Whitehouse, 1983:2). In 1873, large-scale manoeuvres on the Chase were carried out by units of the Regular Army and in 1894 volunteer units (the precursor of the Territorial Army) trained on the Chase with the Staffordshire Volunteer Brigade, joining units from Cheshire and Liverpool. Following the success of these operations the War Office

prepared plans for the construction of a permanent military depot and training facilities on Cannock Chase in 1891, although these plans were subsequently shelved (ibid: 2).

Lord Kitchener had asked for volunteers on 11 August 1914 calling for 100,000 men to enlist; this figure was achieved within two weeks and was followed by several more calls resulting in the creation of several 'New Armies' by December 1914, numbering over one million men. The next issue was to house and train these volunteers; at the outbreak of war camp facilities and accommodation was available for only 175,000, well below the one million men who had enlisted. This necessitated the rapid construction of military camps around the country. It was at this point that the 1891 War Office plans for Cannock Chase are likely to have proved invaluable.

Figure 2. Plan of Rugeley Camp.
© Staffordshire County Council

Construction and Camp Life

The initial logistical problems of constructing two divisional-sized camps on Cannock Chase were immense. Work commenced in the autumn of 1914 and started with the sinking of three boreholes to supply water and the laying of a gravity-fed sewage system across the Chase. Existing tracks were also improved, new roads constructed where required and work commenced on a standard gauge railway to connect the camps with the main London and North Western Railway north of Hednesford. Rugeley Camp appears to have been started first, with Brocton camp laid out in January 1915. Despite numerous industrial disputes Rugeley

Camp was practically complete by March 1915 and Brocton camp not long after.

By the time the camps were completed, Kitchener's divisions were largely engaged on the Western Front and as a result, entire infantry divisions were never housed on Cannock Chase. The initial function of these camps was as transit camps; however, as the war progressed they rapidly developed a considerable training function. As such, by 1916 numerous Reserve Battalions were resident on Cannock Chase; by October 1916, fifteen Reserve Battalions were stationed at Rugeley camp and seven Reserve Battalions at Brocton Camp.

Figure 3. Building the Camps. © Staffordshire County Council

Figure 4. Extent of the Camps. © Staffordshire County Council

Figure 5. Camp facilities included a theatre. © Staffordshire County Council

Designed to hold 40,000 men at any one time, the two camps were each the size of small towns. As such, they were provided with all modern services appropriate to their size. Brocton Camp was provided with a power station, power to the Rugeley Camp was supplied by the nearby Rugeley power Station and a one-thousand bed hospital was located some distance away from the camps and training area. It has also been suggested that further smaller hospitals (triage centres) were located closer to the training areas, although to date the physical remains of these centres have not been located. These centres would stabilise training casualties before their transfer to the main hospital at Brindley Heath.

Surviving camp plans locate five ranges and a 'fire and manoeuvre range were constructed along with pistol ranges (indoor and outdoor) and grenade pits. Postcards (including a series of hand drawn cards by Erskine Williams) also depict barbed wire practice areas and hanging sacks

presumably for bayonet practice. The camp plans also mark out large open surfaced squares presumably for drill practice. As well as these more standard elements of training, several specialist Schools of Instruction were founded on Cannock Chase. These included the first sniping school in the country, and reconnaissance, gas training, Lewis machine gun training and signalling (author J.R.R. Tolkien trained as a Signal Officer for the Manchester Fusiliers on Cannock Chase). Recently several sets of specialist training notes have been deposited with the Staffordshire Record Office including two sniper's manuals (Matthew Blake pers. comm. June 2013).

The War Office also recognised that men stationed on Cannock Chase would require amenities to provide an opportunity to step back from the rigours of military life. Brocton Camp was provided with a Post Office and a Bank. Branches of Boots and W. H. Smith were also set up within the camps (*ibid*:18). The camps were also provided with Y.M.C.A. establishments, tearooms, a theatre (the Empress) and a cinema, not to mention the delights offered by the nearby towns of Stafford and Rugeley. W.H. Smith produced numerous postcards of the Chase; many of these survive providing a valuable record of the camp and the environment of Cannock Chase during the Great War.

German Prisoners on the Chase

At the commencement of hostilities, Lord Lichfield had been adamant that no German prisoners of war would be located on Cannock Chase. However, by 1917, the War Office had allocated A and B lines at Brocton camp (located in Brocton Coppice) as a PoW camp. It would appear that the Brocton PoW Camp was expanded to C and D lines as a separate transit camp, as well as the prisoners housed in A and B lines, and sent out to work primarily on local farms.

This area of the camp pretty much retained its pre-POW camp form although barbed wire and towers topped with machine gun positions guarded the perimeter. Wounded servicemen and those considered unfit for active service due to medical conditions acted as camp guards and eventually became the Royal Defence Corps.

'Lagerstrasse' (the main route through the camp) survives as the main track through Brocton Coppice, flanked by large earthworks and smaller flowerbeds. It is interesting to note that Brocton Coppice, an ancient coppice

woodland, survived the Great War and so the barrack huts and other features must have been erected to respect the historic coppice. Some of the Sessile oak (*Quercus petraea*) trees within the coppice have been aged at *c.*450 years old although one may be over 600 years old (Stephanie Wickison pers. comm. August 2013).

The New Zealanders on Cannock Chase

Towards the end of 1917 the New Zealand Rifle Brigade (NZRB) were moved from their base at Tidworth Pennings to a new Reserve Depot at Brocton Camp. This was to remain their Reserve Headquarters in England until their return to New Zealand in 1919.

Fresh Dominion troops from New Zealand continued to pass through Cannock Chase and early in 1918 the NZRB had a terrain model constructed to train officers and N.C.Os. The model was built using the labour of prisoners of war and was in part an act of commemoration. The model was an exact replica of the NZRB sector in the Battle of Messines (June 1917). This highly successful offensive relied on thorough training (based on accurate mapping and information from RFC aerial photographs) to create three-dimensional models for troops to practice on. This training, combined with the detonation of nineteen mines beneath the German salient, resulted in a substantial Allied victory.

During the battle, the NZRB operated as part of II Anzac Corps and were tasked with the capture of Messines, a key point in the defences and the location of a German headquarters position. It is this sector, which is portrayed on Cannock Chase with the model accurately depicting in concrete German trench lines, trench railways, roads, contours and the village of Messines itself. The model is also accurately aligned to the compass. The model that survives today on Cannock Chase, is the only example of a Great War terrain model in the United Kingdom and one of only a handful built on the Western Front; as such it is considered to be of national, if not international significance.

Decommissioning the Camps

After the end of hostilities, the camps continued to function into the 1920s and indeed, the one-thousand-bed hospital at Brindley Heath housed influenza patients until 1923. After the last patients left, the hospital became home to a small mining village until the 1950s when 'Brindley Village' was relocated.

The huts were dismantled and many were sold at auction. Many left the region although some were re-erected locally; one such hut still survives at Brocton village. Another hut was re-erected at Gayton (Staffordshire) in 1923 to function as the village hall. Following an ALSF (Aggregates Levy Sustainability Fund) grant for a new hall, the old hall was carefully dismantled and reconstructed at Marquis Drive Visitor Centre (where it stands today). It is now a visitor and interpretation centre as well as a base for several Great War living history societies.

Following a series of 'sharp' letters from Lord Lichfield, Cannock Chase was returned to the family in 1924.

Figure 6. Part of the Messines model as it appears today. © Staffordshire County Council

Figure 7. Surviving Practice Trenches. © Staffordshire County Council

Following this it returned to a grouse shooting estate and continued to function as such until it was left to Staffordshire County Council to manage for the people of the West Midlands in 1958.

What Survives of the Cannock Chase Great War Camps?

The single ownership issue for Cannock Chase and its retention as a grouse hunting estate following the end of the Great War has resulted in the relatively good survival of many of the Great War remains on Cannock Chase.

Part of The Chase was purchased by the newly created Forestry Commission during the 1920s. The area purchased included much of the Rugeley Camp footprint and subsequent scarification in advance of tree planting has resulted in the destruction of many of the camp features. Today, the most prominent Great War survivors within Forestry Commission land are the shooting butts and associated features. These in part survive owing to their scale and possibly levels of perceived toxicity as

well as the presence of coal mining fissures across the area; an echo of the area's nineteenth century industrial heritage.

The remainder of the camps lie upon Staffordshire County Council land and it is Brocton Camp and the training landscapes of Oldacre and Sherbrook Valley where the Great War archaeological remains survive best. Here the continued management as a shooting estate (until 1950) meant that earthwork remains and frequently concrete structures were able to survive, gradually reclaimed by heathland vegetation. However, walking over the Chase, once the 'eye is in' the visitor can still make out hut platforms, the line of the railway (and its platforms), coal bunkers, the site of the reservoir, practice trenches and a series of rubbish dumps. Elsewhere in the country, camps often sat on agricultural land or within existing military bases. As their military uses ended, these returned to agriculture or were subsequently built over, thus destroying what were essentially ephemeral, short-lived archaeological sites.

Managing the Camps

Staffordshire County Council (SCC) took ownership of a large part of Cannock Chase in 1950 and at this point were tasked with its management for nature conservation and recreation on behalf of the people of Staffordshire; a responsibility that the Council continues to maintain. The area was designated a country park in the 1970s.

SCC is currently managing Cannock Chase Country Park to return it to an area of lowland heathland (see Sheppard, 2009) – a habitat for which it was awarded SAC status in 2005. Part of this management process requires understanding of the resource be it landscape, biodiversity or heritage assets. With the cultural heritage in mind, SCC have carried out a series of walkover surveys to determine what survives of the Great War within its land holding, in what condition and to identify particular threats. The results of these surveys focused upon what was originally identified in the camp construction plans. However, surveyors were soon recording the positions of small-scale practice trenches across large areas of the country park.

Environmental specialists within the County Council lie within a single group and work closely together on a range of issues but particularly the management of Cannock Chase Country Park. As such, heritage specialists are contributing to the preparation of the latest iteration of the Cannock Chase AONB Management Plan. We also work closely with the SCC Forestry Officer and the Biodiversity Officer when considering tree and scrub clearance informing on the removal of particular trees or areas of scrub and on the methodology for work in sensitive areas informed by the results of historic environment walkover surveys. Most recently (2008) this work has been carried out through the support and funding of the Natural England Higher Level Scheme (HLS) which lasts for 10 ten years. As part of the HLS agreement, tackling scrub on archaeological features is one of the management options, as is the management of trees on archaeological remains.

The results of the archaeological surveys have therefore informed ongoing management across County Council land as well as targeting areas for consideration specifically within the Higher Level Scheme agreement. Beyond the management of dwarf shrub and trees on archaeological features and the aim to return the SAC to heathland, the HLS agreement has provided support for two historic environment capital works projects:

1. The excavation, recording and reburial of the Messines Terrain Model site on Cannock Chase during September 2013.

2. The management and interpretation of one area of the battalion lines at Rugeley Camp to inform visitors to the Chase.

It is anticipated that the excavation and reburial of the Messines model will result in the production of a digital model of the feature. This will facilitate

Figure 8. One of the old huts now resited and converted to a museum. © Staffordshire County Council

its secure reburial with rabbit-proof and root-proof barriers and the reinstatement of a native heather/grass mix on the surface. Shortly after reburial it is anticipated that heather bales will be strewn across the monument to encourage the site's return to heathland where previously it was dominated by brambles, gorse, scrub and trees. Continued management of this site will foster the development of heathland and allow for the removal of any invasive or damaging vegetation before it takes hold.

It is further planned that the removal of scrub and the subsequent interpretation of an area of the Rugeley Camp battalion lines will assist in various SCC education projects during and beyond the Great War Centennial period. A car park is already present near the battalion lines and the area is already serviced with footpaths. It is anticipated that a focus on this area, close to the main SCC visitor centre on Cannock Chase will reduce footfall across more sensitive areas of the camps while providing an excellent opportunity for visitors to appreciate the archaeology of the Great War.

The Centennial and Beyond

Managing visitor use of the Cannock Chase country park is a crucial function of both the County Council and the wider AONB strategies for Cannock Chase, with over two million visitors a year exerting considerable pressures on this fragile and important environment. This situation could potentially become more acute over the next five years with the commemoration of the Great War Centennial. In response to this period of commemoration, Staffordshire County

Council has prepared a Great War Strategy with county-based activities managed by a cross-county steering group, which includes key partners from other organisations (including The National Memorial Arboretum and the Staffordshire Regiment Museum). The County Council also signed up to the Great War partnership managed by the Imperial War Museum. The County has held a number of seminars to date which look to emphasise the role of local societies and assist in the development of more local projects. A *Staffordshire Great War* website has been developed and went live in September 2013 and a *Staffordshire Great War Trail* is being established. It is anticipated that this will appropriately highlight Cannock Chase's role in the Great War, while introducing other venues from around the county for consideration.

Staffordshire County Council will continue to manage the country park, taking into consideration the wide variety of issues and groups who have a stake in the park's future. However, within this, the forthcoming Centennial represents an excellent opportunity to tell the story of a conflict which has traditionally been seen as something which 'happened over there'. Key within this is Cannock Chase and our continuing management will look to emphasise the Great War heritage of Cannock Chase, while looking to manage visitors appropriately, to minimise damage to not only the archaeological remains but also the Chase's rich ecological and landscape heritage. The forthcoming Centennial

therefore provides an excellent opportunity to shine a light on an often-ignored part of our heritage. As such, it is hoped that the impetus provided by this will carry on beyond 2019 to produce a lasting legacy in our understanding and interpretation of the Great War.

References

Greenslade, M.W. (1967) *Forests: Cannock*. In: Greenslade, M.W. & Jenkins, J.G. (eds) *A history of the county of Stafford volume II*. Oxford University Press, London.

Kettle, A. (1979) *Agriculture 1500 to 1793*. In: Greenslade, M.W. & Jenkins, J.G. (eds) *A history of the county of Stafford volume VI*. Oxford University Press, Oxford.

Sheppard, S. (2009) *Cannock Chase Heaths*. In: Rotherham, I.D. & Bradley, J (eds) *Lowland Heaths: Ecology, History, Restoration and Management*. Wildtrack Publishing, Sheffield, 116-122.

Whitehouse, C.J. and Whitehouse, G.P. (1983) *Great War Camps on Cannock Chase*. Staffordshire County Council, Stafford.

Website:

http://www.staffspasttrack.org.uk/exhibit/chasecamps/

THE ILLUSTRATED LONDON NEWS, MARCH 2, 1918.—270

SCIENCE AND NATURAL HISTORY.

SCIENCE JOTTINGS.

STATE-PAID DOCTORS.

FOR some time a rumour has been current in the Medical Press that the setting up of the long-threatened Ministry of Health will be made the occasion to promulgate a great scheme by which the general practitioners throughout the country will be turned into officials paid by the State, and under the rule of the new Ministry. Details of this are necessarily lacking; but the rumour is too persistent to be entirely without foundation, and corresponds well enough with the many leanings towards State Socialism which our present rulers have displayed. It may, therefore, be well to examine as shortly as possible the arguments for and against such a measure.

In the first place, it may be conceded that when the war is happily over, some sort of State aid to the rank and file of the medical profession is, as they would themselves say, indicated. No class of the community has made greater and more willing sacrifices than they; none has worked harder and none has rendered more efficient services to the State. From the first, the great majority of doctors of military age — and a great number who were above it — volunteered for active service, and when accepted have not only ventured their lives as freely as any professional soldier, but have kept our fighting men in such splendid health that the losses from disease, in former wars so formidable as those in the field, have been almost negligible. Yet most of these brave men will come home to find their practices gone, their former patients transferred to others, and themselves under the necessity of starting their careers, but too often with impaired vitality and energy, all over again. Nor have those doctors who, from age or other sufficient causes, stayed at home earned any cause for envy. The absence on service of most of their richer patients, the increasing impoverishment of the middle and professional classes, and the increased expenses that the rise in the price of food — and of petrol — has entailed upon them, have all combined to reduce the value of their practices enormously. It may be doubted if any general practitioner in the kingdom is making half what he did before the war.

On the other hand, there are many reasons why the State relief which is thus due should not take any form which would alter the doctor's present relations with his patients. Before the war nearly all country

and many London practices were run on the old-fashioned principle of average, which, old-fashioned and illogical as it may have been, worked well, as did many other essentially English institutions. Those patients who were well enough off to consult a doctor for their less serious ailments paid fairly for their privilege; while their poorer fellows were attended by him for a minimum fee, which, at any rate, helped

A NEW SUGGESTION FOR "THE DOGS OF WAR": A CANINE AMMUNITION-CARRIER'S EQUIPMENT EXHIBITED IN PARIS.
French Official Photograph.

him to increase his technical knowledge. The effect was to make him the friend of both high and low, to whom both classes looked for relief in their bodily troubles, and tempered his lot with a good deal of pleasant social intercourse. Hence his success, seldom

body, this played no insignificant part in the cure. Are these relations likely to continue when the pleasant, friendly doctor is converted into a State official whose promotion and success will depend on his pleasing, not his patients, but his official superiors?

Candour compels us to acknowledge that they are not. During the war, the public has been treated to a drench of officialism which would have seemed impossible to the happy-go-lucky and freedom-loving Englishman of former times. Ministry after Ministry has been set up, each with its army of highly paid officials, its come-by-chance and cheaply remunerated clerks, and its mass of forms to produce which seems its chief occupation. Has the result been satisfactory? Leaving the older departments out of the question, have those set up to deal with Pensions, Labour, and Food yet proved their value to the taxpayer in efficient administration of the nation's assets? Or have any of them yet succeeded in producing any number of servants of the State in whom the majority of the nation feel confidence? If, as we believe, a plebiscite on these questions would result, in both cases, in a negative answer, what case is that for extending the method to the medical profession?

This is from the point of view of the patient; but how does such a scheme commend itself to the doctor? All previous experience has shown that in State appointments, with the exception of a few experts of such commanding pre-eminence that they cannot be safely ignored, it is the most pushful and those who are most likely to be useful to their departmental chiefs politically or otherwise, rather than those whose only qualification is hard work and a knowledge of their profession, who are likely to be successful. And another element is now entering into the competition. The number of medical women has necessarily increased enormously since the war. Some of these have undoubtedly won their spurs by hard work and intelligence; but in the nature of things, this cannot be the case with all. Yet in many, if not most of these cases, they can command personal or social or political influence which will give them great advantages over the male competitors when appointments come to be made. Neither patients nor doctors can, therefore, look with equanimity on the proposal to turn medical men into State officials.
F. L.

PEAT AS FUEL FOR THE FRENCH ARMY: WORK IN PROGRESS ON A PEAT-FIELD IN ALSACE.
Photograph by Schmier.

very great in a pecuniary point of view, largely depended on the cultivation of a good "bedside manner"; and, as the mind reacts largely on the

Peat as fuel in Alsace, 1918 © Ian D. Rotherham

Ashley Walk Bombing Range, New Forest, Hampshire

Richard Hall
Airfield Research Group

Introduction

In 1939, when war was declared the size and weight of the bombs were a legacy from the 1914–1918 war. Standard weights of 250 lb and 500 lb bombs were common at the onset of the war but larger sizes were slowly becoming available. At this time, Bomber Command lacked a heavy bomber. The front line bombers available to Bomber Command were the Vickers Wellington, Armstrong Whitworth Whitley, Bristol Blenheim and Handley Page Hampden. It was not until the early months of 1941 that Bomber Command received its first operational heavy bombers, these being the Short Stirling, Avro Manchester and Handley Page Halifax. There was also some Boeing B-17 Flying Fortresses on RAF strength. The Avro Lancaster, perhaps the best-known Allied bomber of WWII, was a later addition.

The need for improved accuracy and increased bomb carrying capacity of aircraft soon became evident. Although bombing ranges have existed almost since aeroplanes began dropping bombs, no critical assessment had ever been made as to the accuracy of the claims made by the bomber crews in combat. In August 1941, Cabinet Minister David Bensusan-Butt compiled a detailed, analytical survey of the RAF's target bombing photographs, the Butt Report, which revealed a shocking truth. Early attacks by Bomber Command, upon closer scrutiny, revealed that targets were frequently being missed, sometimes by five miles or more and something needed to be done to improve this situation – it was costly in both men and materials (Hastings, 1999). As a result, bombing ranges with ever more sophisticated targets were built across Britain. Because of their nature, remote areas of land were requisitioned for the purpose, well away from the centres of habitation or agriculture. This often meant that moors, heaths and coastal locations began to feature strange-looking structures and ground-markings. In the New Forest area, Ashley Walk is one particularly good example of a WWII aerial bombing range, which offers a variety of wartime archaeological evidence of its previous use.

Ashley Walk

The New Forest, Hampshire, is now one of Britain's best-known National Parks. It is famous for its ponies and areas of tranquil beauty. With vast areas of tracks and trails, it is a very popular location for those who love the outdoors. Now, if one were to say that amongst all of this outstanding beauty, there exists a German U-boat pen, surprise or disbelief may be the response. Today, the former bombing range at Ashley Walk has now reverted to a quiet heathland landscape, where the skylarks ascend to sing their hearts out and the ponies graze happily. However, the juxtaposition of unfamiliar and unnatural features is the result of Britain's pressing need for military aviation training in WWII, which was set amongst some of the landscapes now held precious as natural resources.

The New Forest was an area that contributed much to the airborne war in 1939–1945. At one time, there were no less than twelve airfields and advanced landing grounds located within its confines. The airfields included such well-known names as Stoney Cross, Ibsley, Holmsley and Lymington.

On 4th December 1939, the New Forest Verderers considered a proposal submitted by the Air Ministry for a bombing range to be built on a temporary basis near Godshill. There was no objection in principle to the proposed range for the duration of the war. However, the Verderers asked that the suggested area be fenced off and to be made man- and pig-proof. In due course, a chain link fence some 6 ft high was erected. There were thirteen access points to the range with the main entrance located on Snake Road. Here, there was a small guardroom building located adjacent to the gate. Although pig-proof, the area did not appear to be small boy-proof and there are tales of the range being much used as a playground during the wartime years by local lads.

The range came into use in 1940 and covered 5,000 acres. Ashley Walk was controlled by the Armaments Squadron of the Aircraft & Armament Experimental Establishment (A&AEE), located at Boscombe Down. The site is quite remote so the personnel operating the range were billeted in purpose-built huts opposite the Fighting Cocks public house in Godshill (Pasmore & Parker, 1995).

There was much in the way of impressive facilities at Ashley Walk; fortunate, as every type of airdropped ordnance used by the RAF, with the exception of incendiary weapons, was tested here between 1940 and 1946. Along with the airdropped ordnance, guns and rockets were also tested and evaluated. These ranged from small anti-personnel types to the 22,000 lb Grand Slam 'earthquake' bomb, designed by Barnes Wallis.

The range was in two parts. The first consisted of a practice area, which had a diameter of 2,000 yards. This was used for dropping inert bombs from a height of 14,000 ft. The range could be used either by day or by night. If night bombing was required the targets could be lit by a diesel generator. It appears that this part was seldom used. This area of the range was controlled by a tower located at Hampton Ridge, which was known as the Main Practice Tower.

The second part of the range was known as the High Explosive Range. This had a diameter of 4,000 yards and was controlled by the North Tower, located near to the road that ran between Fordingbridge and Cadnam.

The High Explosive Range could be used from a height of 20,000 ft for dropping live ordnance.

The towers at both locations were approximately 30 ft high with large observation windows, which afforded a good view of events on the range. The entire facility was under the control of the Range Office. There were two observation huts on the range, one at Amberwood, which still exists, and the other, a filming shelter, adjoining the No. 2 Target Wall.

Transport links to the range were by road but in addition to this, a small airfield consisting of two landing strips was built. The strips were 400 yards long and used by general communications and observation

aircraft such as the Auster AOP IV, which were small enough to operate from such short landing grounds. The strips ran south and south-west from the southern edge of what is now Godshill cricket pitch (all illustrated in Figure 1).

Targeting Facilities

There was a multitude of targets, which included wall targets, air-to-ground targets, a line target, a ship target, a submarine pen (Ministry of Home Security Target), fragmentation targets and a range of custom targets. Evidence of many of these targets can still be seen. This is in part due to the fact that the targets were marked by chalk which is distinctive as it is not part of the geology of the New Forest. The chalk

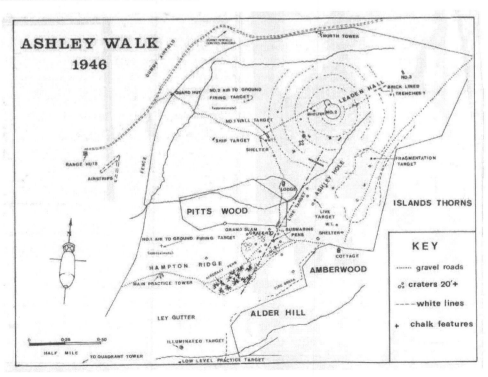

Figure 1. Ashley Walk Range. (Courtesy New Forest Research & Publication Trust)

was imported in to the site to mark targets so they could be seen from the air. The chalk has prevented further native vegetation from growing back; hence, the marked targets can still be clearly seen.

Air to Ground Targets

There were two air-to-ground targets built near the western edge of the High Explosive Range. The targets consisted of yellow and black squares and were used for guns up to 40mm calibre and rockets of 3 inches in diameter.

The Line Target

This target is still very evident today and consists of a 10ft wide line, 2,000 yards in length. The line ended with a white marked cross with arms of 100 yards in length. The lines were created using chalk. The Line Target's purpose was to simulate a railway line and was used to develop techniques to attack railways (or in some cases roads), using rockets or bombs.

Wall Targets

Three Wall Targets were built at Ashley Walk and consisted of the following features:

No. 1 Wall Target

This target was 40 ft wide × 40 ft high and constructed of nine-inch reinforced concrete.

No. 2 Wall Target

This target was the same size as No.1 Wall Target and was built on a nine inch concrete base which was 200 yards in diameter. From an aerial view this target is surrounded by a series of concentric circles which were formed by bulldozing away the top soil to reveal the bleached gravel. These circles were used to provide a guide to impact distances.

No. 3 Wall Target

Very different to the other wall targets, this one was constructed to test 'bouncing bombs' as designed by Dr Barnes Wallis. The wall was 8ft 10in. high × 20ft long and 6ft thick. The wall was faced with two inches of armour plate.

Initially, the smaller Highball bouncing bomb was tested which a de Havilland Mosquito aircraft carried and was intended for use against battleships. In August 1943, the No.3 Wall was extended in length by 90ft to allow testing of the Upkeep (the code-name for the weapon) cylindrical bouncing bomb. This is the bomb that was used during the famous Dambusters raid (Operation Chastise), which took place in May 1943. Specially modified Avro Lancasters were used to carry the Upkeep bomb. It is interesting to note that it seemed that Upkeep was not considered for use after the Dams Raid. However, it would appear from the tests carried out at Ashley Walk it was. It is possible tests were undertaken to ascertain if the bomb could have been used to breach sea wall defences in France; D-Day was approaching.

Ship Target

As the name suggests, the target was designed to represent a ship and was located on flat ground at Cockley Plain. The target was constructed from steel plates and heavy angle iron girders. It was used to test the effectiveness and penetrating powers of 20mm and 40mm cannons, air-to-ground rockets and the 6-pounder anti-tank gun used in the Mosquito.

Fragmentation Targets

Two areas on the range were set aside for the testing of fragmentation bombs. The areas were known as 'A', 'B', 'C' & 'D'. The areas were marked with their designation letters in chalk so they were visible from the air. Sites 'A' & 'B' were located near Alderman Bottom. The area was used to test dispersal areas and the protection they could afford aircraft from fragmentation bombs. A number of aircraft dispersal pens were constructed in line with the design that was used by the Luftwaffe on their airfields. Sites 'C' & 'D' were located to the east of Coopers Hill. This area was used to test fragmentation bombs against surface targets such as trenches and command posts.

Ministry of Home Security Target (Submarine Pen)

A number of theories have been suggested for this target, including testing how well air-raid shelters stood up to the effects of bombing. Alternatively, it has been suggested that the target was used to simulate a German U-boat pen structure.

It became evident that the Germans were building substantial concrete structures on the French coast to house U-boats. The RAF were keen to bomb these targets but needed to evaluate how they could be penetrated. In order to simulate the structures, a replica was built at Ashley Walk in September 1941, at a cost of £250,000. A huge concrete raft 6ft thick and measuring 79 ft ×70 ft was constructed. Supported on five walls 6ft high, the structure was built on a foundation 20 inches thick. The outer walls were 3ft 3in. thick with the inner walls being 1ft 9in. The RAF tried many times to destroy the pen but were not successful. In fact, they had quite an issue with trying to hit the target. The bombs used, 500lb, were also too small to make an impression on such a massive construction. It would not be until later in the war that the RAF managed to penetrate the submarine pens in France. In order to do this, 12,000lb Tallboy bombs were used.

Improving Accuracy

Throughout the tests, as the war progressed, bombing accuracy improved at Ashley Walk. An anecdote from the time relates to the filming of a test drop. Film of an inert bomb approaching a target was required. It was considered that the safest place to put the camera was target centre. This cynical approach cost the ministry one cine camera after the bomb hit target centre fair and square.

Figure 2. 12,000 lb Tallboy, on display at the Battle of Britain Memorial Flight hangar, RAF Coningsby, Lincolnshire

Figure 3. 22,000 lb Grand Slam, on display at the Yorkshire Air Museum, Elvington

Testing of the Big Bombs

The largest air-dropped ordnance used during the war was the 21ft long × 38 inches diameter 12,000lb Tallboy and the 25ft 5in. (plus 13ft tail) × 3ft 10in. 22,000lb Grand Slam bombs (Flower, 2002).

Both weapons were designed by Barnes Wallis and were known as 'earthquake' bombs. There is a good reason for the name – when they landed and detonated, they caused sub-surface effects similar to an earthquake, undermining foundations. The Grand Slam for example, could penetrate up to 120ft deep before exploding. Both types of bomb, inert and live, were tested at Ashley Walk.

Initially, inert Tallboys were dropped into the range. The bombs would have been delivered by Avro Lancasters, whose modified bomb-bay design allowed the dropping of such large weapons. Aside from the inert Tallboys, six live ones were also dropped. Starting in June 1944, 9 Squadron and

617 Squadron (the latter of Dambusters fame), went on to use Tallboys to attack such targets as V1 & V2 rocket sites in France and Holland, U-boat pens on the French coast, the Dortmund-Ems Canal, the battleship *Tirpitz* and even the *Berghof*, Hitler's mountain retreat in Bavaria (Middlebrook & Everitt, 1985).

Following the Tallboy trials, a larger variation of the bomb, the 22,000 lb Grand Slam, was tested. A series of inert Grand Slams were dropped into Ashley Walk. The Grand Slams' development was halted in September 1944, as it was considered that the war would be over by Christmas of that year. However, after the failure of *Operation Market Garden* (the attempt by the Allies to capture and cross the bridges over the River Rhine at Arnhem, Holland), development was resumed. After the inert tests on 13 March 1945, Lancaster PB592/G of the A&AEE, flying at 18,000 ft above Sandy Balls, released a live Grand Slam, which impacted near Pitts Wood (Pasmore & Parker, 1995). The bomb buried itself deep into the ground and then exploded producing a crater 30ft deep ×124ft in diameter. The local residents were not informed prior to the test; they did not see it but would certainly have felt it as the earth moved.

The exercise was deemed a success and the following day, 28 Lancasters dropped Tallboys and a Grand Slam in an attack on the Bielefeld and Arnsberg viaducts, in north-west Germany. The 617 Squadron Lancaster piloted by Squadron Leader C.C. Calder dropped his Grand Slam at Bielefeld, which resulted in 100 yards of the viaduct collapsing due to the earthquake effect of the bomb. The Arnsberg viaduct was later found to be undamaged. However, the Arnsberg viaduct was again attacked on 19 March 1945, when 617 Squadron dropped six Grand Slams, blowing a 40 ft gap in the structure. In total, 42 Grand Slams were dropped by 617 Squadron Lancasters before the war ended (Flower, 2002).

What Remains on the Ground Today

Ashley Walk today is a very quiet place with acres of beautiful Hampshire countryside just waiting to be explored by anyone who enjoys a good walk and wants to find a piece of local history. The sounds of the Merlin and Centaurus engines are long gone. However, evidence of the wartime activities are very easy to find although some of them take a little looking for. The following information, set out below, gives an indication of what survives as standing remains and earthworks. Live ordnance is still occasionally unearthed on the range and care should be exercised if anything suspicious does come to the surface.

Bomb Craters

Bombs craters are still very evident today and parts of the range resemble a lunar landscape. The main part of the range is littered with bomb craters; many now have become artificial ponds, as detailed in Figure 4. Grid Reference SU 2019 1550.

Figure 4. One of the surviving bomb craters, typical of many at Ashley Walk

Figure 5. Piles of chalk evident and numerous at Ashley Walk

Figure 6. The Line Target, marked out in chalk

Chalk

As can be seen in Figure 5, chalk is still much in evidence at the range even after all these years of closure. Today, where the chalk was used native plants do not grow, hence why the target markers have not become overgrown and remain clearly visible. Grid Reference SU 1977 1525.

The Line Target

The Line Target (Figure 6) is still very much in evidence although it does become difficult to trace after it has passed over the Submarine Pen. The target's termination is easily identifiable

as a large white cross again marked by chalk (Figure 7). Parts of the target resemble a long, straight footpath cutting across the range. Grid Reference SU 1995 1396.

Wall Targets

With all the Wall Targets, there is no effective way to photograph the remains in a way that gives much meaning. Therefore, OS grid references have been used. It is suggested that systems such as Google Earth be used in conjunction with maps to understand the layout of the range and its surviving structures today.

Figure 7. The cross at the termination of the Line Target (Grid ref. SU 2041 1505)

Figure 8. Concrete base of the Ship Target

Figure 9: The odd fragment of metal plate visible on the ground

Figure 10. The chalk remains of Target 'C', the identification letter clearly visible

No. 1 Wall Target

Not much evidence can be seen of this target at ground level; however, from Google Earth, its base impression can still be discerned at ground level. Grid Reference SU 1983 1532

No. 2 Wall Target

This now appears on the ground as a large circle of ground that looks out of place to its surroundings. Again, Google Earth shows the target very clearly as a large, sand-coloured disc. The target is very large and there is no effective way to photograph it from ground level. Grid Reference SU 2052 1565

No. 3 Wall Target

This now appears only as a long low mound of earth. The mound is marked by gorse bushes (*Ulex* sp.) growing along it and evidence of rubble. It is understood that the wall was undermined along its length and then simply pushed over and buried.

Ship Target

The remains of this target are still visible in the form a concrete base and some concrete foundations with metal bolts still in place (Figures 8 & 9). Grid Reference SU 1927 1522

Figure 11. Ministry of Home Security (Submarine Pen) target

Figure 12. Tallboy crater and Submarine Pen

Fragmentation Targets

Grid Reference 'A' & 'B' Target Area - SU 1964 1136

Grid Reference 'C' & 'D' Target Area - SU 2085 1467

All of the letters 'A', 'B', 'C', & 'D' can still be seen on the ground although a GPS device is recommended to effectively locate them. Figure 10 shows Target 'C'.

Ministry of Home Security Target (Submarine Pen)

This is still very much in evidence as a large mound of earth that covers the concrete structure. It was massively built and demolition was not considered to be an option after the war. It was therefore simply covered over with earth. Concrete is starting to show through where erosion of the earth is taking place. Many people walk past this mound oblivious to its former function. Grid Reference SU 2002 1412.

Tallboy Crater

This crater was created by a 12,000 lb bomb and now resembles a small lake. It is often now used by New Forest ponies as a watering hole. This is the most obvious crater of its type. Incidentally, the one and only live test Grand Slam crater was back-filled, post-war. The photograph in Figure 12 shows the Tallboy crater with the Submarine Pen, visible as a large earth mound (see Figure 11), in the background. Grid Reference SU 1995 1407.

Other Remains

Observation Hut

This is located near Amberwood and is one the few remaining above ground standing structures on the range. Close observation of the end wall of the hut reveals an enterprising bricklayer has formed the letter 'V' (Figure 13). Grid Reference SU 2194 1640.

Figure 13. Observation hut

Figure 14. Display panels, the Main Observation Tower

Detail of the line display panels at the remains of the Main Practice Tower located on Hampton Ridge (Figure 14). Grid Reference SU 1882 1360.

Located next to the Main Practice Tower is a large white concrete direction arrow (Figure 15), which points towards Ley Gutter, where an illuminated target was located. Grid Reference SU 1883 1359.

Figure 15. Target direction arrow

The remains of a cast concrete light box at the Illuminated Target location below Ley Gutter are shown in Figure 16. Grid Reference SU 1913 1279.

Figure 16. Cast concrete light box, Illuminated Target

Conclusion

Therefore, in conclusion, Ashley Walk has gone from one extreme to another and then back again. Today, all is quiet and nature has reclaimed its land back from the days of noise, explosions and flying shrapnel. It is hard now to consider what went on at the range but the evidence is there.

From the early days of Bomber Command's less-than-successful attempts to the end of the war, bombing ranges played a vital part in the on-going training, both general and specialized. The Butt Report clearly troubled the Air Ministry and can be seen as a contributory factor in the increased and more sophisticated efforts in the training of bomber aircrews. Progress was rapid as the war continued with aircraft, bomb design, bomb aiming, navigation and electronic aids becoming far more effective. Ashley Walk played its part in this fast moving arena by being the place that the aircraft tested their ordnance to ensure its design and effectiveness were such that it could be taken to war. Ultimately, the biggest airdropped conventional ordnance of the war was tested at

Figure 17. Fragments of shrapnel are frequently seen on the surface

Ashley Walk, this being the 12,000 lb Tallboy and the 22,000 lb Grand Slam 'deep penetration' bombs.

With attacks by the RAF at night and the USAAF by day, the bombing campaign continued throughout the war and wreaked havoc against the Third Reich. There were huge losses on all sides and much controversy surrounds the campaign and whether it was justified in the way targeting was conducted. However, at the time the allies were locked in a life and death struggle and had to use all weapons and tactics at their disposal. The sky over north-west Europe was the battle ground and the airfields of Britain were effectively the front line. Around 125,000 aircrew served with Bomber Command during WWII, and 55,573 died, a loss-rate of almost 50%. By anyone's standards, that is a staggering number and unacceptable today, a statistic that should not be forgotten.

Thankfully, the crews have at last been recognized with the dedicated of the Bomber Command Memorial in Greene Park London in 2012 (Flagg (Ed.), 2012). It has been a long time for the men of Bomber Command to receive national recognition but it is here now. Along with many of the other aviation-related sites of WWII across Britain, Ashley Walk stands as quieter place of reminder and remembrance to those days; their remains add a subtle layer of archaeology to a landscape already rich in history and protected for its natural beauty.

Figure 18. A peaceful scene more familiar with the New Forest today – a far cry from the short, busy and often noisy period between 1940–1945

References

Delve, K. (2005) *Bomber Command 1936–1968*. Pen & Sword, Barnsley.

Flagg, R. (ed.) (2012) Memorials – Round-up. *Airfield Review*. **135**, p. 20. Airfield Research Group

Flower, S. (2002) *A Hell of A Bomb*. Tempus Publishing, Stroud.

Garbett, M. & Goulding, B. (1979) *Lancaster at War 2*. Ian Allan, London.

Hastings, M (1999) *Bomber Command*. Pan Macmillan, London.

Middlebrook, M. & Everitt, C. (2nd ed. 2011) *The Bomber Command War Diaries – An Operational Reference Book 1939–1945*. Midland Publishing, Hersham.

Pasmore, A. & Parker, N. (1995) *Ashley Walk – Its Bombing Range Landscape and History*. New Forest Research & Publications Trust, Fordingbridge.

Bogs as defence in the seventeenth century Dutch Republic

Michiel Gerding
Historisch Adviesbureau Drenthe

Introduction

Natural barriers against enemy attacks surrounded Friesland, Groningen and Drenthe, the three northernmost provinces of the Netherlands. To the west and to the north they bordered the sea (Zuiderzee and Waddenzee), to the east and to the south the border areas consisted of vast, mostly inaccessible, peatlands (mires, bogs, moors). These moors played an important role in the defence of the Dutch Republic.

The exact border between The Netherlands and Germany (Lower Saxony) was not fixed until 1825. On both sides the peatlands extended kilometres into the hinterland. They were part of the Bourtanger Moor, which covered an area of 140,000 hectares (ha).

Only at certain points, where sandy ridges penetrated the morass, were there crossings and fortresses or sconces could easily defend these places. The most important of these was the fortress

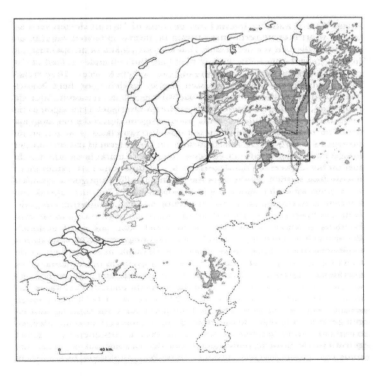

Figure 1. Peatlands in seventeenth-century Netherlands. Bogs in the west, moors in the north

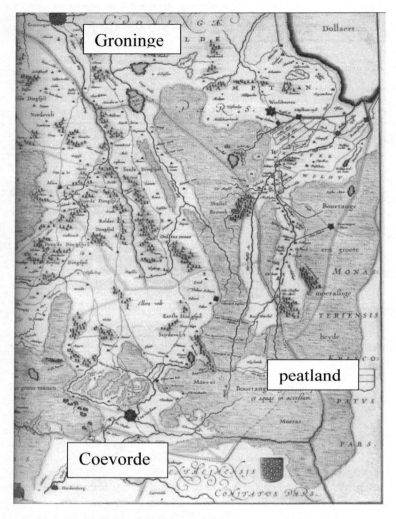

Figure 2. The Bourtanger Moor in the seventeenth century (the green-yellow area)

Coevorden (which translates into English as Oxford) in the southeast of the area. Ever since the eleventh century, it was the north's most strategically important place. The ruler who controlled Coevorden commanded the complete northern region. That is why the fortress was besieged innumerable times. Once past Coevorden the whole area lay open for the traveller, especially the main route to the most important city of the north, Groningen.

Peat as fuel

From the sixteenth century onwards, peatlands played an ever-increasing role in the Dutch economy. It was by far the most important fuel for industry and households. Therefore, in the economic upsurge of the Dutch Golden Age more and more peatland areas were began to be exploited. Two main methods of peat extraction can be distinguished. One was *dredging* and the other was *digging*. The method depended on the location of

Figure 3: Production of dredged peat. From front to back: dredging, spreading, cutting, and drying.

the peatland. In Dutch, the distinction is made between *laagveen* and *hoogveen*. There is no adequate English translation for these two concepts but *bog* for the first and *moor* for the second might come closest.

Bogs were found mainly in the low-lying western parts of The Netherlands (the provinces of Holland and Utrecht), the moors in the north. In the bogs, the peat mud was dredged from under the surface into small boats, spread out in an even layer on a field and after sufficient drying-out cut up into bricks of peat. This type of extraction left behind a steadily expanding lake causing a threat to the surrounding villages and countryside.

In the case of moors the peatlands, which consisted of about 90% water, had to be drained first. A main canal had to be dug to drain the peat area and get rid of the excess water. The draining had to be a very precise process to prevent the moors from washing away. The second indispensable function of the main canal was to offer a transport axis for the dried peat. Once a main canal reached a moor area, the waterways branched out to open up the complete production site. This process could take centuries. Once a plot had been drained sufficiently to a percentage of about 60% it could be cut up into bricks to be spread out on a field for further drying.

Once dried a brick of peat no longer soaks up any water (irreversibility), but it is essential that the peat is dried before the wet season starts. That is why peat production was a seasonal activity: dredging and digging during spring, drying during summer.

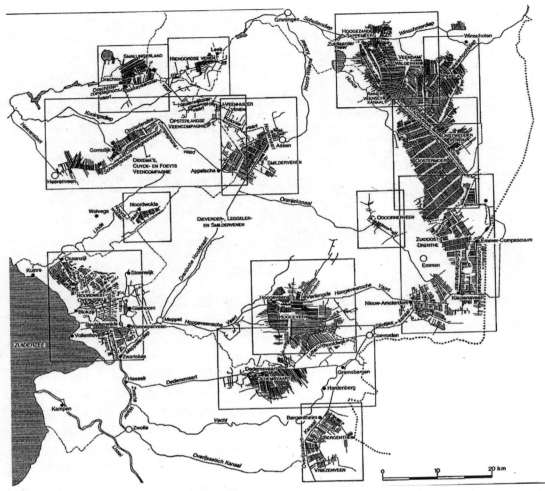

Figure 4. Production areas of peat digging 1550-1950

Figure 5. A peat digging production site. The peat is cut out of the bank in layers

Figure 6. One of the entrances to the fortress of Bourtange, 2012

The ever-increasing demand for fuel made investing in the moors in the north an attractive option for the wealthy Dutch merchants. Companies sprang up to build canals and open up moor areas. The most accessible areas of the moors first of course, so that over the centuries one can ascertain a trend from accessible to more remote.

Dutch Revolution

When the revolt of the Dutch provinces (gewesten) against their Spanish sovereign Philip II broke out in 1568, the main goals of the conflicting armies in the north were the fortress of Coevorden and the city of Groningen. In fact the first battle in the war was waged in the province of Groningen (Battle of Heiligerlee), won by the Dutch. The war would last for 80 years and ended with the treaty of Munster in 1648. In the first decades of the war, until the beginning of the seventeenth century, the north formed the main battleground with the occupancy of

Coevorden as the foremost objective. This caused much suffering in the surrounding countryside, which was plundered and put to ransom by both parties. At the beginning of the seventeenth century, 30% of all the farms in Drenthe had consequently been abandoned by their owners. From 1580 the fortress of Coevorden was strengthened by the Spaniards but after a siege of six weeks the Dutch conquered the, by then destroyed fortress. After the siege, not only Coevorden was rebuilt as the main stronghold but all along the edges of the moors, on the borders, entrenchments and sconces were erected, 10 in total. There was also one other fortress, Bourtange.

The moors were formed after the last Ice Age (10,000 years ago) when the climate became substantially warmer and wetter (Holocene). Over the centuries thick layers of peatlands arose, here sometimes more than 10 metres thick. The subsoil under the moors

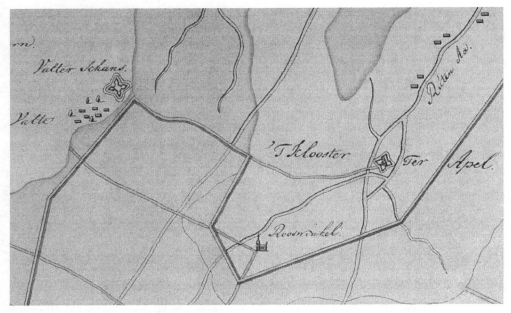

Figure 7: Seventeenth-century map of the Valther entrenchment and dike

consisted mainly of sand and boulder clay and was not completely flat. Where there were sandy ridges the moors would dry sufficiently in summer to make them passable. A few developed into regular passageways, sometimes strengthened into dikes or tracks fit for carts.

The entrenchments were located at the end of these passageways across the moors. They consisted of a simple earthwork in the form of a square in which a company of soldiers and guns could be stationed. The attacker coming across the moor would be highly exposed, with no means to take cover or spread out across the field. If he tried, he would drown in the morass.

The moors were an obstacle not only for attackers but for the local people as well. That is why we find wooden trackways in lots of places, dating back to prehistoric times. The tracks

consisted of tree trunks or planks. In The Netherlands, dozens have been identified, in Germany hundreds and in Ireland more than a thousand. The moors were also put to use by local farmers wherever that was possible. This was to obtain their own fuel of course, but more importantly for growing buckwheat. By draining the moors, a little the topsoil would dry out enough so they could set fire to the vegetation on it. In the ashes, the buckwheat was sown which in the right weather conditions would result in a high yield. The authorities considered this process to be a direct threat to the defensive qualities of the moors.

Bombing Berend

After the peace treaty of 1648, it was not long before the Dutch Republic was under attack again. Its supremacy in the sea trade was threatened by the English, which led to wars between 1652-1654 and 1665-1667. During the second English war, the belligerent bishop of Munster Bernard von Galen (nicknamed *Bombing Berend*) grabbed his chance and attacked the country from the east, concentrating on the northern provinces. His main force tried to break through form the south where he had occupied the provinces of Gelderland and Overijssel, while 500 of his soldiers attacked from the east. Helped by local knowledge they succeeded in crossing part of the moors to reach TerApel. From there they advanced along the Valtherdijk, one of the important passageways across the moors, to reach the centre of Drenthe. However, they did not get far because a company of only fifty local soldiers managed to stop them from the entrenchment of *Valtherschans* at the end of the dike.

The other entrenchments further north proved equally effective. The main army from Munster tried to break the defence from the south at the *Ommerschans*. With wooden planks and doors ripped from houses in the vicinity of Bommen Berend created a passageway across the moor. This was in vain, as fifty of his carts were blown from the improvised bridge by the guns in the entrenchment. Finally, he succeeded further to the west, mainly because Dutch troops could not get there in time. With 8,000 soldiers, he crossed Drenthe leaving a trail of destruction behind. He did not dare lay siege to the city of Groningen because his support from the east had not arrived. He holed up twenty-five kilometres east of the city, near the town of Winschoten. There he was closed in by Dutch troops. His army

Figure 8. Map of the fortress of Coevorden in the seventeenth century

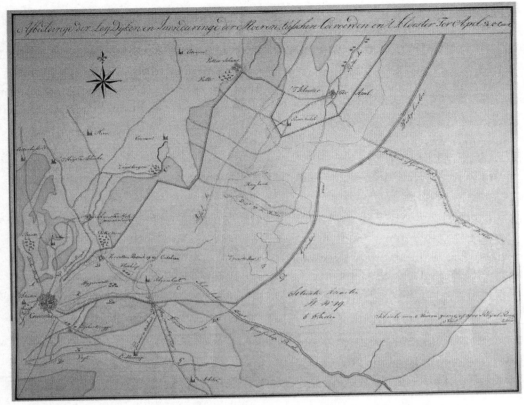

Figure 9. Map of the proposed defence system 1681. The moors in the grey area are bordered by dikes to keep the water in.

met with food shortages, disease and desertion. By the end of 1665, the Bishop realised that his position was hopeless and he pulled back across a specially created five-metre wide dike across the moor, built by thousands of farmers from Munster.

If anything, this experience made Bishop Von Galen more eager to teach the Dutch a lesson. His chance came in the *Rampjaar* (Disaster year) 1672 when the Republic was attacked from all sides by all the major European powers and the country was *reddeloos, redeloos en radeloos* (beyond saving, beyond reason, beyond hope). Again, Bommen Berend attacked the north. This time in July, he succeeded in

conquering Coevorden quickly, and within a month, he laid siege to the city of Groningen. The city however was well prepared with fortifications all around the city walls. The frequent bombardments of the Bishop's guns (that is why *Bombing Berend* got his name) could not reach the northern part of the city. Nightly sorties from the city laid waste to trenches etc., so all his efforts came to nothing. He had to admit failure with half of his soldiers sick and deserting and on the 25th of August, he began to pull back. This was a great morale boost for the country in distress, the more so when by the end of that year he was chased out of the fortress of Coevorden as well.

Figure 10. Katshaar entrenchment from the air on google earth 2013

Figure 11. Entrance to the Katshaar entrenchment, 2012

Strategic peat

In the aftermath of the Rampjaar, the authorities realised once more the strategic importance of Coevorden and the string of moors. The fortress was further strengthened according to the latest concepts and a plan was made to keep the moors as wet as possible. It was proposed to build an extensive system of small dikes (*leidijken*) to keep the water in and maintain the system of entrenchments. Farmers were expressly forbidden to make cuts in the *leidijken* to get rid of excess water.

After 1672, the moors gradually lost their meaning as a defence system. During the following century, there were no attacks on the country, which lost its dominance in international politics. The maintenance of the defence line became more and more of a burden and one which nobody was prepared to carry. When later on the need for fuel rose, again the moors literally went up in smoke.

Only a few entrenchments remain as witnesses of those enervating times.

Bibliography

Gerding, M.A.W. (1995) *Viereeuwenturfwinning. De verveningen in Groningen, Friesland, Drenthe en Overijsseltussen 1550 en 1950.* Wageningen.

Gerding, M.A.W. (2013) *Geopark de Hondsrug. Expedition Traces of battle.* Borger (in preparation).

Versfelt, H.J. (2012) *Venen en schansen.* In: *Nieuwe Drentse Volksalmanak 2012*, pp. 51-96.

Versfelt, H.J. (2004) *Kaarten van Drenthe 1500-1900.* Groningen.

The battlefield at Northampton (Wars of the Roses, 1460)

Peter Burley

The Battlefields Trust

Abstract

The exact site of the battle of Northampton (10 July 1460, Wars of the Roses) - and of the Lancastrian field defences around which it was fought – are a matter of academic controversy with two rival sites. This new interpretation of the battle (and the campaign leading up to it) uses fresh thinking about the topography of the River Nene's floodplain, and about the weather in early July 1460, to suggest redrawing the map of the battlefield. This new landscape seeks to make more sense of the events on the day and reconcile all the contemporary accounts. The enquiry also serves to focus attention on the most likely areas in which to concentrate efforts to find the Lancastrian camp.

Keywords: Wars of Roses, Northampton, flood plain

Introduction

The work here has been carried out under the aegis of the Battlefields Trust (BT). The Trust is a national charity (Registered No. 1017387, www. battlefieldstrust.com) whose aims are to save battlefields from destruction by motorways, housing developments etc., provide a range of battlefield-related activities and information, including the quarterly journal *Battlefield*, battlefield walks and conferences, liaise with local and national organisations to preserve battlefields for posterity and improve the interpretation and presentation of battlefields.

A team from the Trust (Peter Burley, Michael Elliott and Harvey Watson) was commissioned about ten years ago to take a fresh look at the battles of St Albans (1455 and 1461 in the Wars of the Roses) with an emphasis on detailed knowledge of the topography of these two battlefields. This led to the publication of a book in 2007. Colleagues in Northampton liked what they read and asked the team to take the same approach to their battle of 1460 in the Wars of the Roses. The work here is the result of a team effort. It is currently on hold and will be integrated in due course with a project on all of the Wars of the Roses battlefields which is being compiled at the University of Huddersfield. This present paper presented at the War & Peat conference in September 2013 gives an opportunity to draw attention to our specific work.

There has been a great deal of interest in the land (posited as the location of the battlefield) between the Delapre golf course (most clearly shown in Figure 6 below) and the River Nene in recent years for development proposals of various types, but all involving disturbance of the top soil. This has generated much academic study of the whole area between Hardingstone in the south and the river in preparation for the publication by Foard & Partida of a *Northampton Battlefield Conservation Plan* and a *Northampton Battlefield Assessment* – both awaiting publication as at 2013 and drawn on throughout this paper by kind permission of the authors. The Plan and the Assessment will form the yardstick against which future development proposals will be judged for their impact on the archaeology of the battlefield.

This paper is a suggestion about avenues of future enquiry about the battlefield with the focus on locating the exact site of the Lancastrian artillery camp. This was the seat of most of the fighting, the point of departure for the rout that followed the battle and in which most of the casualties incurred. It starts with an appraisal of what is known about the Lancastrian camp, and moves on to an assessment of the weather conditions in the days before the battle (6 to 9 July 1460) and how that affected both the movements of the armies and the landscape. The paper then speculates on the state of the ground south of Northampton on the day of the battle (10 July 1460) and how that might have affected the deployments and the subsequent action. Despite a great deal of published information on the battle and the battlefield, there are some key questions apparently still unresearched.

Another dimension to this enquiry is to look at the apparent contradictions between the written chronicles as to where the battle was fought. The suggestion made here may help to resolve this problem.

Finding the Lancastrian camp will not just be an important academic and archaeological achievement, it will also be of great value to local tourism, sharpen up the heritage protection of the battlefield, and allow better commemoration of those who gave their lives in this battle.

Two examples of the team's methodology used in a different context for the work on the Battles of St Albans may be helpful. Firstly, conventional wisdom had it that the Abbot of St Albans' account of the First Battle of St Albans (1455) was suspect because, in some passages, although he used identifiable Latin words in grammatical Latin sentences, the words seemed to make no sense. The team took one of the suspect passages (about events in the Abbey after the battle) and commissioned its own translation with strict instructions that the translators did not attempt to impose any meaning of their own on the words. This translation was then read against the known layout of the Abbey and its out-buildings in 1455. Seen through the lens of this detailed topographical information, the Abbot's words were terse but accurate and informative. What was surprising was the Abbey's layout rather than the words the Abbot had used to describe it.

The second was that none of the chronicles mentioned the weather on the day of the second Battle (17 February 1461). This was unusual and it made us feel we were missing a trick. We contacted the Meteorological Office to access their database of historic weather records. They were able to tell us that if it was not raining on that day, then rain would have been threatening. This explained the pattern of use and non-use of longbows that day. Longbows cannot be allowed to get wet. In the morning's fighting, Yorkists under cover had been able to shoot at Lancastrians in the open, who had not been able to shoot back. In the open air fighting in the afternoon, neither side used longbows. Now we knew why, the likely weather conditions were not favourable.

The Campaign and the Battle

A brief account of the campaign and the battle is needed for context. The whole theatre of war stretched from Ireland to Calais, but focused on a corridor from Sandwich in Kent to Coventry in the East Midlands.

The Yorkist army under the Earl of March (the future Edward IV), the Earl of Warwick ("Warwick the Kingmaker") and Baron Fauconberg landed at Sandwich from Calais on 26 June 1460. They reached London on 2 July after a triumphal march through Kent. Here they besieged the Lancastrian garrison in the Tower of London but nearly doubled their numbers with new recruits

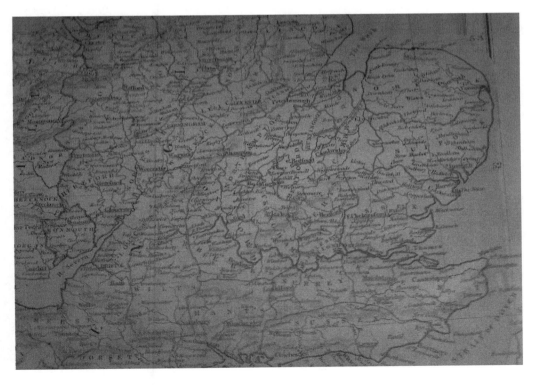

Figure 1. The theatre of war © Peter Burley

and were able to dispatch most of their troops northwards on 5th July leaving the Tower to wither on the vine.

The Lancastrians had been expecting the invasion, but did not know until the end of June if it would be from France, or Ireland where the Duke of York was based. To cover all options, the Royal Family, the Court and their army had moved to Coventry. The one chronicler who addressed their strategy was Bale, who said that they planned to fall back to the redoubt of the Isle of Ely while seeking to give battle on favourable terms if they could. This explains their line of march due eastwards from Coventry when news of the Yorkists' capture of London reached them (probably on 4th July).

On 5th July the Yorkists left London to march up Watling Street (the A5). The Lancastrians, led by the Duke of Buckingham, had a powerful artillery train with them, and this slowed their march. It was clear that they could not outpace the Yorkists and the two armies would encounter each other somewhere in the East Midlands even though the Lancastrians had less ground to cover. This suited Buckingham well because his tactic would be to fortify strong ground and invite the Yorkists to launch a suicidal attack against his artillery. This was the tactic the French had used against the English to devastating effect at the battle of Castillon in 1453. Buckingham was an experienced – even if not very successful – soldier and he

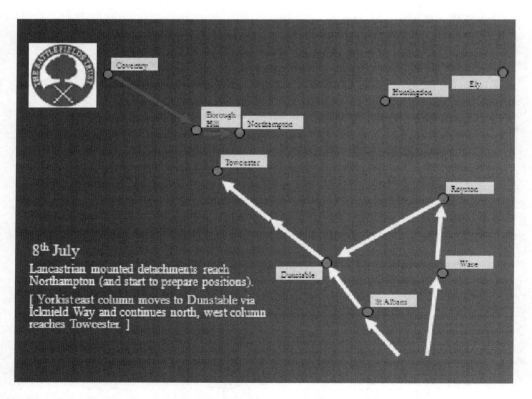

Figure 2. The movements of the armies before the battle © Battlefields Trust

had most likely reconnoitred the route from Coventry to Ely to identify the good defensive positions along it.

For their part, the only successful outcome for the Yorkists was to defeat and kill or capture Henry VI. Not attacking the Lancastrians was not an option. They had, however, an ace up their sleeve in the form of Lord Grey of Ruthin, one of the Lancastrian commanders, who had already agreed to turn whatever position the Lancastrians held as soon as the Yorkists attacked it. Thus both sides thought they had a winning strategy and the behaviour of both armies (and their commanders) makes sense. The Yorkists had the advantage here because they knew that the Lancastrian army was fatally compromised while their enemies did not.

By 6th July the Lancastrians had reached, according to Cardinal Coppini, their chosen position to make a stand. This was in the valley between Borough and Beacon Hills just east of Daventry where the Iron Age "Burnt Walls Fort" on the valley floor appeared to offer the perfect and unturnable defensive position. At this point the weather took a hand. According to Coppini, "Fortune", who favoured Warwick, sent so much rain (on the 7th) that the Lancastrian position became untenable and they had to abandon it.

The Trust's team put some store by Cardinal Coppini's account because he presented the campaign as a moral tale of divine providence. It would have been positively counter-productive for him to have fabricated evidence. What lay behind Coppini's account was that the Yorkists had done a deal with the

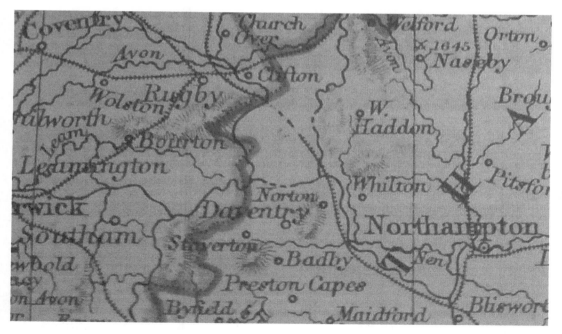

Figure 3. The first Lancastrian position between Beacon and Borough Hills © Peter Burley

Papacy whereby they would join a crusade to recover Constantinople in return for the Lancastrian army being excommunicated. The Yorkists carried Papal Bulls with them designed to be read just before battle commenced. This theological twist to the campaign and the battle was to have other implications, but the one that matters here is the added credibility it gives to Coppini's evidence.

The flooding forced the Lancastrians to use a Roman road on higher ground (and a bridge over the Nene/Avon River kept in good repair in the Middle Ages) running east to Northampton from the north of Daventry. Their army reached Northampton in two columns on the 8th and 9th and, literally, started digging in and preparing their artillery camp to await the inevitable Yorkist attack. They may have been using a pre-existing

landscape feature that lent itself to being adapted readily as a field fortification.

The Yorkists paused at Towcester and then pressed on to Northampton to reach it early on 10th July. After the customary exchange of heralds, the Yorkists deployed off the London Road (from Towcester) and attacked the Lancastrian artillery camp. The Lancastrians had time to fire one salvo of artillery before, again, the weather took a hand. All the chroniclers agree that there was a cloud-burst as the Yorkists charged the camp. It rendered the Lancastrian gunpowder useless, it would also have written off using their longbows, it caused a small watercourse beside the camp to burst its banks and flood their entrenchments and it turned the approach to the camp into a sea of mud.

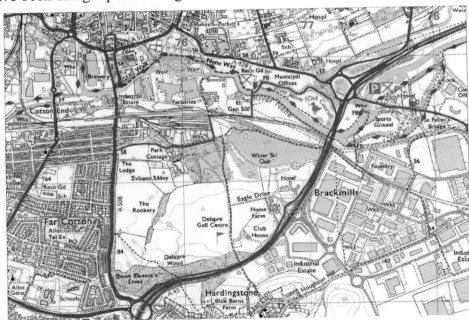

Figure 4. The Registered Battlefield (continuous red line) as identified by English Heritage by kind permission of Glenn Foard and Tracey Partida from Foard &Partida (2013) *Northampton Battlefield Assessment.*

The Yorkists pressed home their attack in the mud and were, exactly on schedule, helped to scale the field work's ramparts by Lord Grey of Ruthin's men. There was a sharp hand to hand fight inside the camp. Those Lancastrians who stood and fought, which included Buckingham and several of their commanders, were killed; Henry VI was captured and most of the rest fled north towards the illusion of safety behind the walls of Northampton. It was here that the heaviest casualties were incurred when most of the fugitives drowned trying to cross the River Nene.

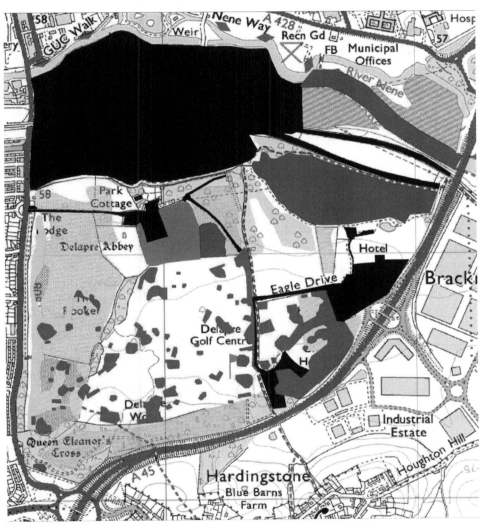

Figure 5: Location map for the areas also showing approximate extent of destruction and disturbance within the Registered battlefield (Black: developed; Grey: garden; Blue: quarried/new river channel; Red: golf course tees, bunkers and related earthmoving; red stipple: ridge and furrow levelled; red hatched: water; yellow: bunds; green: surviving ridge and furrow from lidar data), by kind permission of Glenn Foard and Tracey Partida from Foard &Partida (2013) *Northampton Battlefield Assessment.*

The Lancastrian Artillery Camp

What are we actually looking for and what are the parameters for its location?

The artillery camp had to be between Hardingstone and the River Nene and east of the London Road. It had to be near enough the London Road, and on firm enough ground, to bring heavy artillery to it. It would also make more sense if it was near enough to the London Road to bring it under artillery fire. It had to be on firm dry ground at no immediate apparent risk of flooding in order to protect the gunpowder that was an integral part of the Lancastrian plan. The ditches were reported as being dry at the start of the battle but becoming flooded during it. This suggests a location where the water-table was well below the normal ground surface. It also had to enjoy clear fields of fire in all directions. This meant it could not be in a wood or next to a large building.

The structure was described in some detail in the chronicles. It was surrounded by trenches deep enough for sharpened stakes to be buried in them. It had ramparts too tall for a man to climb. This suggests ditches about around six feet deep with the soil making ramparts around six feet high from ground level. The ramparts had to be stout enough to mount artillery. The overall structure needed to accommodate, if not all, then at least enough of the Lancastrian army to be able to win the battle. This figure is going to be measured in thousands rather than hundreds of men.

Conventional archaeology and related disciplines will be used in due course to try to find this structure, but there is one other factor to be taken into account. At most, the Lancastrians only had 48 hours to prepare this position. The smart money is on them using some pre-existing feature whereby most of the digging had been done by someone else already and they only had to embellish and fortify it. (This was exactly what the Earl of Warwick was to do with an Iron Age earthwork at St Albans only six months later at the Second Battle of St Albans on 17 February 1461). Using a known and reconnoitred position makes far more sense than the Lancastrians wandering round the countryside hoping to find the ideal site by chance.

No trace of such an earthwork is visible today, but the same is true of scores of English civil structures of a similar size and shape as the Queen's Sconce at Newark. This structure is the size of a castle, but built entirely of earth.

The disputed Locations

There is no dispute that the battle took place south of Northampton, but the exact location of the Lancastrian camp is still not settled.

There are two schools of thought, both based on the landmarks provided by the chroniclers. These landmarks, from north to south, are the Nene, Delapre Abbey, the Eleanor Cross on the London Road and the village of Hardingstone. The "traditional" school, for want of a better term, puts the greatest weight on the comment made by many chroniclers that the camp had the river to its back, and must, therefore, have been located on the (present day) south bank of the river. The other interpretation gives greater weight to those chroniclers who place the camp nearer to Delapre Abbey, the Eleanor Cross and Hardingstone than to the river. They appear to be mutually contradictory. For completeness, English Heritage has favoured a more southerly location on the basis of textual analysis but covered its bets by registering much of the ground between Hardingstone and the river.

The Trust's team looked for some way to square this circle, and we explored the implications of the weather between 7th and 10th July for the terrain.

The Weather 7 – 10 July 1460

We have seen that Coppini reported a deluge in the area on 7th July. De Waurin in his account of the campaign recorded rain on 8th and 9th July. Everyone recorded a cloud burst and flooding on 10th July.

The team wanted to explore the implications for the rest of the Nene's river system of the area occupied by the Lancastrian camp outside Daventry, being flooded. We were helped by the eminent military historian, local resident and expert, Martin Marix Evans. He had identified the valley between Borough and Beacon Hills as the only position matching (and matching exactly) Coppini's brief description. This identification requires a leap of imagination in the abstract, but is utterly obvious when the site is visited. This valley is drained by the WeedonBec, a tributary of the Nene meeting it at

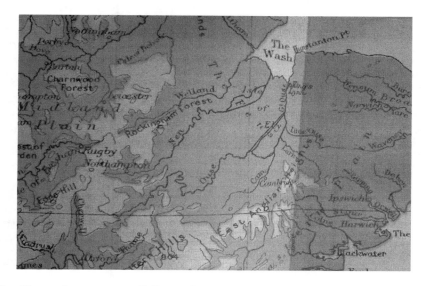

Figure 6. The Nene river system © Peter Burley

Weedon, which is the watercourse that must have flooded out Burnt Walls Fort. Weedon is still a high flood risk area, with serious flooding as recently as 1998.

If more rain fell on 8th and 9th July, then the summer of 1460 looks very like the summer of 2007 (where extensive and severe flooding occured after prolonged intense rainfall). The effect would be to overload the river system and innundate the floodplains with water, with a final surge arriving actually during the battle on the 10th.

The Landscape South of Northampton on 10 July 1460

A simple question is whether the ground between the Nene and Delapre Abbey was an active floodplain in 1460. This is where the scientific archaeology runs out. A look at the contour lines and the current flood risk assessments suggests that it was, but a counter argument is that the current flood risk has been created by subsequent flood prevention measures further downstream. There is also some inconclusive evidence of medieval buildings in this area, but were they built to withstand seasonal flooding? We do not know. The way to settle this is to establish whether this ground was used as seasonal water meadows in the Middle Ages. This is where the team suggests that research might most usefully be focused.

What would be the implications of filling this floodplain with water on 8th to 10th July 1460? It would not have prevented movement across this landscape either by wading or by using the causeways across it. It would, though, have ruled out any military engineering work in it. The relevant contour line runs just north of Delapre Abbey, so sunken trenches and serious digging would only have been viable south of the Abbey.

This is perhaps even better illustrated by one of those lovely Victorian maps using shading to represent contour lines (Figure 8).

The most interesting – and, for us, compelling – implication is that this potential flooding moves the Eleanor Cross and river (or its south bank) much closer together. The statements that the Lancastrian camp was near the Eleanor Cross and that it had its back to the river cease to be mutually exclusive. Everyone may have been right after all. It also gives the floodplain a more poignant status on the battlefield. Many of those who drowned in the river may not have done so in the main stream below the town walls, but in the wide expanse of flooded meadows leading to the river's normal channel. It is worth remembering that the flight from the Lancastrian camp was a panicked stampede with men in armour falling over each other.

There is one piece of evidence that may be relevant here. There is an unsubstantiated report in the nineteenth century of bodies, weapons and armour being found when the piers for a railway viaduct were built across the flood plain. This cannot be Lancastrians fleeing from a camp on the present day river bank – they would be running towards the Yorkists and not away from

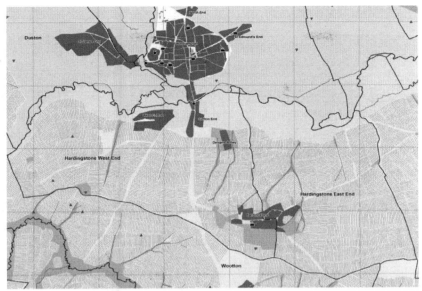

Figure 7. The Nene Flood Plain and its Environs, by kind permission of Glenn Foard and Tracey Partida from Foard & Partida (2013) *Northampton Battlefield Assessment.*

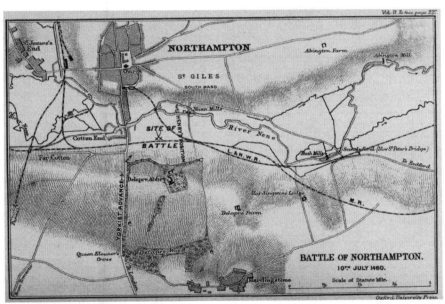

Figure 8. The area with contours shown by shading and railway lines in the Victorian period by kind permission of Glenn Foard and Tracey Partida from Foard & Partida (2013) *Northampton Battlefield Assessment.*

them. It is also most unlikely that it can be the site of the Lancastrian camp because all the bodies in it were removed and buried elsewhere shortly after the battle. What it could be is a site of mass drowning in the flooded meadows where the bodies – with their weapons and armour – would have been hidden from view under water.

Conclusion: Why Worry about the Location?

Finding the Lancastrian camp is the key to understanding the battle and to understanding the chronicles about it. As well as helping with battlefield interpretation and local tourism, finding the camp provides the point of departure for looking for any surviving human remains. This is important for honouring the fallen and giving them a proper commemoration, which they still do not enjoy.

The team addressed this same issue at St Albans. We located the main burial site for the Second Battle of 1461 and found that the 2,500 or so people buried there had been deliberately interred without Christian rites. This is not the place to explore the theological implications, but the local vicar held a very moving Requiem Mass for their souls in 2011 – a mere 550 years late! - as the finale to a two-day academic conference about the battle. Were human remains to be found at Northampton then they, similarly, could be laid to proper rest.

We suggest that a reinterpretation of the battlefield and of the chronicles in the light of topographical and meteorological information may help point future archaeologists in the most profitable direction.

Lastly, this project illustrates the work of the Battlefields Trust, not just to collaborate with English Heritage to locate battlefields more securely, but also to understand them better and to honour the memory of those who gave their lives on them.

Acknowledgements

This project and research would not have been possible without the support of the Battlefields Trust and colleagues in it, the generous sharing of their knowledge by Glenn Foard and Tracey Partida and the local wisdom and expertise of Martin Marix Evans.

Bibliography

Foard, G. & Partida, T. (2013) *Northampton Battlefield Conservation Plan*. Northampton Borough Council.

Foard, G. & Partida, T. (2013) *Northampton Battlefield Assessment*. Northampton Borough Council. (This assessment contains a comprehensive account of all the primary sources for the battle and the campaign, and these are set out as an appendix below. It also contains a comprehensive bibliography of secondary sources on the battle and the campaign and on local archaeology and geography, which is not set out separately).

Battlefields Trust (2010) *Proceedings of the Battlefields Trust Conference on the Battle of Northampton, 1460, held at Northampton Museum on 10 July 2010 to make the 500th Anniversary of the Battle*. On-line publication only at http://www.battlefieldstrust.com/page78.asp

APPENDIX: PRIMARY SOURCES

This appendix is a comprehensive compilation of the primary sources for the battle with relevant extracts. With some additions, it is taken directly by kind permission from Foard, G. & Partida, T. (2013) *Northampton Battlefield Assessment*.

A Short English Chronicle

'*...Erle of Marche, and the Erle of Warwyke, the Lord Faconbryge, the Lorde Bowser, and his sonnes, with myche other pepull of Kent, Southesex, and Esex, tawarde the Kynge with grete ordenaunce; and the Erle of Salysbury, the Lorde Cobham, and Sir John Wenlock, were lefte in the cite of London with the meire. And forthe with the Lord Cobham and the shoreffes went and laide grete ordenaunce a yenes the Toure on the townesyde, and Sir John Wenlok, an[d] Harow mercer, kept on Seint Katerynes side, and myche harme done on bothe parties. And in all placis of London was gretewatche for doute oftresoun. And then they skyrmysed to gedir, and myche harme was done dayly. And on the Thorsdye, the ixth (fn. 23) day of Julle, was the bataylle be syde Northhampton in the Newfelde be tween Harsyngton and Sandyfforde, and ther was the kynge take in his tente. And ther was slayne the Duke of Bockyngham, the Erle of Shrovysbury, the Vycounte Bemonde, the Lord Egremonde, and Sir William Lucy, and many other knyghtes and squyers, and many comyners were drowned. And than the Erle of Marche, and the Erle of Warwyke, with oþerlordis, brought the kynge to Northampton with myche rialte.*'

(J. Gairdner (ed.) *Three fifteenth-century chronicles: With historical memoranda by John Stowe*, Camden Society 1880. http://www.british-history. ac.uk/report.aspx?compid=58661 Date accessed: 22 March 2013)

An English Chronicle

'*The kyng at Northamptone lay atte Freres [Friars], and had ordeyned there a strong and a myghty feeld, in the medowys beside the Nonry, armed and arayed wythe gonnys, hauyng the ryuer at hys back.*

The erles with the nombre of lx Ml, as it was sayd, came to Northamptone, and sent certayne bysshps to the kyng besechyng hym that in eschewyng of effusyone of Crysten blood he wolde admytte and suffre the erles for to come to his presence to declare thaym self as thay were. The duk of Bukynghame that stode besyde the kyng, sayde unto thaym, 'Ye come nat as bysshoppes for to trete for pease, but as men of armes;' because they broughte with thayme a notable company of men of armes. They answered and sayde, 'We come thus for suerte of oure persones, for they that bethe aboute the kyng by the natoure frendes.' 'Forso the,' sayde the duk, 'the erle of Warrewyk shalle nat come to the kynges presence, and yef he come he shalle dye.' The messyngers retorned agayne, and tolde thys to the erles.

Thanne the erle of Warrewyk sent an herowde [herald] afarmes to the kyng, besechyng that he myghte haue ostages of saaf goyng and commung, and he wolde come naked to his presence, but he myghte nat be herde. And the iiide tyme he sente to the kyng and sayde that at ii howres after none, he wolde speke with hym, or elles dye in the feeld.

The archebysshoppe of Caunterbury sent a bysshoppe of this lond to the kyng with an instruccione, the whyche dyd nat hys message indyfferently, but exorted and coraged the kynges part for to fygte, as thay sayde that were there. And another tyme he was sent to the kyng by the commones, and thanne he came natayene [again], but pryuely departed awey. The bysshop of Herforde, a Whyte Frere, the kynges confessoure, ded the same: wherfore after the batayle he was commytted to the castelle of Warrewyk, where he was long in pryson.

Thanne on the Thursday the Xth day of Juylle, the yere of oure Lorde Mlcccclx, ay ii howres after none, the sayde erles of Marche and Warrewyk lete crye thoroughe the felde, that no man should laye hand vpponne the kyng ne on the commune peple, but onely on the lordes, khyghtes and squyers: thenne the trumpettes blew vp, and bothe hostes countred and faughte togedre half an oure. The lorde Gray, that was the kynges vawewarde, brake the feelde and came to the erles party, whyche caused sauacione of many a mannys lyfe: many were slayne, and many were fled, and were drouned in the ryuer.

The duk of Bukyngham, the erle of Shrouesbury, the lorde Beaumont, the lorde Egremount were slayne by the Kentyssh men besyde the kynges tent, and meny other knyghtes and squyers. The ordenaunce of tyhe kynges gonnes avayled nat, for that day was so grete rayne, that the gonnes lay depe in the water, and so were queynt and myghte nat be shott.'

J S Davies (ed.) *An English Chronicle of the reigns of Richard II, Henry IV, Henry V and Henry VI,* Camden Society 1856, 96.

Gregory's Chronicle

'...so forthe to Northehampton. And there they mete with the kynge and foughte manly with the kyngys lordys and mayny, but there was moche favyr in that fylde unto the Erle of Warwycke. And there they toke the kynge, and made newe offycers of the londe, as the chaunceler and tresyrar and othyr, but they occupyde not fo[r]the-with, but a-bode aseson of the comyng of Duke of York owte of Irlonde. And in that fylde was slayne the Duke of Bokyngham, stondyng stylle at hys tente, the Erle of Schrovysbury, the Lord Bemond, and the Lord Egremond, with many othyr men. Ande many men were drownyd by syde the fylde in the revyr at a mylle. And that goode knight Syr Wylliam Lucy that dwellyd de Northehampton hyrde the gonne schotte, and come unto the fylde to have holpyn [t]e kynge, but the fylde was done or that he come; an one of the Staffordys was ware of hys comynge, and lovyd that knyghtys wyffe and hatyd hym, and a-non causyd hys dethe.'

There is a further reference in Gregory's chronicle to one single salvo of artillery having been fired.

J. Gairdiner (ed.) *The Historical Collections of a Citizen of London in the Fifteenth Century* Camden Society, new series XVII, 1886 (http://www.british-history.ac.uk/report.aspx?compid=45559 Date accessed: 22 March 2013).

John Bennet's Chronicle

'*Et juxta Northampton Castra metatus est rex in campo inter vill amque vocatur Hardyngeston et domummoni alium que voatur de Pratis cum 20,000 hominum bellatorum, versus quem venit Comes Marchie, Comes Warwyci et dominus la Faucumbrege cum 60,000 men. Et vi Idus Julii (10th July 1460) pro tunc die Jovis pugnabant. Etibi interfectus est dux Bukynggamir et Comes Salope et eciam dominus de Bellomonte scilicet Bewmont et dominus la Egremont et multi alii ex parte regis circa numerum quad ringentorum. Et sic Comes Marchie et Comes Warwici expectavertunt cum regeapud Northampton. Et EpiscopusWyntonensis Cancellarius, scopus Dunolmensis clericus privatis igilli, fugerunt. Et comes de Wyltshyre latenter et alii qi multa sinimicicias fecerunt contra ducem Eboraci et dominum ....*'

Harriss, G.L. and Harriss, M.A., (eds.) *John Benet's Chronicle for the Years 1400 to 1462 Camden Miscellany, Vol. XXIV*, London, Camden Society, Fourth Series, vol. 9,1972, 225-6.

Waurin

'*De la bataille de Northampton ou fut princ le roy Henry et le duc de Buckingham, le comte de Beaumont et autres grans seigneurs, des quelz aulceuns furent a prez de capitez .....et autres qui aussi es toient assamblez a Northampton, a la garde de la quele ville es toit commis de par le roy de seigneur de Greriffin avec de trieze a quatorse cens hommes, et le roy et son ost es toient en ung parc qoultre la ville sue une petite riviere, Lors le comtes de La Marche et de Warewic tyrerent vers la ville de Northampton, venans de Callaic oui lza voient fait leur assemble ella que le ville de Northampton qui estune des fortes ville d'Angleterre, qui, ce non obstant, fut emportee dassault aprez que le capittaine les rut escarmuchies lespace de heure et demie, syduar alassault environ demye houre depuis quel edit seigneur de Greriffin se futretrait a la porte, avec lequel entrerent par force sesannemus, quy pillerent la ville en passant oultre et aprochant lost du roy prochain de la, qui ortiffies sur la dite riviere merveilleusement et fait un tre fort parcq, lequel incontinent ilzassaillirent tresasprement. Si dura peu ledit assault, car it avoit en la compaignie due royde dens le parcq plusieurs quy estoient Warewics en corage, et mesmes le canonniers, quy par chete maulvais en avoient mis nulles pierres en ursengiens, parq uoywuantilz bouterent le feude densnen saillirent que les tampons, laquele chose parchevant les seigneurs quy dedens le parcq estoient, par maniere subitterom pirentung quartier dudit parcq purissir et sen fuyrent en Northumberland. Si fuerent illec prins le roy, le duc de Buckingham le seigneur de Beaumont .....'*

William Hardy and E L C P Hardy (eds.) *Recuiel des Croniques et Anchiennes Istories de la Grant Bretagne, a present nomme Engleterre,* (Rolls Series 1891) V, 322-3.

'... and on that, without waiting any longer, they sent their men forward in good order to invade their enemies. Soon after the said herald had left, the Duke of Buckingham called together all the lords who were around the King and said to them: 'Good lords, today it is necessary for us to fight, because our enemies are marching forward', and they all replied 'we will stand our ground, because there are enough of us', which there were, around 50,000 [Waurin had already computed the Yorkists as 80,000 strong]. And to him who says that those who reckon without one's host customarily reckons twice over; I say to him that it is very difficult to guard against a traitor, as you can hear, because before going into battle the Earl of Warwick had ordered his war chiefs to warn their men that all who bore the ravestocnoue [the black ragged staff the badge of Grey of Ruthin] were to be saved, for it was they who were to give them entry to the park. After the Earl of Warwick had had his men instructed in what they must do, he sent forward the advance guard, commanded by Lord Fauconberg, which descended to the bottom of the valley; and the earls of March and Warwick led the [main] battle, which pushed so far forward that they came to fight hand to hand in a great struggle which lasted three hours and would have lasted much longer had Sir Ralph Grey not betrayed the Duke of Buckingham by allowing the Earl of March inside the camp on his side, as a result of which there was much killing. King Henry was captured by an archer called Henry Montfort and the Duke of Buckingham, Lord Chursbury, Viscount Beaumont, Sir Thomas Fyderme and many other great lords were killed. In this defeat the dead numbered 12,000 and the prisoners were a great multitude.'

Translation from National Army Museum report 1994.

Also, on page 196, Waurin records that it rained on the 8th and 9th of July 1460 while the Lancastrians were preparing their position at Northampton.

John Stone's Chronicle

'...*iuxtae andem villa merat bellum in campo, And for the feldys name of that oon parte on the northest syde it is callyd Cowe medewe. And that othir parte is I callyd Menthyn feld. And for the othir part is I callyd of tyme Sandyng ford bregge nexte the towne. On the estsyde there is a water melle [that] is called Sandford melle'.*

He also states that the Archbishop viewed the battle from the hill *'qui vocatur Crux sine capite'*

W.G.Searle (ed.) *The Chronicle of John Stone* (Cambridge 1902)

Whethamstede

The Lancastrians had a strongly fortified camp equipped with engines of war : '*Dominus Rex suam posuerat castra metationem' and 'tam de machinis suis bellicis, et fortitudine castra metationis'*.

H.T. Riley (ed.) Register in Registra quorundam Abbatum Monasterii S Albani, Rolls Series 1872, 372-4.

Bale's Chronicle

'*And on the friday and Saterday suyng they brake agein and departed in two weyes that is to wite oonwey toward Seint Albons and that other wey toward Ware because that the seid lordes wold mete wt the king and countre wt his ost and lett and stopp them their entre into the Isle of Ely, wher then the kings counceill hadde proposed as was seid to have left the king and for their strength and saufgardther to have hiden. But in as moche as the kings counseill might not opteyn that purpose they set a feld beside Northampton and the dir cam the seid lordes and their peple departed in iiii Batailles and ther was nombred than of them C lx M and of the kings Ost xx M. And on the thursday was Bataill in which wer slain in the kings Ost the Duk of Buk, the ErleShrovesbury the lord Beaumond the lorde Egremond and many other gentiles and of other to the nombre of l [50] persones and on the other partie not over viii persones...*'

On page 151 Bale describes the Lancastrian strategy of seeking to fall back on the Isle of Ely.

Ralph Flenley (ed) *Six Town Chronicles Of England* , Oxford 1911, 151 (copy from National Army Museum report 1994)

William of Worcester

J. Stevenson, (ed.) *Letters and Papers illustrative of the Wars of the English in France*, Rolls Series 2:2 1861-4, ii, 773.

Polydore Vergil

'*Then Warwick, seeing that his enemies posed no danger, crossed over to Ireland to the Duke of York and consulted, dealt, and deliberated with him about what to do. This done, he promptly returned to Calais and reported to his father and Earl Edward of March that the duke's opinion that they should cross over to England with a ready army and, omitting no opportunity for successful action, to trouble King Henry with their fighting until he himself could come to their aid with a large number of soldiers. They liked this plan, and, coming over to England, set out for London. For this city was not strengthened by any garrisons, nor did it abound in equipment for war, and so it was of necessity open to all comers. Here they armed men of the lower classes and whoever else came running to them, prepared the other things needful for war, then with their assembled army they marched on Northampton, where the king had come a little earlier. The queen, learning of these things, and aided by the resources of the Dukes of Somerset and Buckingham (since she was more concerned about things of this kind than was the king, for he acquiesced in her decisions alone), assembled an army with high spirits, summoning nobles of her faction from all over, who each made his appearance with a company of armed men, and in a short time she assembled her forces. The king, after discovering that, thanks to the efforts of the queen and the dukes, he was in possession of no mean army, decided to come to blows with his enemies, and encamped outside the town in the nearby meadows, along the river Nene. And when he had learned the enemy was at hand, he went to meet them and gave the signal for battle. The enemy did not shun a fight. The battle was joined early in the morning, and it was now noon when the king was defeated. A little less than 10,000 died in that fight, including Duke Humphrey of Buckingham, John Talbot Earl of Shrewsbury, an outstanding young man who resembled his ancestors, Thomas Lord Egremont, and very many others. And the number of those captured was very great, because many horsemen had elected to send away their horses and fight on foot, as was their habit. Above all, King Henry fell into his enemies' clutches, a man born for human misery, calamity, and woe. The rest of the nobles who escaped this catastrophe, together with the queen and Prince Edward, fled to Yorkshire, and thence to County Durham, so that there they might rebuild their army, or, if there was no hope for renewing the war at present, continue on to Scotland, there to await until a better opportunity for success was offered. The victorious earls led Henry to London as a captive.*

Then they convened a parliament and arranged for his deposition. The Duke of York, assured of this victory, immediately appeared out of Ireland, and, entering the parliament, sat in the king's chair.'

Polydore Vergil *Anglica Historia*, 1555 (http://www.philological.bham.ac.uk/polverg/ accessed 26/03/2013)

Edward Hall, *The Union of the Noble and Illustre Famielies of Lancastre and York*, London 1809, 244-5 (http://openlibrary.org/books/OL7060976M/Hall's_chronicle)

Leland

'There was a great bataille faught in *Henry the vi. tyme at Northampton on the hille withoute the Southe Gate, where is a right goodly crosse, caullid, as I remembre, the Quenes Crosse, and many Walsch men were drounid yn Avon (sic) Ryver at this conflict. Many of them that were slayn were buried at de la Pray : and sum S.John's Hospitale.'*

Toulmin Smith, L. (ed), *The Itinerary of John Leland in or about the years 1535-1543*, 1907-10,I, 8.

Milanese State Papers

"When the King heard of Warwick's arrival, he betook himself to a valley between two mountains, a strong place. But Fortune, who throughout showed herself so favourable to Warwick, willed that it should rain so heavily that they were forced to come out of that place and encounter Warwick."

Calendar of State Papers and Manuscripts existing in the Archives and Collections of Milan, Vol. 1, ed. A.B. Hinds. London 1913 (and published in translation), page 27. (Cardinal Coppini to the Duke of Milan on 6 August 1460).

Venetian State Papers

Reference on pp 92-3 to the Lancastrians being deemed to have been excommunicated at the time of the battle.

Calendar of State Papers and Manuscripts relating to English Affairs existing in the Archives and Collections of Venice, Vol 1, ed. R Brown. Longmans 1864 (and published in translation).

Dancing the Highland Fling in the face of the enemy on the Western Front, 1916. © Ian D. Rotherham

In to the bog: 'Silently and in good order. German fashion...'

Chris Burgess
Flodden 1513 Archaeological Manager

Abstract

Whilst there is some limited truth in the notions that the Scots were ill prepared and ill equipped for the Battle of Flodden, most of the accounts have reached us via the filter of Victorian romanticism and for the most part nothing could be further from the truth. This paper looks at the modern re-evaluation of the Battle and shows how the local terrain and the characteristics of the bog at the foot of Branxton Hill was an unforeseen but key component leading to the Scottish downfall.

Keywords: wetland environments, military actions, Flodden, Early Modern Europe

Introduction

On the 22nd August 1513, a Scottish army estimated to include between 7,500 and 10,000 people (men, women and children) crossed the English border along an eight-mile front between Wark Castle in the west and Norham Castle in the east. Their strategic aim was to draw an English Army commanded by Henry VIII back from France and onto English soil.

Though the English government was not aware of the invasion for a further three days, the response, once news of the invasion reached the south was swift, as James' attack had been anticipated. The English commander, Thomas Howard, the Earl of Surrey had been preparing throughout the summer. From his headquarters at Pontefract Castle, he ordered a muster near Alnwick for the 5th of September and began the journey north.

Fifteen days later James IV, King of Scotland, lay dead on the Battlefield at Flodden Field along with more than 100 of the senior nobles and clergy of the Scottish state. Yet any visitor to Flodden Field wonders how a superior force (the Scottish combat contingent included 32-33,000 men to an estimated English force of 25,000) fighting from a superior position with time, equipment and tactics on their side, not only lost the day but also were so tragically routed.

It has been argued the Scottish army came to England with the wrong cannon, the wrong infantry weapon (the 18-ft Swiss Pike), that they had no answer to the English long bow, that they were poorly disciplined and poorly trained, that their King made bad decisions, which led them to the most terrible defeat in their history. Yet while there is some limited truth in part of this, most of it has reached us via the filter of Victorian romanticism and for the most part nothing could be further from the truth.

The Latest Research

Renewed combined archaeological and historical study is beginning to demonstrate a broader understanding of the battle. This work clearly shows that James should have won, and may well have done so if it was not for the unforeseen factor of the bog at the foot of Branxton Hill.

Recent publications by Professor Paul Younger on the hydrology of the site have pointed to the presence of several water table convergence zones that saturated the soil regardless of the prevailing weather. This effect created a bog, which would not be particularly visible to the naked eye and which when walked through might leave wet feet but with nothing to be concerned about. It has been suggested that it was the form of the Scottish divisions or scheltrons, squares or columns 80-100 wide and 80-100 deep (8,000-10,000 men) closely packed together, marching in serried ranks, which broke the surface tension of this saturated ground. This caused a wet surface to become a mire which could cripple an army.

This work, combined with recent archaeological metal detecting surveys and an assessment of the landscape has been combined with the reappraisal of the two primary documentary sources. These publications are the *Articles of Bataille* (written by Thomas Howard

Jnr the day after the battle) and the *Trewe Encounter* (written by an unknown Northumbrian shortly thereafter) provide a picture of a well ordered Scottish force. The Scottish army may not have been as expert with the pike as the Swiss mercenary armies who developed the weapon, but they were well enough practiced and familiar with it to advance down Branxton Hill towards the English forces 'silently and in good order'.

Their effectiveness and capability were ably demonstrated on their left flank (the west side of the battlefield) where the unit commanded by Lords Hume and Huntley advanced first, leading James' echelon assault. They passed completely by luck, through a gap in the bog, an area where the water table was not converging with the surface and where the ground was relatively firm and dry. Reaching the foot of the hill they then advanced *'pikes charged'* (lowered for combat) on the English right, commanded by the Earl of Surrey's youngest son Edmund Howard.

The effect of this body of pikemen, imbued with the momentum of descending the steep slopes of Branxton Hill was clearly devastating. The locations of burial pits recorded during the late nineteenth century demonstrate where approximately the battle line on this part of the field was. The Scots managed to either push the English back to their start line or cross the open ground quickly enough to engage them before they could advance. Their attack proved deadly, overwhelming Edmund

Figure 1. Looking down the hill into where the bog used to be towards Branxton Hill and towards the monument that marks the English battle line.

Figure 2. Looking down the hill into where the bog used to be towards Branxton Hill and towards the monument that marks the English battle line.

Figure 3. Looking south (opposite direction to Figures 1 & 2) towards the hill where the Scots army descended (the bog was in the bottom).

Howard's forces and led to an early deployment of the English reserve to stop the Scottish turning that part of the English line.

As the second, third and fourth Scottish units began in turn their decent of Branxton Hill they must have felt some certainty in the potential outcome of their advance. This however was soon to change as first the centre-left, then the centre-right and finally their right flank units all successively marched into the convergence zones at the foot of Branxton Hill. As each in turn stalled in the bog the major weakness of the pike as an infantry weapon came to have a deadly effect. At 18 feet in length, these overlong spears are only effective if delivered in an ordered mass and with momentum. In a bog, with all forward movement halted and the pressure of their countrymen pushing forward from behind, the pike lost all of its effectiveness. The front rows probably died from suffocation and the English forces closed to join battle with an enemy that was unable to move, uncertain of what was happening and incapable of effectively defending itself.

James IV went to death and to the defeat of his nation not because of hubris, or poor tactics and certainly not due to the poor training of his army, but because of a landscape condition, a convergence zone between the water table and ground surface. This condition and the effects of a body of men marching in unison across the surface could not reasonably have been foreseen, but which, over two hours in

the failing light of evening on the 9th of September 1513, was fatal for James IV and 10,000 of his countrymen.

References

Howard, T. (Lord Admiral) (1513) *Articles of Bataill or Account of the Battle of Flodden*. In: Brewer, J.S., Gairdner, J. & Brodie, R.H. (eds) (1862) *Letters and Papers foreign and domestic in the reign of Henry VIII. 1509-1547*. **Vol. 1**, HMSO, London.

Petrie, G. (1867) *A Contemporary Account of the Battle of Flodden 9th September 1513 (also known as the 'TreweEncountre')*. In: *The Proceedings of the Society of Antiquaries of Scotland*, **Vol. VII**. March 1867, Society of Antiquaries of Scotland, Edinburgh, pp141-152.

Younger, P.L. (2012) *Crouching Enemy, Hidden Ally: the decisive role of groundwater discharge features in two major British battles, Flodden 1513 and Prestonpans 1745*. In *Geological Society London: Special Publications*, **362** (1), Geological Society, London, pp19-33.

The effect of marsh, bog and moor environments on the execution of warfare, with particular reference to the Early Modern period in Britain and Europe

Sean Bell
Independent Historic Environment and Archaeological Consultant

Abstract

Throughout the history of warfare, terrain and landscape have had a great effect on the course of conflicts at both a strategic- and a tactical-level. This paper examines a number of general trends related to how wetlands in particular have affected not only the tactics and strategies involved but also the mind-set of those involved in armed conflict and military campaign, with particular consideration given to the Early Modern period (*c*. AD 1480-1720) in Britain and Europe.

Areas of difficult or rough terrain, such as extensive areas of wetland, have often been viewed in defensive terms. As such, forces at a disadvantage through numbers, technology or composition have favoured them. Though the defensive benefits of wetlands are clear, it is important to consider how these environments can also aid an attacking force. For example, there are instances where the perceived safety of the terrain was used to deceive and execute an innovative, attacking plan. This raises questions concerning the psychological effect of terrain and whether the perceived defensive benefits of a terrain system can actually be considered detrimental to a military commander's ability.

The Civil Wars in Britain are of particular note as many of the pitched battles are named with the appellation '*Moor*', particularly in the north. Is this a reflection of the predominant terrain feature in the geography of the war, or does it reflect the choice of a military commander to make a stand, or to launch an attack? On the other hand, did the nature of that war create circumstances, or even a mind-set that funnelled military action onto moorland? These points are considered in this discussion.

It is concluded that the effects of wetland in the execution of a military campaign can be both complex and subtle. Its effect also requires further study not only in terms of technology and the execution of war, but also particularly in terms of the psychology of war for those who lead, and those who are lead.

Keywords: wetland environments, military actions, Early Modern Europe

Introduction

The aim of this paper is to present an overview of the role played by marsh, bog and other wetland environments on the execution of warfare, with particular examples taken from military actions during the Early Modern period (*c.* AD 1480-1720). This overview will examine the general trends of interplay between these environments with, not only, military strategies, tactics and technology, but also the effect of these environments on the perceptions and assessments of those individuals leading or participating in military operations.

The Terrain as Defence

Areas of difficult or rough terrain, such as extensive areas of wetland, are usually viewed and assessed in defensive terms. Common considerations are the methods by which the terrain can be used to protect a military force; which aspects of the terrain can be used to negate any shortcomings a military force may have through, for examples, its composition of troop-type or technological aspects. In the event of an enemy attack, common considerations would be about how the terrain will break-up an enemy's approach or funnel his avenues of approach and lines of attack. Further considerations would take into account any advantages that the enemy forces possess and how the terrain can be used to nullify these.

Military Campaigns

In terms of campaigns, the use of these environments would be favoured by forces at a numerical or technological disadvantage compared to their opponent, or at least the perception of their opponent. This is probably greatest in forces which are conducting a guerrilla-style campaign such as the Soviets in 1941-44, the Water Margin of Sung Dynasty-China and Alfred the Great's campaigns against the Danes. This last example shows a combination of using wetland terrain to create a fortification, as a means to protect a mobile force and to refuse battle against its opponent. The ability of a mobile military force, that is one which is not primarily a garrison, to protect itself and be able to refuse battle at its own discretion is important. In these situations, the force lacks a particular element, which then renders it vulnerable to a better-equipped enemy, or the force is too small to create an effective defensive perimeter even when their numbers are equal or greater than their opponents.

There are a number of examples of this situation during the British Wars of 1638-1652 (commonly referred to as the English Civil War) particularly amongst those forces that operated in the Celtic realms of Ireland and Scotland. The growth of firearms as the decisive factor on the battlefield led to a technological separation between the abilities of various forces, but with it came a need for greater investments in training, drill and experience, which could exacerbate any technological shortcomings. These could be exploited by any mounted elements, and the need to protect a force from being overly exposed to enemy horse was a considerable factor in the use of terrain features during the Early Modern Period.

It should also be noted that many of the pitched battles in the Civil Wars in England are named with the appellation 'Moor' or 'Heath', particularly in the north. Is this a reflection of the predominant terrain feature in the geography of the war, or does it reflect the choice of a military commander to make a stand, or to launch an attack?

The ultimate expression of the defensive capabilities of wetlands has been through their incorporation within systems of fortification, such as the large Vauban-style forts around settlements within the Bourtange Moor of the eastern Netherlands, which protected both the settlements and the routes through this peatland, and played an important role in the conflicts of seventeenth- and eighteenth-century Europe.

The Terrain as Attack

Though the defensive benefits of wetlands are clear, it is important to consider how these environments can also be used to aid an attacking force. One disadvantage of using bog, marsh and wetlands as a defensive anchor is that the terrain can also hinder your own ability to manoeuvre in response to the enemy's movements. Furthermore, they may hinder capability if the situation changes sufficiently for a force in a defensive posture to assume

offensive actions. At Benburb in 1646, the Irish commander used the surrounding watercourse and associated wetlands, not to aid his own defence, but to place his Scots opponents in a position, which severely limited their ability to manoeuvre.

One of the classic examples of Napoleon's genius was the Battle of the Bridge at Arcole, in November 1797. Here he used the marsh terrain to limit the movements of his Austrian Hapsburg opponents to allow him to both defend against one Austrian force whilst simultaneously assaulting another.

In considering the Battle of Blenheim of 1704, we also see another aspect in which the perceived safety of the terrain was used to deceive and execute an offensive plan of some daring and indeed risk. The French had sought to protect their front with a watercourse and adjacent wetlands, but John Churchill whilst appearing to be forced to funnel his attack to the flanks actually launched the bulk of his Allied Army across the wetlands against a French centre, which had been significantly weakened by the removal of troops to the flanks. This raises the question of whether the perceived defensive benefits of a terrain system can actually be considered detrimental to a military commander's ability. Marlborough's tactics at Blenheim relied to some extent on the French commander being unable to perceive the threat across the marshland in the centre of his front. However, is the effective offensive use of such terrain an indicator of outstanding military ability on one hand, or of military incompetence on the other? Recent theories consider that Parliament's victory in the Great Civil War (1642-1646) was due, not to material advantage or the justness of its cause, but to the generally higher quality of its leadership.

During the Great (English) Civil War, there are examples, such as Staveley Hall and, possibly Crowland Abbey, of fortified positions being easily captured by an assault being launched from an area of wetland, which the garrison commander had considered impenetrable. In these cases it sems that the terrain had clearly created a false sense of security, and is a point worth considering in relation to other armed conflicts.

Conclusion

The effects of wetland in the execution of a military campaign can, therefore, be both complex and subtle. These effects require further study in terms of the technology and the execution of war, but also particularly in terms of the psychology of war for those who lead, and those who are lead.

Bibliography

Chandler, D.G. (1995) *The Campaigns of Napoleon*. Simon & Schuster, New York.

Kenyon, J. & Ohlmeyer, J. (eds.) (1998) *The Civil Wars: A Military History of England, Scotland and Ireland 1638-1660*. Oxford University Press. Oxford.

Lavelle, R. (2012) F*ortifications in Wessex c. 800-1066*. Osprey Publishing. Oxford.

Lenihan, P. (2001) *Confederate Catholics at War 1641-1649*. Cork University Press, Cork.

Reid, S. (1998) *All The King's Armies: A Military History of the English Civil War 1642-51*. Spellmount Ltd., Staplehurst, Kent.

Stone, B. (1992) *Derbyshire in the Civil War*. Scarthin Books. Cromford, Derbyshire.

Wanklyn, M. (2006) *Decisive Battles of the English Civil War*. Pen and Sword Books. Barnsley, South Yorkshire.

Young, J.R. (1997) *Celtic Dimensions of the British Civil Wars*. John Donald Publishers Ltd. Edinburgh.

The impact of the Falklands War (1982) on the peatland ecosystem of the islands

Jim McAdam

Queen's University Belfast and United Kingdom Falkland Islands Trust

Abstract

Although the Falkland Islands (52°S) are relatively small (12,000km^2), they are a globally important peatland resource. Most of the soils are classified as peat that has been formed under a unique set of climatic conditions and location-specific circumstances. Their estimated carbon stock is equivalent to 66% of the UK total and more than that of Ireland. Most of the land activity of The Falklands War in 1982 was essentially fought on peatlands though the main battles approaching Stanley were on the quartzite hilltops. However the timing of the action (winter), the relatively short duration of the land conflict and the unpreparedness of the combatants for the peatland conditions, meant that the overall impact on the ecosystem was minimal. A small but significant area of minefields is an unwelcome human legacy (which may have some ecosystem benefits) but a greater number of military and other tourists visiting the main battle sites have the potential to increase awareness of the peatland ecosystem.

Keywords: climate change, overgrazing, farm restructuring, minefields, military tourism, ecosystem services

Introduction

The Falkland Islands

(i) Background

The Falkland Islands are an archipelago of 782 islands (Woods, 2001) situated in the South Atlantic Ocean between latitudes 51°S and 53°S and longitudes 57°W and 62°W. They cover an area of *c.*12,200km^2 (almost exactly the same as Yorkshire or Northern Ireland), and are approximately 500 kilometres from the nearest point on mainland South America. The climate is cool/temperate, oceanic and is characterised by its lack of extremes. Temperatures are maintained at a moderate level with a mean for January of 9.4°C and a mean for July of 2.2°C, and ground frosts can occur throughout the year. Rainfall is low with a mean annual precipitation at Stanley of 640 mm. Rainfall distribution is associated with the main mountain ranges to the north of both main islands and tends to decline towards the south and west. Rainfall is lowest in spring and this, combined with strong winds, reduces plant growth (McAdam, 1985; Summers & McAdam, 1993). Climatic variation across the Falkland Islands archipelago is poorly understood.

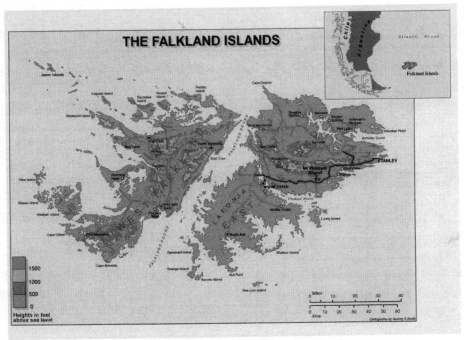

Figure 1. The size and location of the Falkland Islands

(ii) Soils and Vegetation

The topography of the islands is not extreme with the landscape being generally hilly, the tallest mountain, Mt Usborne on East Falkland, is 705m high. The underlying geology is quartzite, sandstones and shales. During the Quaternary, although the islands experienced cold conditions, the only glaciers were those that formed the small cirques on the highest hills. The rest of the land surface was subjected to periglacial, tundra conditions and deep weathering was more-or-less in situ. Many areas of exposed, fractured rocks were left which gave the unique landscape feature of periglacial blockfields, locally referred to as "stone runs". A typical Falkland soil comprises a shallow (usually no deeper than 30cm) peaty horizon overlying a compact, poorly drained, silty clay subsoil. Mineral soils occur in areas

wherever the underlying geology is exposed, particularly on mountaintops and in coastal areas. Falkland soils generally are shallow peats (less than 30cm deep) but in places, deposits of 11-12m have been recorded. They have a pH in the range 4.1 to 5.0 and are deficient in calcium and phosphate (Cruickshank, 2001). The main vegetation types are acid grasslands dominated by *Cortaderia pilosa* (Poaceae) and dwarf shrub heathland dominated by *Empetrum rubrum* (Ericaceae), but other vegetation types of more limited extent may be locally important, particularly around the coasts. Scrub communities dominated by *Chiliotrichum diffusum* (Asteraceae) or *Hebe elliptica* (Plantaginaceae) would have been much more widespread before the introduction of livestock as was a coastal community dominated by the tall grass, *Poa*

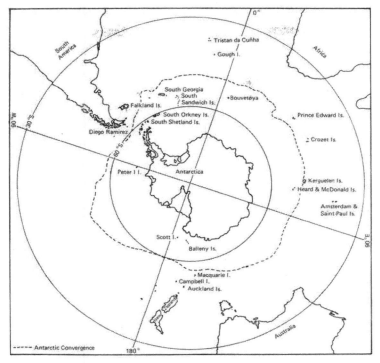

Figure 2. The circumpolar location of the Falkland Islands

flabellata (Poaceae), which today survives mainly on small offshore islands. There is no native tree cover.

(iii) Land Use

The islands had no indigenous human or large ungulate populations and human impact on the landscape only began with the first settlement approximately 250 years ago, when cattle, pigs, sheep and goats were first introduced by French settlers (Summers & McAdam, 1993). Sheep were farmed commercially from the 1860s, numbers increasing up to a maximum of 800,000 in the early 1900s. Stock density declined to about 600,000 by 1930 and remained relatively constant (at a mean stocking density of approximately 1 sheep per 2ha) until early in the 1980s when a programme of farm sub-division was introduced (McAdam,1984a;

Summers & McAdam, 1993). Since then sheep numbers have increased by approximately 20% (Summers, Haydock & Kerr, 1993; Department of Agriculture, 2012). Some reseeding has been carried out using introduced European forage species but most of the grassland is extensively grazed. Since the late 1990s, there have been moves to increase the numbers of cattle on the Islands. The rural population is small (3-400 people) and though most are still engaged in agriculture, farm-based tourism has steadily increased in popularity in recent years and become economically more significant than sheep farming on several islands. A rural roads programme, commenced in 1985 with over 900kms having been built to date, has made access to the countryside more widespread.

Peatland in the Falkland Islands

(i) Definition

The IUCN define peatlands as 'areas of land with a naturally accumulated layer of peat formed from carbon-rich dead and decaying plant material under waterlogged conditions'. Joosten & Clarke 2002, define peats as 'sedentarily accumulated material consisting of at least 30% (dry mass) of dead organic material'. However, in the Falkland Islands, where the soils can clearly be defined as peats, the rainfall is very low for what would conventionally be regarded as peat formation. Only limited areas are permanently waterlogged. This would suggest that either there was an earlier very wet period (and the pollen record does not indicate this) or peat has formed/is forming in the absence of waterlogging but low temperatures are the factor significantly reducing soil microbial activity. Most soils in the Falklands come under the definition of peat as they have a fibric surface horizon >20% organic C in the upper layers (this is more than the 30% definition of organic material above). In reality, no proper soil survey of the Falklands has been carried out.

All soils in the Falklands have been subject to a long period of chemical weathering, which makes geological differences in soils virtually zero (Cruickshank, 2001).

(ii) Classification

1. Permanently water-logged

Vegetation:

Cushion or Bryophyte clump peatland.

Mat forming cushion plant (*Astelia pumila*) usually dominates.

Extent of Sphagnum (e.g. *S. magellanicum*; *S. fimbicatum*) usually restricted to small patches.

These can form mosaic communities with graminoid peatland.

2. Permanently or temporarily waterlogged forming either peat soils or soils with varying organic content.

Vegetation:

a. Graminoid peatland

Tussac grass – dry coastal habitats.

Acid grassland.

Neutral grassland.

Marshy grassland (e.g. with high *Carex* proportion).

Fen/ Marginal. Very restricted.

b. Dwarf shrub heath

Dwarf shrub heath – *Empetrum rubrum* dominates with *Baccharis magellanica*. In waterlogged areas, there can be rushes and Sphagnum.

c. Shrub

e.g. with *Chiliotrichum diffusum*.

Figure 3. Acid Grassland dominated by *Cortaderia pilosa* is the dominant vegetation type on the islands

(iii) Extent

Although the land area of the Falklands is not large; given its very high proportion of peat cover (Table 1), it is a globally important resource.

The estimated carbon stocks (m ton C) of the Falklands in 2008 was 1151, compared to 1745 for UK and 1130 for Ireland (Joosten, 2010).

Table 1. Peatland occurrence in selected countries (International Mire Conservation Group, Global Peatland Database, 2010).

Country	Peatland area km^2	Global Ranking	% Land area	Global Ranking
UK	17,113	18	9.5	22
Falklands	11,408	26	93.7	11
Ireland	11,090	27	15.8	13
Chile	10,996	28	-	-

Table 2. CO2 emissions from degraded peatlands (1990 status) – Falkland Islands (Joosten, 2010)

Total Area	12,173 km2
Peatland Area	11,500km2
Peat Carbon Stock	11,150MtC
Total emissions	1.1 Mt/C/yr

(iv) Use for fuel

The first settlers on the islands, a small French colony in 1764, record using peat for fuel (Pernety, 1769). Governor Moody imported a peat stove in 1842- the first record of a stove for burning peat in the islands (Dickson *et al.*, 2001). Subsequent locations for farm settlements around the islands were based on the availability of peat for cutting (Miller, 2006). One of the reasons for choosing to move the small settlement from Port Louis to Stanley in 1843 was because it was thought there was about 100 years of peat on the common land at the south of the harbour. Each house in Stanley was issued a peat bog from which they could cut peat for domestic use.

All peat was cut by hand until the early 1950s (the Government used to employ hand peat cutters) when the Falkland Islands Company imported a peat-cutting machine from Ireland. The cutter was used for a few years but proved unsuccessful as the peat deposits in the Falklands were not of the raised bog type found in Ireland (Miller, 2006). Subsequently different machines were tried, the most successful being a *"McConnell Arm"* a back-mounted tractor attachment. There are no figures available for the amount of peat used for fuel locally (the 2012 Census records that only 4% of households now use peat to heat their properties – a decline of almost 90% since 1991) but it must be noted that no peat was ever exported and the population of the islands has never exceeded 3,000 people. For most of their history, it has

been much lower than that. Hence, the amount of peat extracted for fuel, while significant in some locations has been inconsequential given the dispersed and sparse network of small farm settlements. In 2001, the children of North Arm School record the settlement changing to diesel from peat-fuelled stoves in the late 1990s. This was because of the increasing distance from the settlement the workers had to travel for good peat, the cost of fuel and labour (Dickson *et al.*, 2001). Gradually, over the past fifty years, most homes and settlements increasingly used oil for fuel and since about the 1980s there has been a steady rise in the use of wind turbines for energy on farm settlements. The town of Stanley now generates over 40% of its electricity use from six wind turbines.

(iv) Ecosystem services provision

The peatlands in the Falklands deliver a clean water supply to the population, store an estimated 11,150 MtC (Table 2) and support most of the biodiversity associated with the islands.

There are 363 species recorded as growing wild in the Falkland Islands' vascular flora and listed in the checklist (Broughton & McAdam, 2005). Of these 178 species are native and 200 species non-native and naturalised (Broughton & McAdam, 2002c; Lewis, 2012; Upson, 2012a, b).

The Falkland Islands are currently considered to have fourteen endemic species. These are *Chevreulia lycopodiodes, Erigeron incertus, Gamochaeta antarctica, Hamadryas argentea, Leucheria suaveolens, Nassauvia falklandica, Nassauvia gaudichaudii, Nassauvia serpens, Nastanthus falklandicus, Phlebolobium maclovianum, Plantago moorei, Senecio litorali, Senecio vaginatus* and *Calceolaria fothergilli.*

As would be expected the native flora shows strong affinities with that of southern South America. Thirty-four species (19%) have a *"circum-Antarctic"* distribution occurring in some part of the sub-Antarctic zone, New Zealand or south-eastern Australia, and sixteen species (9%) have a bipolar distribution, being found also in higher latitudes of North America and to a slightly lesser extent, Europe (Moore, 1968). The juxtaposition of the islands between Antarctica, South America and often remote South Atlantic islands gives them high bio-geographic importance. Nationally, five threatened species are restricted to peatlands: *Alopecurus magallanicus, Carex banksii, Carex macloviana, Carex magellanica,* and *Carex sagei* (R. Upson, pers. comm.).

Threats to the Peatlands

(i) Reform of rural infrastructure.

Land reform in the 1980s has resulted in farm subdivision and increased stock numbers. In many cases, this has been accompanied by fencing, pasture improvement and greater stock control but overgrazing and erosion of some of the shallow, fertile soils has occurred. Agricultural research has greatly contributed to an understanding of the sustainable management of the rangeland vegetation (e.g. Kerr, 2003). Other rural development activities related to oil, fishing, aquaculture and tourism have had limited impact.

(ii) Plant introductions.

Introduced plant species will affect the peatland ecosystem to a greater or lesser extent. The total number of non-native species (200) exceeds the total for native taxa (178 species) (Broughton & McAdam, 2002c; Lewis, 2012; Upson, 2012). Taxa come from 46 families of which the Asteraceae (24 species and 12% of the non-native flora) and the Poaceae (30 species and 15% of the non-native flora) are undoubtedly the most important. Most non-native species, (174 taxa and 87% of the non-native flora), show an association with human habitation and other built environments. Of these approximately 18% are dependent upon such habitats, reflecting the requirement of many non-natives for open, disturbed or nutrient enriched ground. Other species associated with habitation are more widespread and can also be found in naturally open and disturbed habitats such as beaches and seabird colonies, or in vegetation that has been modified by domestic animals. However, the association of some species with habitation is equally a reflection of their horticultural and agricultural origins and some species, particularly the trees and shrubs, are merely relicts surviving where settlements and gardens have been abandoned.

Most non-native taxa were rare or local in occurrence and so probably do not have the competitive ability to spread far in the harsh environment of the Falklands peatlands (Broughton & McAdam, 2002c). As man's activities continue to expand and diversify in the Falkland Islands the non-native flora can also be expected to expand and to become more prominent. A similar trend has already been noted in Tierra del Fuego, where the increasing activity of man has undoubtedly extended the area of many non-native taxa (Moore, 1983). *Cirsium vulgare*, for example, arrived in Tierra del Fuego prior to 1917 but was not common for many years. During the 1960s, however, it became more widespread, particularly along roads.

(iii) Countryside access.

Building a rural road network commenced in 1985, before then there were virtually no roads in the Falkland

Islands. Now a sparse network of roads exists, giving more people from Stanley (the only town) access to the countryside. This, coupled with more leisure time, a greater interest in wildlife, and the growth of the tourism industry has put more pressure on coastal and other sensitive habitats. A road network allows weed species to expand their range. This has already happened with *Senecio sylvaticus* and *Cirsium vulgare* may follow the same expansion pattern as on Tierra del Fuego.

(iv) Fire.

As vegetation emerges from the winter it has accumulated a high proportion of dead matter which creates a fire hazard, particularly in the dry windy spring and summer (McAdam, 1984b). The peat soils that dominate much of the landscape are also vulnerable to fire particularly following prolonged periods

Figure 4. It has been common practice to burn some peatlands in spring

of dry weather or drought. It was common land management practice to burn pasture in spring to remove this dead material and to make the greener leaves below more available to sheep, but this practice is used less often nowadays. Repeated burning may have some detrimental effect on the flora but this is not clearly known. Fires can also occur through carelessness and from lightning strikes.

(v) Climate change.

On a more global scale, climatic change may have a significant effect on the ecosystems within the Islands (Bokhorst *et al.*, 2007; Sear *et al.*, 2001; Wadhams, 1993). There is evidence that summer rainfall is slowly declining and sunshine increasing (Hoppe & McAdam, 1998; McAdam & Upson, 2012) and there are periods when ozone depletion is particularly evident over the islands. A combination of these processes may well have a significant effect on the peatland ecosystem and this is currently being investigated (McAdam & Upson, 2013). A combination of these processes may well have a significant impact on the flora.

Hence it can be concluded that, although relatively small in area, the Falkland Islands do constitute a significant and unique global peat source.

What has been the impact of the Falklands War (in 1982) on the peatland ecosystem?

Figure 5. The thin layer of peat is vulnerable to erosion in many areas

The Falklands War

The Falklands War (1982) has been analysed in great depth both from a military, geopolitical, strategic and personal perspective. There is a huge volume of literature on the subject and while many of the (particular personal) accounts refer to the effects of the terrain (peatlands in most cases) on combatants and their equipment, not one refers to the impact on the peatland ecosystem.

(i) The course of action

The War (technically it was a conflict as Britain and Argentina never actually declared war) insofar as it impacted on the Islands started on 2nd April 1982 when Argentine invading forces landed and, after a brief battle, captured the Islands capital, Stanley. The initial landing by Argentine special forces was very close to the capital at Port Harriet a few kilometres to the south east.

Subsequently, Argentine heavy armament and vehicles landed on Cape Pembroke about 3km to the north east of Stanley and had only limited peatland to cover. The peat was dry, shallow and well disturbed anyway in this area so overall the initial landing had little environmental impact.

Subsequently the Argentine garrison was strengthened around the Islands at key coastal locations – Fox Bay, Port Howard, Pebble Island on West Falkland and Darwin/Goose Green on East Falkland as well as other locations. As there was no road network in the Islands, these garrisons were established by sea so there was little effect on the peatlands. Argentine forces commenced a programme of "digging in" around key locations to repel any land invasion but such "dugouts" and "fox holes" were largely hand dug and insignificant in area. Overall Argentine forces concentrated approximately 70% of their troops in defending Stanley so

Figure 6. Most initial damage was around the Cape Pembroke area.

most disturbance was in an area already heavily disturbed. Minefields were established. The land battle on the Falklands commenced on 1st May and ended on 14th June so was for a relatively short period.

Most of the initial action was around Cape Pembroke Peninsula, an area already severely eroded and disturbed by human activity due to its proximity to Stanley (McAdam, 1981). On 1st May a Vulcan bomber dropped twenty-one 1,000lb bombs on the area and there were subsequent intensive Harrier aircraft raids. All this served to further damage an already eroded area. On 22nd May the main landing of British forces occurred – on the west side of East Falkland at San Carlos. This was the commencement of a land battle during which most damage to the peatlands occurred. There was limited land action around the bridgehead at San Carlos,

and at Goose Green, and virtually none on west Falkland apart from a raid on the grass airstrip on Pebble Island.

From 9th May onwards, British warships were shelling the Falklands from up to 13 miles offshore. Their targets were usually Argentine positions in the hills immediately surrounding Stanley. These are rocky areas interspersed with grassy heath. This shelling continued intermittently for the next month. On 28th May the 2nd Battalion, the Parachute Regiment captured Goose Green after an intense land battle. The shallow peat around the battle site was little disturbed, a gorse hedge was set on fire but it was raining heavily during the battle and there was little fire spread. Over late May and early June many troops "yomped" across East Falkland, 3rd Battalion the Parachute Regiment arriving at Teal Inlet on 26th May. There were some smaller vehicles with the troops who

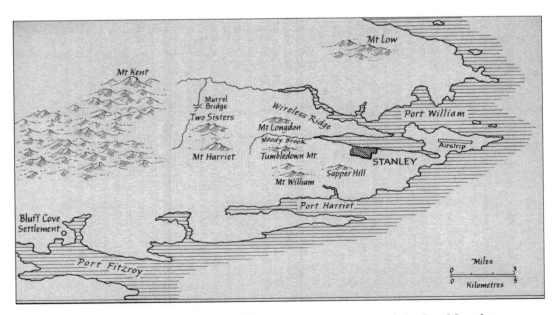

Figure 7. The area immediately west of Stanley, sites of most of the land battles.

marched across East Falkland, but much gear and heavy guns were transported by helicopter so the effect on the peat was minimal. There are substantial areas of deeper, wetter peat in the area around Teal Inlet, the Malo River etc.

From 10th June onwards the British were in command of high ground around Stanley and commenced an intensive 3-day fire period on the area with 105mm guns. This created further disturbance of the peatland in the area west of Stanley though much action and effort was directed to the quartzite ridges on the hills overlooking Stanley. Further naval bombardment of this area occurred immediately prior to the final attack (there are numerous accounts of all these actions by strategists and the men who fought in them. For an analytical time line see Cordesman & Wagner, 1990).

(ii) Timing of the war.

Overall, the impact of the Falklands War on the peatland as an ecosystem was very limited. Deliberate fires to "rejuvenate" grasslands in the Falklands used to be common in the spring when the dry, strong winds and strong sun create much more inflammable conditions. These could be environmentally deleterious, particularly if the shallow peat became ignited. However, this was a *"Winter War"* (Bishop & Witherow, 1982) and while it was an average winter, the peat is at its wettest, the vegetation damp, and the winds moist, and the risk of fire minimised.

No major peat or vegetation fires occurred as a direct result of the action. The time involved in actual on-the-ground fighting was relatively short so had little lasting effect.

Figure 8. The "Winter War "so damage from fire was minimal. Mount Longdon –typical of the quartzite ridges which saw the fiercest action (Photograph. Julian Thompson)

Figure 9. Argentine helicopter completely burnt out in 1982. This photograph, taken in 1983, shows that the fire damage to peatland had been minimal

Figure 10. Driving on the soft terrain can be hazardous (Photograph: A. Moffat)

(iii) Logistics.

Driving across the Falklands' countryside in winter was a skilled operation requiring the correct weight of vehicle, appropriate tyres and a knowledge of ground terrain – none of which either sides' forces had in great amount. Neither side was adequately equipped for the peatland conditions found in the islands so there was little heavy vehicle incursion, particularly into wetter areas. The most versatile cross-country vehicles the British had were tracked versions of the Combat Vehicle Reconnaissance (CVR) fast flexible gun platforms –the Scorpion and Scimitar. Due to doubts about their suitability for the islands terrain, only four of each were shipped down and deployed, mainly for ferrying supplies forward to advancing troops. In the end, the Argentine tanks and armoured vehicles played no part in the land battle so damage to the ground was minimal. Therefore, most of the fighting and technology involved lighter equipment or men on foot, both of which had minimal impact on the peatland. That is not to detract from the unpleasantness and misery of the conditions underfoot for those involved in the conflict.

(iv) Impact on wildlife.

The Falklands have no naturally occurring forests or woodland and most of the large numbers of seabirds, will have been at sea during the winter, only returning to the Falklands to breed in spring (Sept - Oct) by which times activity was long gone. None of the ground traversed and disturbed could be classified as threatened or fragile habitat, particularly in winter.

(v) Minefield situation.

From the start of the invasion, Argentine forces laid minefields on the islands to help protect them from invading British forces. Small areas of mines were laid around the major settlements at Port Howard, Fox Bay and Darwin but most were around Stanley, particularly on or above beaches where an attack was perceived.

In most cases, these areas were well mapped and are still clearly marked permanently and reasonably securely fenced in the islands. The area of these known minefields totals about 1,300ha of peatland (0.1% of the land area). Although four minefields have been cleared since 2009, most have largely remained untouched since 1982.

It could be argued that they are an (albeit unwelcome) form of protection of peatland habitat as people and grazing animals are excluded and flora can get a chance to proliferate. Of more concern initially was the much larger area around Stanley where large amounts of dumped and/or unexploded ordnance existed and which initially posed a real threat to the public. While not excluding the public from such areas, there were very rigorous warnings and maps distributed to walkers and travellers in the countryside urging extreme caution and warning not to touch items found. Over a period of years, these areas have gradually been cleared of all but very minor risk and no attention is drawn to them anymore. In some ways, their presence did reduce the enthusiasm of locals and military personnel for leisure or unnecessary travel in the countryside for quite a few

Table 3 Minefield areas in the Falkland Islands (2002)

Land classified as "Dangerous"	1,314.9ha
Sub-classified as :-	
No landmines – change status	577.5ha
Mined areas – high hazard	57.5ha
Mined areas – Low hazard (7750m from settlement or 100m from road)	664.8ha
Cannot be cleared easily	17.9ha

Figure 11. One current minefield area showing the quartzite ridges where the final battles for Stanley were fought

years after the conflict. This probably reduced the foot and vehicle pressure on the affected peatlands.

From a survey of feasibility of minefield clearance (Cranfield, 2007) the clearance of mines from all areas on the Islands currently classified as 'minefields' or suspect areas is challenging but technically feasible. The clearance work will have some environmental impact however *"considering this in a timescale of many years of grazing and the likely future effects of climate change this will be minimal. Some environmental remediation will be required"*.

Post-war effect on the peatlands

(i) Farm development.

Since the war, investment in the islands and farm subdivision because of an island-wide ownership transfer process

has resulted in some redistribution of grazing pasture. Farms have been encouraged to reseed, albeit on a limited scale and sub-divide their large paddocks to exert greater grazing control. There has been more understanding of pasture dynamics to minimise the risk of overgrazing and erosion and there is less enthusiasm for burning the grasslands. The Falklands peatlands are relatively fragile though and extreme care will need to be taken in encouraging further pastoral intensification.

(ii) Peat cutting for fuel.

There was a surge in peat cutting immediately after the conflict and the Falkland Islands Development Corporation funded the importation of a peat-cutting machine. This was used extensively for a few years mainly around Stanley and is still used but increasing prosperity has meant that bottled gas and fuel oil have taken over. Once again, the small population and localised use meant that this venture has had a very limited impact on the resource.

(iii) Travel and transport.

The commencement of a rural road programme from 1985 further reduced the pressure to drive across peatlands and indeed their condition now is probably better than it was pre-conflict. Vehicle off-roading and motorcycle scrambling has become popular in the Islands since the conflict but it is very restricted in area given the low population density.

(iv) Military activity.

There are still military firing ranges in the hills. The area around Mount Pleasant Airfield is disturbed but there is also a perimeter fence, which excludes livestock from a substantial area of peatland.

(v) Tourism.

Increased awareness and involvement by landowners has resulted in a sustainable tourism, which has no significant negative effect. In the thirty-one years that have elapsed since the Falklands conflict, Islanders have always made "veterans" of the action and their families very welcome to the Falklands. In most cases, these people have wanted to visit the primary sites of the action and have had to traverse the peatlands. In some cases, access to the sites is a problem and more hard-surface track provision would help reduce the damage to the peatlands. Many soldiers/relatives return to mount plaques or leave mementoes to recall their experiences or to honour fallen comrades. All of these events, while each minor in their own way are extremely important to people and, in a more diffuse way could be used to increase their appreciation of the landscape and peatlands of the Falkland Islands.

Figure 12. New roads have helped reduce the impact of vehicles on the peatlands

Figure 13. Soldiers of the Green Howards at Captain John Hamilton's grave, Port Howard, East Falkland, December 2012. (Photo: Andrew Roe)

Personal observations

The author worked in the Falkland Islands from 1975-1978 on a UK Government, Overseas Development Administration funded project to set up the first permanent agricultural research station on the islands. This gave him a chance to travel widely around the islands and observe the peat at first hand. He returned in 1983 in an agricultural consultancy and advisory capacity and has visited the islands almost every year since. Hence, he has been in an almost unique position to observe the state of the peatlands before and after the conflict. His overall observation is that the effects were minimal – for the reasons given above - with the only lasting legacy the minefields. There is a great awareness among the population of their countryside, an active local conservation organisation (Falklands Conservation) and an Environmental Officer in the Falkland Islands Government who are targeting resources from both without and within the islands to better understand the ecosystem services delivered by the peatlands and how best to sustain them.

Acknowledgements

The author is grateful to Phil Stone, Rebecca Upson, David Tatham, Tim Miller, Emma Jane Wells and Nick Rendell for helpful comments on, and additions to this paper. Andrew Moffat kindly permitted the use of some of his photographs for the oral and written presentations. Other photographs are the author's unless acknowledged otherwise. The United Kingdom Falkland Islands Trust (www.ukfit.org) funded most of the visits that led to the observations recorded in this paper.

References

Bishop, P. & Witherow, J. (1982) *The Winter War: The Falklands*. Quartet Books, London, Melbourne, New York.

Bokhorst, S., Huiskes, A., Convey, P. & Aerts, R. (2007a) The effect of environmental change on vascular plant and cryptogram communities along a latitudinal gradient from the Falkland Islands to the southern Maritime Antarctic. In: Bokhorst, S. (ed.) *Functioning of terrestrial ecosystems of the Maritime Antarctic in a warmer climate*. Thesis 2,117-150, Institute of Ecological Sciences, Vrije University Amsterdam.

Bokhorst, S., Huiskes, A., Convey, P. & Aerts, R. (2007b) External nutrient inputs into terrestrial ecosystems of the Falkland Islands and the Maritime Antarctic region. *Polar Biology*, **30**, 1315-1321.

Broughton, D.A. & McAdam, J.H. (2002a) *The vascular flora of the Falkland Islands: an annotated checklist and atlas*. Unpublished report to Falklands Conservation. The Queen's University of Belfast, Belfast.

Broughton, D.A. & McAdam, J.H. (2002b) A Red Data List for the Falkland Islands vascular flora. *Oryx*, **36**(3), 279-287.

Broughton, D.A. & McAdam, J.H. (2002c) The non-native vascular flora of the Falkland Islands. *Botanical Journal of Scotland*, **54**(2), 153-190.

Broughton, D.A. &McAdam, J.H. 2005. A checklist of the native vascular flora of the Falkland Islands (Islas Malvinas). New information on the species present, their ecology, status and distribution. *Journal of the Torrey Botanical Society*, **132**(1),115-148.

Cordesman, A.H. & Wagner, A.R. (1990) *The Lessons of Modern War. Volume III. The Afghan and Falklands Conflicts*. Westview Press, Boulder and San Francisco.

Cranfield University (2007) *Field Survey to examine the feasibility of clearing landmines in the Falkland Islands*. Field Survey Report 2007, University of Cranfield, Bedford.

Cruickshank, J.G. (2001) *Falkland Soils – origins and prospects*. Unpublished Report to the Department of Agriculture, Stanley. Department of Agriculture for Northern Ireland, Belfast.

Department of Agriculture (2012) *Agricultural statistics, 2010-11*. Department of Agriculture, Falkland Islands, Port Stanley.

Dickson, J., Velasquez, E., Faria, S., Tellez, T. & Velasquez, K. (2001) Good -bye peat stoves. *The Falkland Islands Journal*, **7**(5), 124-130.

FIG (1999) Conservation of wildlife and nature ordinance 1999. *The Falkland Islands Gazette Supplement*, **10**, 2-18.

Hoppe, G.M. & McAdam, J.H. (1992) Management of a tussac grass community for wildlife, tourism and agriculture. *Aspects of Applied Biology,* **29**, 413-418.

Hoppe, G.M. & McAdam, J.H. (1998) Is the Falkland Islands climate really changing. *Wool Press*, N° **109**, 7-10.

Hoppe, G.M. & McAdam, J.H. (1999) Precipitation in the Falkland Islands 1874 to 1996. (Abstract) *Irish Journal of Agricultural Research*, **79**.

Joosten, H. (2010) *The global peatland CO2 picture. Peatland studies and drainage related emissions in all countries of the world.* Wetlands International; UNFCC Barcelona.

Joosten, H. & Clarke, D. (2002) *Wise use of mines and peatlands – Background and principles including a framework for decision making.* International Mine Conservation Group/ International Peat Society 304pp.

Kerr, J.A. (2003) A history of grazing management in the Falkland Islands. *Falkland Islands Journal*, **8**(2), 94-106.

Lewis, R. (2012) *Checklist of Falkland naturalised vascular plants.* http://www. falklandsconservation.com/wildlife/ plants/native-vascular-plant-checklist

McAdam, J.H. (1981) Uncontrolled grazing and vegetation removal in the Falkland Islands. *Environmental Conservation*, **7**, 201-202.

McAdam, J.H. (1984a) Recent changes in Falkland Islands agriculture. *Interciencia*, **9**, 307-310.

McAdam, J.H. (1984b) The introduction of *Holcus lanatus* by direct drilling following burning of native grassland in the Falkland Islands. *Research and Development in Agriculture*, **1**,165-169.

McAdam, J.H. (1985) The effect of climate on plant growth and agriculture in the Falkland Islands. *Progress in Biometeorology*, **2**, 155-176.

McAdam, J.H. & Upson, R. (2012) *Peatlands in the Falkland Islands – Origins, status and threats.* IUCN UK Peatland Programme/British Ecological Society Symposium, Bangor Wales. p15.

McAdam, J.H. & Upson, R. (2013) *Climate Change in the Falkland Islands.* The Wool Press. Department of Agriculture, Falkland Islands Govt. April. 278, 13-15.

Miller, S. (2006) Peat. *The Falkland Islands Journal*, **8**(5), 124-134.

Moore, D.M. (1968) The vascular flora of the Falkland Islands. British *Antarctic Survey Scientific Reports*, N°**60**, 1-202. NERC, London.

Pernety, A.J. (1769) *Histoire d'un voyage aux Iles Malouines fait en 1763 et 1764 avec des observations sur le Detroit de Magellan et sur les Patagones.* Paris.

Sear, C., Hulme, M., Adger, N. & Brown, K. (2001) *The impacts of global climate change on the UK Overseas Territories. Tyndall Centre for Climate Change Research*, Natural Resources Institute, pp 50.

Summers, R.W. & McAdam, J.H. (1993) *The Upland Goose*. Bluntisham Books, Bluntisham.

Summers, O., Haydock, W.J.R. & Kerr, J.A. (1993) *Land subdivision in the Falkland Islands*. Proceedings of the XVII International Grassland Congress, New Zealand, 812-814.

Upson, R. (2012a) *Checklist of Falkland native vascular plants*. http://www.falklandsconservation.com/wildlife/plants/native-vascular-plant-checklist

Upson, R. (2012b) *Important Plant Areas of the Falklands*. Unpublished report to Falklands Conservation.

Wadhams, P. (1993) *How the polar regions affect climate change*. The Falkland Islands in the 1990s. Proceedings of a seminar. The Falkland Islands Association, Cambridge, pp 37-40.

Woods, R.W. (2000) *Flowering Plants of the Falkland Islands*. Falklands Conservation, London.

Woods, R.W. (2001) A survey of the number, size and distribution of islands in the Falklands archipelago. *Falkland Islands Journal*, **7**(5), 1-25.

Aviation archaeology: A legitimate branch of archaeology? Its development and path to professional standards

Graham R. Chaters
British Aviation Archaeology Council

Abstract

This paper endeavours to clarify the origins and development of aviation archaeology as a distinct part of the aviation preservation and restoration movement. The roots, motivations, and links with mainstream archaeology are considered in the light of the development of the aviation preservation movement in the 1960s. The wider awareness of aviation archaeology through popular television programmes is also considered. The tripartite development of aviation preservation, airfield archaeology and aviation archaeology and the development of codes of conduct for aviation preservation and aviation archaeology are described as is the development of a national body for aviation archaeological research and excavation. Consideration of the need for the air war to be fully investigated and the importance of using archaeological techniques to preserve artefacts for future generations are considered likewise are the wider aspects of community and military archaeology. Legal aspects and the development of the licensing system are then explored as is the role of the British Joint Casualty Compassionate Centre (JCCC) and the US Joint POW/MIA Accounting Command (JPAC) teams. A practical stance is then presented with the focus on how aviation archaeologists follow professional standards to investigate, excavate and present aircraft remains and their narrative to enthusiasts and the general public alike. Case studies illustrate the investigative process from research, through excavation to public display of artefacts.

Keywords: *aviation archaeology, history*

Aviation archaeology's roots, motivations, and links with mainstream archaeological enquiry

Aviation archaeology might be a contradiction in terms to some observers. This is because the archaeology is less than 100 years old and often has been the result of a violent impact with *terra firma* following an all too violent engagement in the air war. In investigating the developments of the specialism, it is clear that there have been many problems with the very terminology, with individuals involved in the recovery of aircraft wreckage being labelled anything from wreckologists, wreck-hunters, grave robbers, to aviation archaeologists, aviation enthusiasts, etc. As shall become apparent this special interest group of individuals has over the past 30 years carved themselves a particular niche in aviation preservation, which now prides itself in developing a professional and polished approach to investigation and excavation of aircraft crash sites.

Schofield draws attention to the fact that collections of militaria '*are often considered to sit rather uneasily on the fringes of credible conservation efforts*' (Schofield, 2005 pg 63) whilst acknowledging at the same time that that the meaning and sense of authenticity (of these artefacts) '*to the often now rather ephemeral and fragmented places of conflict*' (ibid). He also highlights that the values and importance of crashed military aircraft has received greater articulation following research by Holyoak (2001, 2002) and English Heritage (2002). As a result English Heritage's approach to aviation archaeology is to encourage excavations of an acceptable standard and ensure that the recording of the excavations is in sufficient depth to benefit future historians (Holyoak, 2002).

A second and more poignant aspect of crash sites and the recovery of artefacts is the act of commemoration, both for the crews and their relatives and the local communities. The renewed focus on the Second World War from

the huge interest in genealogy as well as the National Curriculum has seen a greater awareness and interest in wartime occurrences. With the numbers of living participants in the 1939-45 conflict fast dwindling, families are researching their wartime pasts and learning far more of events than was ever made available at the time. One case in point being the family of a Wireless Operator killed on a training flight in April 1944, his family only learning more of the accident after stumbling across photographs of a memorial dedicated to the crew at the crash site near Boston when searching Google.

Figure 1. Memorial to the crew of Lancaster ND820, Bicker, Lincolnshire

The development of aircraft preservation and aviation archaeology

With the embryonic pre-war Shuttleworth, Nash and Imperial War Museum collections being accentuated by service based collections (such as the Fleet Air Arm Museum and the RAF collections at St Athan and, Cosford), the 1960s was a catalyst in the development of the aircraft preservation movement. The volunteer-led collections (such as the Newark Air Museum, the Lincolnshire Aircraft Preservation Society, and the Northern Aircraft Preservation Society), also contributed to the impetus. By 1967, there was sufficient interest for the British Aircraft Preservation Council (BAPC) to be formed with thrity-one delegates starting what Brew describes as 'a body of lasting importance and relevance in the world of aircraft preservation' (Brew, 2003, pg 28). The relevance of the BAPC to wreckologists / aviation archaeology is that many of the member organisations embodied this within their wider remits of aircraft preservation and restoration. At present the BAPC has 106 member organisations of which eleven groups are also members of the British Aviation Archaeology Council (BAAC) more of which later.

The activities of the BAPC include:

- Quarterly Council Meetings hosted by member organisations.

- Maintaining the BAPC Logbook which contains contact information, advice etc.

- Organizing a Parts Finder (Wants and Disposals) system.

- Maintaining The National Aviation Heritage Register.

- Maintaining the 'BAPC Register of Anonymous' Aircraft.

- Developing and implementing a National Aviation Heritage Strategy.

- Organizing "Stopping the Rot" conferences and seminars dealing with preservation issues.

- Providing contact information for access to specialist help.

- Publications about Britain's National Aviation Heritage and how to preserve it.

- Providing free / low cost training courses for member organisations' volunteer staff.

A third strand related to aviation history and archaeology is provided by the Airfield Research Group (ARG) (http://www.airfieldresearchgroup.org.uk/). The Airfield Research Group has enjoyed a continuous existence since it was formed in the late 1970s. The non-profit organisation is made up of like-minded people and its aims are to research, record and to report information and material related to the history, architecture, current status, and use of military and civilian airfields throughout the United Kingdom.

Individual member preferences are wide ranging and include researching all aspects of architecture associated with aviation, individual airfield histories, technical innovations related to aviation, archaeology and memorials. In order to disseminate this information the Group publishes a quarterly journal, *Airfield Review*. The journal is recognised throughout aviation circles as a first class product, with high quality content. ARG publications also include a series of books, which focus on twentieth century military archaeology. Again as with the close links between the BAPC and the BAAC, many members of either or both of these organisations also have individuals who are members of the ARG.

As with the aircraft preservation movement, aviation archaeology has its roots in the 1960s in a growing interest in the air battles of the Second World War. Indeed the release of the United Artists film *Battle of Britain* in 1968 served as a catalyst to yet more groups. These pioneering groups of individuals gained a range of reputations, the worst excesses leading to the movement being collectively labelled as '*relic hunters and grave robbers*' (de la Bédoyére, 2000). In his preface de la Bédoyére likens the emergence of more responsible 'professional' aviation archaeologists as a modern day equivalent of the late nineteenth century '*weekend barrow-digging antiquarian vicars*' (ibid pg.9). Further support is provided by Moshenska, who identifies aviation archaeology as one of the '*oldest and best established aspects of the archaeology of the Second World*

War'(Moshenska, 2012, pg.99), and that aviation archaeology groups have developed a high level of expertise over the years – with teams developing a detailed knowledge of geological and technical aspects (ibid). It is this realignment of the aviation archaeologist that forms the basis of this paper, demonstrating that the aviation archaeology community is indeed generally a respectful and professionally aspiring group of individuals, aiming to follow best practice as laid down by professional archaeology bodies such as the Institute of Field Archaeologists. As shall be seen further on in this paper, the last two decades has seen a greater focus on developing a professional approach.

In his preface to *Final Flights* (1989) Ian McLachlan traces his deep interest in the air war and aircraft back to childhood days engrossed in making plastic model kits before moving on to investigating East Anglian crash sites having been spurred on by local eye witness accounts of air operations. McLachlan makes an important point, one that resonates through the BAAC membership that it is not the digging of the aircraft, although the fragments add to the history of the time, which is so important. Rather that it is the crews who flew, and often died, that really is central to his motivation. McLachlan goes on to add that regardless of the size of findings, the aviation archaeologist (and through their work, the community local to the crash site) ensure that the passing of these men is preserved in local history. Moshenska, in his preface to his book (2012, pg.

xiii) emphasises that ' *the duty of archaeologists is to bring the traces of the Second World War to life again to illuminate the lives and experiences of the people who worked, fought and died among them*'. Crash sites yield not only aircraft components, small and large, but also the minutiae of air war. These include equipment, maps and, occasionally, flying clothing, the latter normally associated with a body *in situ*. However, there are exceptions (for example: an excavation of a Lockheed P-38 Lightning which crashed at Walcot, near Sleaford, revealed the pilot's flying helmet which he left in the cockpit when abandoning the aircraft.).

This thread links neatly to the wider archaeological idea, that of community archaeology. Whilst Moshenska is at pains not to define community archaeology, he nevertheless points to the common threads such as cooperation between professional and non-professional archaeologist, he goes on to consider a community as being based, '*on locale, class, interests, ethnicity, hobbies, language, sexuality and any number or combination of other factors.*' (Moshenska & Dhanjal, 2012, pg 1).

The focus of investigations is on the period 1939-1945 as this saw the most intense air activity over the United Kingdom. Aircraft losses both Allied and Axis, whether on operational sorties or on training flights, amounts to over 10,000 aircraft (Holyoak, 2002). The sheer magnitude of airframes is also compounded by the advances in aircraft construction – metal structures as opposed to the wood, canvas and wire of First World War and inter-war period designs. Whilst there have been a limited number of digs on First World War sites, they generally lack any real scope for artefacts other than turnbuckles or (very rarely) engines, the bulk of the structure being lightweight and of easily corrodible materials. Examples of such digs include Dr Neil Faulkner's excavation of Zeppelin L48's crash site at Croft's Field, Thurberton, in 2006, and an excavation by the local aviation enthusiasts of the area immediately around one of the seaplane jetties at North Killingholme, on the River Humber, in the early 1970s. However, there have been a number of post-war excavations. As peace-time recovery teams usually had more time, these sites generally have been cleared of most if not all the wreckage, although there are exceptions.

Amateur groups exist in Britain and on the Continent, with the aim of researching and recovering the remains of crashed historic aircraft. Most of these aircraft are military aircraft lost during the Second World War and, in some cases, circumstances led to substantial remains being left buried. Today wartime relics are becoming increasingly rare, indeed Holyoak highlights that of the 576 aircraft known to have been lost over the UK during the Battle of Britain, at least 250 have had archaeological interventions of one form or another (Holyoak, 2002).

The increase in awareness and interest in aviation archaeology has also been mirrored by an increase in the public's awareness. This is not only through commemorative events and inclusion of the Second World War in the National Curriculum, but also through a number of TV documentaries and programmes. In 1981, BBC2 covered the recovery of the Loch Ness Wellington, whilst four years later Ulster Television commissioned a documentary on the work of the Royal Dutch Air Force in recovering aircraft and human remains from the Ijsselmeer as the polders were drained. Between 1999 and 2008, there was a variety of programmes ranging from *Time Team* investigating a number of crash sites both in the UK and Europe, to *Timewatch*. They addressed such diverse topics as the First World War Zeppelin raids, through to the search for the P-38 in which maverick Malta photo-reconnaissance ace Adrian Warburton went missing, to the work of JPAC (see below). *Wreck Detectives* has covered the partial recovery of items from a Short Sunderland flying boat, which sank at Pembroke Dock. As well as three *Time Team* digs, Channel 4 has also covered the search for Douglas Bader's Spitfire. Channel 5 has covered the live dig, over a bank holiday weekend, of a Battle of Britain Hurricane in Central London and a dig in France on the last of the 'Dambuster' Lancasters (lost some months after the Dam's raid after being returned to standard specification). Most recently, the BBC has brought not only aviation archaeology to the public attention but also military and maritime archaeology through the *Dig WW2* series.

The role of British Aviation Archaeological Council (BAAC)

The BAAC is the official national body in the United Kingdom for aviation archaeologists and researchers of historic aircraft crashes. Founded in 1978, the aims of the council are:

- To establish and maintain ethical standards.

- To provide a forum for discussion.

- To provide advice for member groups.

- To liaise with national and international bodies.

- To promote the preservation of aircraft relics and relevant historical documents.

The majority of the BAAC's membership, some thirty-five groups, is actively involved in research and recovery, however, these are augmented by seven UK based research members and five international associates spread across Europe and North America. UK membership ranges (quiet literally) from Wessex Archaeology to the Dumfries and Galloway Aviation Museum. BAAC groups are encouraged: to research the background of each incident; display relics in the context of their local history and; to commemorate those who, all too often, died in the crashes. The BAAC publishes an in-house magazine,

Aviation Archaeologist: The Journal of the British Aviation Archaeology Council, 3 to 4 times a year.

The inspiration for the BAAC's inception came from the success of the BAPC in developing both a technical and a lobbying voice with both government departments (such as the MoD, the Royal Air Force, etc.) and influential bodies (such as English Heritage, the Heritage Lottery Fund, etc.) There is mutual support between both umbrella organisations, for example the BAAC Code of Conduct providing a model of best practice for the BAPC when they developed their own code of conduct.

The BAAC Code of Conduct provides a guide for best practice for aviation archaeology and covers the following two broad aspects:

1. Legal requirements:

- Compliance with the Protection of Military Remains Act;

- Land owners permission;

- Consent of other interested bodies – i.e. the Environment Agency; Natural England; the receiver of Wrecks, etc.;

- Full compliance with the MoD 'Notes of Guidance' as regards the discovery of human remains and/or ordnance; and

- Necessary precautions to ensure the safety of individuals working on crash sites.

2. Requirements for the investigation of aircraft crash sites. This includes as detailed and thorough research prior to the excavation and as detailed recording as possible of the excavation itself.

Getting down to the practicalities

Having outlined the development of aviation archaeology and the principal aviation organisations behind it, our attention is turned to how BAAC groups go about identifying, researching and organising a dig.

As with any project that might be likened to a huge jigsaw with many missing / hidden pieces, the mantra is 'Patience is a virtue – assume nothing'. Each project starts with a comprehensive trawl for information, and to this end, the particular BAAC group will have established comprehensive records over the years. These records will be drawn from the following: contemporaneous official reports (RAF accident reports; squadron operational record books (ORBs); RAF station ORBs; combat reports; local police 'Daily Situation Reports', etc.); local newspaper reports; eye-witness accounts / local knowledge; squadron associations; photographic evidence; map references; Google Earth images; and wide and varied internet sources.

Initial investigations

Once the initial research has been collated the next phase is to obtain permission from the landowner to carry out a field walk. 'Mark One Eyeball' combined with hand held metal detectors enables an initial assessment to be made. Legally, no penetration of the ground surface below 18 inches is permitted without a MoD licence. However, ploughing and general surface movement often brings to light small artefacts such as fragments of airframe, components, spent bullet cases, etc. Hedgerows and ditch bottoms can also prove a surprisingly rich harvest of finds. Larger ground penetrating detectors such as a Forster magnetometer / gradiometer or radio locators (such as a Fisher or a Whites) are used to identify large magnetic/ electrical resistance anomalies beneath the surface. Small items are removed by hand with the assistance of a small trowel with the item recorded photographically. Often small parts will yield manufacturing stencils, parts numbers or quality inspection stamps – all of which can clarify the aircraft type (for example a Handley-Page Hampden component produced by the manufacturer has the prefix 52 (The HP type number of the Hampden) with subsequent groupings identifying specific sub-assemblies.

Figure 2. Manufacturer's plate for Handley-Page Hampden AE436 – the second (lower) set of numbers (E.E.P. 19540) identifying this as an English Electric built airframe from the Preston production line

Excavation of crashed military aircraft within the United Kingdom

All military aircraft crash sites in the United Kingdom (UK), its territorial waters, or British aircraft in international waters, are controlled sites under the Protection of Military Remains Act 1986 (PoMRA). It is an offence under this Act to tamper with, damage, move or unearth any items at such sites, unless the Ministry of Defence (MoD) has issued a licence authorizing such activity. Consequently, anyone wishing to recover a military aircraft, or excavate a military aircraft crash site in the UK is required to obtain a licence from the Joint Casualty and Compassionate Centre (JCCC). A licence is required irrespective as to whether the aircraft was in the service of the British, American, German or other nation's armed forces.

The Joint Casualty and Compassionate Centre (JCCC)

The Joint Casualty and Compassionate Centre (JCCC) provide a reporting centre for all UK Armed Forces. Any casualty whether a fatality or injury is supported by this dedicated team, which is part of the Service Personnel and Veterans Agency (SPVA) based at Innsworth in Gloucestershire. Neither the Commonwealth War Graves Commission (CWGC) nor the JCCC actively seek the remains of British casualties from past conflicts. Today, remains of the war dead are now usually discovered in connection with road works, the excavation of foundations for buildings, archaeological digs, farming activity or metal detecting and battlefield research / "scavenging" by private individuals. (Indeed it was private research that resulted in a 'lost' grave-pit of 400 Australian soldiers being discovered at Fromelles, on the Somme, in 2007.) Any such finds are reported to the police, who would contact the local coroner or equivalent authority. Once the coroner is satisfied that the remains are those of a British or Commonwealth serviceman, the British Embassy or High Commission or CWGC would be contacted. The Defence Attaché/CWGC then in turn alerts the JCCC, who then co-ordinate attempts to identify the remains, using an extensive range of forensic techniques, as well as archive resources such as contemporary accounts, battalion war diaries, unit histories etc. This process will often involve the relevant Service historical branch or regimental association. Where positive identification is possible, the JCCC then attempts to trace the family, initially by writing to the home address given on the personal record of the casualty but local media appeals will also be made and the aid of regimental and squadron associations sought.

Before a licence can be issued, applicants are required to research and supply to the JCCC all relevant information on the aircraft they wish to recover including: location of crash site; the fate of the crew; supporting evidence from official sources; eye-witness accounts; initial field walk results (i.e. geo-physical readings); presence of small surface debris; etc.

The JCCC provides further support and guidance in the form of a comprehensive booklet "Crashed Military Aircraft of Historical Interest – Notes for Guidance of Recovery Groups". This also includes sample copies of the relevant forms.

On receipt of a licence application, the JCCC checks the information supplied against official records held with the MoD, Air Historical Branch, CWGC and where appropriate with the German or American authorities. These enquiries often take several months to complete. As such, applicants are required to apply for a licence at least 3 months before they intend to commence work. The information held by the MoD is far more detailed than anything within the public domain (extensive medical and personnel files as well as detailed recovery / salvage reports). Once the JCCC has completed its initial investigations it will arrive at a decision, which will also take into account the following considerations:

- A licence will not be issued if human remains are likely to be found at the site;

- A licence cannot be issued if significant amounts of unexploded ordnance (bombs / explosive ammunition / pyrotechnics) are believed to be present at the site; and

- All applications for a licence require the written support of the landowner to the excavation taking place.

The Joint Prisoner Of War / Missing In Action Accounting Command (JPAC)

Figure 3. The badge of JPAC

The JCCC has an equivalent organisation within the United States military, although its remit is far more proactive, US Congress decreeing that every casualty would be accorded the right to be repatriated and buried in US soil. This responsibility is tasked to the Joint POW/MIA Accounting Command (JPAC), which conducts global search, recovery, and laboratory operations to identify unaccounted-for Americans from past conflicts in order to further this goal. (http://www.jpac.pacom.mil/)

Located on the island of Oahu in Hawaii and employing more than 400 joint military and civilian personnel, JPAC continues its search for the more than 83,000 Americans still missing from past conflicts. The laboratory portion of JPAC, referred to as the Central Identification Laboratory, is the largest and most diverse forensic skeletal laboratory in the world.

The core of JPAC's day-to-day operations involves researching case files, investigating leads, excavating sites and identifying Americans who were killed in action or died on active service, but were never brought home. This process involves not only close coordination with U.S. agencies, but also routine engagement in technical negotiations and talks with representatives of foreign governments. JPAC works closely with JCCC as regards applications for licences to excavate USAAF aircraft, which lie within the UK. In the very rare event that human remains are discovered during an excavation, control and responsibility for the investigation passes to JPAC. The work of JPAC in co-operation with the Lincolnshire Aircraft Recovery Group in its recovery of a P-51C Mustang can be found on the Lincolnshire Aviation Heritage Centre's associate's Silksheen Photography website (http://silksheenphotography.co.uk/resident-aircraft/mustang-42-103007-gallery-history/.)

Licence application, approval and excavation: the process

In addition to the strict licence guidelines required by the JCCC, local Councils may impose additional requirements or limitations in respect of archaeological activity within their area of jurisdiction, particularly if the crash site is in an area where other historical artefacts may be disturbed. Applicants for a licence under the Protection of Military Remains Act 1986 need to check with the Council or local Sites and Monuments Records Officer in advance, or at the same time, as applying for a licence from the MoD. The MoD reserves the right to deploy its representatives to witness any excavations approved under the Protection of Military Remains Act.

Outside the United Kingdom, International or British territorial waters, the PoMRA does not apply, with excavations of crash sites of British aircraft being subject to the laws of the country concerned. However, MoD policy is to discourage disturbance of

such sites unless necessary in respect of host Government approved activities, such as land reclamation or construction.

Additional requirements may have to be met before a licence is issued to excavate a crash site in a National Park or designated Site of Special Scientific Interest. For example the map below shows the disposition of 176 aircraft from 170 Peak District crash sites.

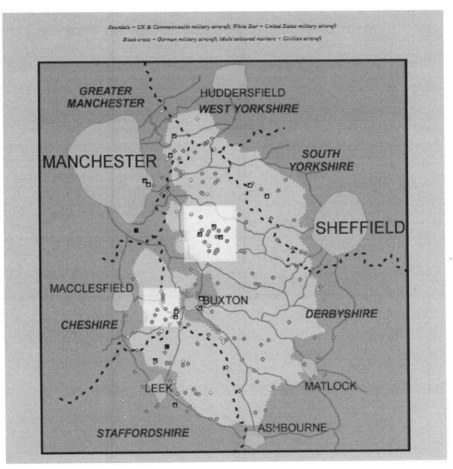

Figure 4. Map showing the location of Peak District aircraft crash sites
http://www.peakdistrictaircrashes.co.uk/pages/pdmap.htm

Project design

The project design is very specific in its format, and has been developed by JCCC specialists. It must include the following:

- Location – 6 digit map reference, general area described.

- Aircraft details.

- Aircrew details.

- Date and time of crash.

- Historical background.

- Previous work on site.

- Site description.

- Extent of excavation work.

- Documenting the excavation.

- Conservation and display of artefacts.

- Appendices (usually BAAC Code of Conduct).

Legal requirements include compliance with the following: the provisions of the Protection of Military Remains Act; the MoD licence; land owner's permission; and where appropriate the requisite approval from the National Trust, English Heritage, Natural England, and Environment Agency etc. Consultation with the relevant County Archaeologist is also required.

LINCOLNSHIRE AIRCRAFT RECOVERY GROUP

MEMBER
B.A.A.C.

MEMBER
D.A.P.C.

PROJECT DESIGN FOR PROPOSED EXCAVATION OF
HP HALIFAX V EB185

HP Halifax V of 1663 Heavy Conversion Unit [HCU] (Representative aircraft)

A planned excavation by the
Lincolnshire Aircraft Recovery Group

Under the supervision of

David Stubley, Lincolnshire Aircraft Recovery Group [LARG] Secretary
33, Grosvenor Road, Frampton, Boston, Lincolnshire. PE20 1DB

June 2009

Figure 5. LARG Project design front cover for the excavation of Handley-Page Halifax V Serial No. EB185

Other important information includes: Investigation of crash site; Detailed pre-excavation research; Evidence / observations / findings during excavation / photographic and / or video record; Stabilisation of finds; Restoration of site after completion; Documentation, conservation and display of artefacts; The completion of a return for JCCC; and A full report to JCCC (a copy going to the County Archaeologist).

Figure 6. Halifax EB185 Initial excavation based on readings from metal detectors (Photograph: G R Chaters)

Figure 8. Propeller boss showing, to the left and right of the resting gloved hand, the wooden propeller bladestubs (Photograph: G.R. Chaters)

Case study: a Handley Page Halifax V EB185, No. 1667 Heavy Conversion Unit, RAF Faldingworth

On the 16th December 1943 at 23:25, whilst on a night training exercise, this aircraft crashed approximately 2 miles northeast of the airfield, on land close to Newton Ings Farm. The cause of the crash could not be ascertained. All seven crew lost their lives and are buried at various locations in the UK.

Figure 7. Part of propeller blade complete with laminate covering (Photograph: G.R. Chaters)

Figure 9. Reinstating the site after closing down the excavation (Photograph: G.R. Chaters)

Weather played a significant contribution to the loss of 26 heavy bombers on this night, with dense fog carpeting much of Yorkshire, Lincolnshire and East Anglia in time for their return from bombing Berlin. Add to this a further three HCU aircraft, including EB185, the total carnage for the night was 29 aircraft lost and over 340 aircrew killed.

LINCOLNSHIRE AIRCRAFT
RECOVERY GROUP

MEMBER
E.A.A.C.

MEMBER
B.A.P.C

REPORT ON THE EXCAVATION OF
HANDLEY PAGE HALIFAX V EB185

HP Halifax V of 1663 Heavy Conversion Unit [HCU] (Representative aircraft)

A report on the excavation by the
Lincolnshire Aircraft Recovery Group

Under the supervision of

David Stubley, Lincolnshire Aircraft Recovery Group [LARG] Secretary
33, Grosvenor Road, Frampton, Boston, Lincolnshire. PE20 1DB

June 2010

Figure 10. Cover of the Excavation Report for Handley Page Halifax Mk V EB185. (Source: Lincolnshire Aircraft Recovery Group)

Following the completion of the dig a return is made to JCCC. This is followed by a report which is forwarded to JCCC with an additional copy passed to the relevant County Archaeologist. The reports contents are: 1 Background; 2 Summary; 3 Permissions/Licence; 4 Location; 5 Locating; 6 Recovery; 7 Results; 8 Conclusions; and 9 References.

Ownership of items recovered

According to the JCCC's notes of guidance all items recovered remain the property of the Crown although this was not established by the PoMRA or by any case law. This includes items recovered from crashed British aircraft outside the UK (for which a licence is not required). Excavations are licensed on the understanding that the Ministry of Defence may require the licensee to surrender all items recovered to the Department without compensation. On expiry of the licence, or completion of the excavation if earlier, licensees are required to file a report to the JCCC, listing all items found and if appropriate request transfer of ownership. Transfer of ownership is not guaranteed, but in practice ownership of most items recovered, including parts of the aircraft may be transferred to the licensee. However, the following items have to be surrendered to the Ministry of Defence:

- All personal items belonging to the crew (which will be returned to the next of kin or crew member if still alive).

- All official documents / records.

- Items assessed as being of historical interest (The Ministry of Defence seeks the views of the Royal Air Force Museum on the historical value of items recovered).

Should the Ministry of Defence learn that not all items recovered have been declared, or items have been recovered or disposed of contrary to the terms of the Protection of Military Remains Act 1986, the licensee or individual concerned will be liable to be prosecuted.

Case Study B: Consolidated B-24J Liberator Serial No 43-50907 'LilyMarlene' USAAF 755th Bomb Squadron of the 458th Bomb Group. Crashed 9th September 1944 7 killed, 2 survived.

This aircraft, based at Horsham St Faith (now Norwich airport) was engaged on a night cross-country flight to Shrewsbury when it got into difficulties over the Lincolnshire Fens. The cause of the crash was not determined, although it is known from the navigator, Glenn Allen (who along with Bombardier Jack Hibbs were the only crew to escape) that at around 23:30hrs the aircraft became uncontrollable and the pilot sounded the 'Bail out' warning bell. Theories proposed include that either the B24 flew through the prop-wash of another aircraft, or it encountered a down draft that made the aircraft uncontrollable; or that there was a malfunction with the autopilot (which was engaged at the time). As the aircraft's altitude was only around 3,800 feet, there was precious little time for the pilot to take corrective action. Details regarding this incident were collated from the survivors' testimony and witness testimony on the ground – the bomber falling on the crew yard and outbuildings at Fleet Hall Farm, Crowland Common. Local sources included Mr and Mrs Maddison, who

with their son, George, were lucky to escape the wreckage falling around them, and the local ARP Warden, Jack Wheat. The hastily gathered civilian rescue party could do nothing for the rest of the crew – the impact having torn the aircraft apart and causing the fuel tanks to rupture, igniting the contents.

The remains of the seven airmen were collected over the next few days and it was to be several weeks before the local AFS fire crew could declare the fire to be extinguished – much of the fuel having permeated the peat layer beneath the surface. This was confirmed during the dig when a 'fired' layer of clay was uncovered beneath the few remaining pieces of wreckage.

Figure 11. B-24J Liberator Serial No 43-50907 'Lily Marlene' (Photograph: Lincolnshire Aircraft Recovery Group)

Once the site has been closed down all artefacts are recovered to the LARG workshop at the Lincolnshire Aviation Heritage Centre at East Kirkby. Each bag / container of finds is sorted and categorised. Normally, small, non-descript or heavily corroded (but insignificant) pieces are consigned to the local scrap recycling facility. All other items are stabilised. The LARG team follow the guidelines set out in the

Standing: Daniel Peller– Tail Gunner, William Casey – Top Turret Gunner, Jack Zonker–
Radio Operator, William Nobles – Nose Turret Gunner, Robert Leake– Ball Turret Gunner,
Ulysses Seymour – Engineer.
Kneeling: Glen Allen - Navigator, William Frederick - Pilot, Lawrence Doelling– Co Pilot,
Jack Hibbs– Bombardier.

Figure 12. Lily Marlene's crew (Photograph: Lincolnshire Aircraft Recovery Group)

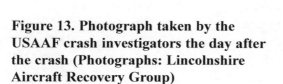

**Figure 13. Photograph taken by the
USAAF crash investigators the day after
the crash (Photographs: Lincolnshire
Aircraft Recovery Group)**

**Figure 14. Photograph taken by the
USAAF crash investigators the day after
the crash (Photographs: Lincolnshire
Aircraft Recovery Group)**

Figure 15. Image showing the area investigated – arrow shows direction of photograph in Figure 16
https://maps.google.co.uk/maps?hl=en&q=crowland+common&ie=UTF-8

Figure 16. One of the few artefacts recovered; a propeller boss with one of the three blades still attached (Photograph: G.R. Chaters)

Figure 17. Site after back filling of the excavation by LARG (Photo: G.R. Chaters)

Figure 18. Comparison photograph taken by the USAAF crash investigators the day after the crash (Photograph: Lincolnshire Aircraft Recovery Group)

RAFM Cosford Michael Beetham Conservation Centre guidance on Cleaning Artefacts and Preserving Existing Paint Finish. Metal items, if deemed suitable for display are cleaned and coated with a mixture of varnish and engine oil. Some items will be coated, if appropriate, with Renaissance Microcrystalline wax. Once stabilising and conservation has been accomplished, a display cabinet is constructed and the artefacts along with narrative and photographic interpretation are put on display.

Further examples of aviation archaeology displays and excavations

The following examples illustrate the range of projects undertaken by aviation archaeology groups.

Figure 19. Artefacts and story of Lily Marlene on display in the hanger at the Lincolnshire Aviation Heritage Centre, East Kirkby (Photograph: G.R. Chaters)

Figure 20. Spitfire Vb BL655 engine and cockpit display Lincolnshire Aircraft Recovery Group (Photograph: G.R. Chaters)

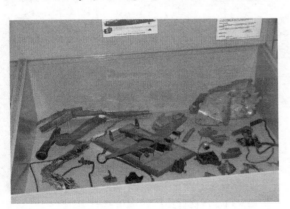

Figure 21. Typical small artefact display - in this instance for 100 Squadron Lancaster ED583, which suffered a catastrophic structural failure whilst on air test 5th October 1943 (Photograph: G.R. Chaters)

Figure 22. General view of LARG displays at East Kirkby (Photograph: G.R. Chaters)

Figure 23. General view of LARG displays at East Kirkby (Photograph: G.R. Chaters)

Case Study C: Brian Nicholls Hampden Project

Figure 24. Handley-Page Hampden AE436 (Photograph: Brian Nicholls Hampden Project)

In September 1942, Handley-Page Hampden, AE436 was flying from the Shetlands to Russia to take up convoy protection duties. Due to technical issues, the aircraft could not maintain height and crashed on Mount Tsasa in Sweden, killing three of the five aircrew on board.

The wreckage lay undisturbed until the long hot summer of 1976 when the snow line retreated far higher up the mountain than normal. Two hikers came across the site and the Swedish Air Force recovered the bodies of the three crew members for burial. Much of the wreckage was then returned to the RAF who in turn donated it to serving RAF armourer Brian Nicholls. Brian started a rebuild but unfortunately succumbed to a terminal illness in May 1996. His name is perpetuated in the title of the project. The following images show steps in the recovery and rebuild. This project also highlights the links between aviation archaeology and aircraft preservation and restoration, as opposed to conservation and interpretation of artefacts.

Figure 25. AE436 in situ Mount Tsatsa, Sweden August 1976 (Photograph: Brian Nicholls Hampden Project)

Figure 27. Sweden August 1976 tail section in the foreground (Photograph: Brian Nicholls Hampden Project)

Figure 28. Cockpit showing instrument panel and control column. (Photograph: Brian Nicholls Hampden Project)

Figure 29. Tail surfaces as part of a larger display at East Kirkby (Photograph: G.R. Chaters)

Figure 30. Forward lower fuselage under construction – upper forward fuselage in background (Photograph: G.R. Chaters)

Figure 31. Interior view showing refurbished original instrument panel (Photograph: G.R. Chaters)

Case Study D: Midland Aircraft Recovery Group (MARG) Vickers Armstrong Wellington Mk IV Z1206 No.104 OTU

This bomber was found buried in a beach on the Isle of Lewis and salvaged in 2002 - the culmination of five years of work and planning. It is the sole surviving Mk IV - the fastest of all the Wellingtons, with Pratt & Whitney Twin Wasp engines. Built at Chester (Hawarden) in 1941, Z1206 flew 14 operational sorties with 142 (City of Worcester) Squadron. Coded QT-F (F for Freddie), it was based at Binbrook and Waltham (Grimsby) in Lincolnshire.

By 1943, Z1206 was with 104 Operational Training Unit at Nutts Corner, Northern Ireland. On 26th January 1944, Z1206 ran short of fuel whilst on a navigational exercise and was ditched at UigBay, Isle of Lewis. It was washed up onto the sand and then lay buried for over fifty years. The front fuselage of the Wellington is being conserved and will be rebuilt for display. MARG aims to display it surrounded by photographs and anecdotes relevant to the men of 142 Squadron and 104 OTU. (http://www. aviationarchaeology.org.uk/marg/ projects.htm)

Figure 32. General view of site (Photograph: Mark Evans, MARG)

Figure 33. Selective enlargement of Figure 32– Z1206 was buried at the water line just below the small headland bisecting the beach (Photograph: Mark Evans, MARG)

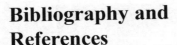

Figure 34. Lower half, front fuselage (turret bottom left) during excavation (P Photograph: Mark Evans MARG)

Figure 35 Brooklands museum Wellington R-Robert (recovered from Loch Ness) – comparison photograph of lower front fuselage (Photograph: G.R. Chaters)

Bibliography and References

Airfield Research Group http://www.airfieldresearchgroup.org.uk/ accessed 17/07/2013 20:04

Blackamore, I. (2002) *Metal Birds: Stories from Lincolnshire's Air War, Book Three*. I. Blackamore, Boston.

Brew, A. (2003) *Vampires and Fleas: A History of British Aircraft Preservation*. The Crowood Press, Marlborough.

British Aviation Archaeology Council (2000) *British Aviation Archaeology Council Code of Conduct*.

British Aviation Preservation Council http://www.aviationarchaeology.org.uk. Accessed 18/07/2013 14:40

de la Bédoyére, G. (2000) *Battles over Britain: The Archaeology of the Air War*. Tempus Publishing, Stroud.

Clarke, B. (2008) *The Archaeology of Airfields*. Tempus Publishing, Stroud.

Crossland, J. (1990) To Dig or Not to Dig? *History Today*, **40**(12). http://www.historytoday.com/john-crossland/dig-or-not-to-dig accessed 02/07/2013 20:10

English Heritage (2002) *Military Aircraft Crash Sites: archaeological guidance on their significance and future management*. English Heritage, London.

Faulkner, N. and Durrani, N. (2008) *In Search of the Zeppelin War: The Archaeology of the First Blitz*. Tempus Publishing, Stroud.

Hood, J. (2012) *Dig WW2: Rediscovering the Great Wartime Battles*. Conway, London.

Holyoak, V. (2002) Out of the blue: assessing military aircraft crash sites in England, 1912-1945. *Antiquity*, **76**, 657-63.

Joint POW Casualty / MIA Accounting Command http://www.jpac.pacom.mil/index.php?page=mission_overview&size=100&ind=0 Accessed 17/07/2013 21:47

McCarthy, M. *Historic aircraft wrecks as archaeological sites* http://wamuseum.com.au/collections/maritime/march/fallenangels/macs.html Accessed 02/07/2013 08:22

McLachlan, I. (1989) *Final Flights: dramatic wartime incidents revealed by aviation archaeology*. Patrick Stephens Limited, Cambridge.

Midland Aircraft Recovery Group www.aviationarchaeology.org.uk/marg/projects.htm Accessed 18/07/2013 15:10

Moshenska, G. (2012) *The Archaeology of the Second World War: Uncovering Britain's Wartime Heritage*. Pen and Sword, Barnsley.

Moshenska, G. & Dhanjal, S. (eds.) (2012) *Community Archaeology: Themes, Methods and Practices*. Oxbow Books, Oxford.

Parry, S. (2010) *Spitfire Hunters: The Inside Stories Behind the Best Aviation Archaeology TV Documentaries*. Red Kite, Walton on Thames.

Peak District Air Crashes *http://www.peakdistrictaircrashes.co.uk/pages/pdmap.htm* Accessed 20/3/13 20:53

Reffrew, C. & Bahn, P. (2000) *Archaeology: Theories, Methods, and Practice 3rd edition*. Thames & Hudson, London.

Robertson, B. (1978) *Epics of Aviation Archaeology*. Patrick Stephens Limited, Cambridge.

Robertson, B. (1983) *Aviation Archaeology: A Collectors' guide to aeronautical relics*. 2nd edition, Patrick Stephens Limited, Cambridge.

Sarkar, D. (2006) *Missing in Action: Resting in Peace?* Ramrod publications, Worcester.

Schofield, J. (2004) *Modern Military Matters: studying and managing the twentieth-century heritage in Britain: a discussion document*. Council for British Archaeology, York.

Schofield, J. (2005) *Combat Archaeology: Material culture and Modern Conflict*. Duckworth, London.

Silksheen Photography http://silksheenphotography.co.uk/resident-aircraft/mustang-42-103007-gallery-history/

Veronico, N.A., Davies, E., Grantham, A.K., Kropp, R.A., Massagli, E., McComb, D.B., McCmob, M.B., McGarry, T.W. & Wetz, W. (2011) *Wreck chasing 101: A Guide To Finding Aircraft Crash Sites*. Stance & Speed – no place of publication given.

War in a Wetland, cartoon illustration from World War 1. © Ian D. Rotherham

Radionuclide sorption on the peat

Andris Abramenkovs[1], Maris Klavins[2], Janis Rudzitis[1] and Andris Popelis[1]

[1]Latvian Environment, Geology and Meteorology Centre
[2]University of Latvia

Abstract

The emission of radionuclides in the environment during the last 70 years is a global phenomenon and arises because of nuclear weapons tests, emissions from different nuclear facilities, especially during severe nuclear accidents like Chernobyl, 1986 or Fukushima, 2011. It was found (Lidman, 2009; Le Roux, 2010), that the bog's peat accumulates the radionuclides, which significantly influences the bog's ecosystem. On the other hand, organic sorbents like peat can be successfully used for purification of radioactive wastewaters due to economic and technical considerations. This study examines the sorption of radionuclides ^{137}Cs, ^{55}Fe, ^{63}Ni and ^{60}Co through peat samples from different bogs in Latvia. The initial radioactivity of the peat samples was studied before the experiments.

The samples were oven dried over a period of 24 hours at 105°C, ground and sieved using a sieve shaker to obtain peat fractions with sizes: <0.25 mm, 0.25-0.5 mm, 0.5-2.0 mm and >2.0 mm. Radionuclides' solutions were prepared using deionised water and appropriate radionuclide composition from the Salaspils research reactor's stock water. The solution's pH and conductivity were controlled during the experiments.

Batch mode studies were performed in isothermal conditions at temperature 20±0.1°C. Flow experiments were performed using a sorption column with a 50g peat load. An Ortec gamma spectrometer with high purity germanium probe was used for the measurement of the concentrateion of gamma radionuclides in solutions and peat samples. Radioactivity of beta radionuclides was measured using the liquid scintillation counter HIDEX.

It was found that the main natural radionuclides in the peat samples were ^{210}Pb, 40K and ^{214}Bi, but artificial radionuclides ^{152}Eu, ^{137}Cs and ^{60}Co were also detected in the peat. Experimental results indicated that the near surface peat samples have the increased radioactivity of ^{137}Cs and ^{60}Co radionuclides.

Batch, sorption, mode studies indicated that during the first five hours of the experiments, the initial radioactivity of the solution decreases in the case of radionuclides ^{63}Ni, ^{60}Co and ^{55}Fe within a factor of 4 to 20. The same results were observed in case of the flow sorption mode experiments. It was shown, that the radionuclides ^{137}Cs and ^{60}Co sorption ability by the peat samples significantly depends on the solution pH. It shows that peat can effectively remove the radionuclides from radioactive water solutions. The role of humic substances in the immobilization of radionuclides is discussed.

Keywords: peat, radionuclides, sorption

Introduction

The emission of radionuclides in the environment during the last 70 years is a global phenomenon and arises because of nuclear weapons' tests and emissions from different nuclear facilities, especially during severe nuclear accidents like Chernobyl, 1986 or Fukushima, 2011. Different studies have shown that peat and peat-bogs function as an important factor for environment protection (Nifontova *et al.*, 1987; Ritchie *et al.*, 1990; Ibrahim *et al.*, 2005; Convey *et al.*, 2011). It has been stressed that due to the low salinity of bog water and humic acids the peat is capable of extracting caesium, strontium, and other radioactive elements (Jantulen *et al.*, 1991; Jungner *et al.*, 1995; Gallagher *et al.*, 2000; Lubyte *et al.*, 2004; Lidman, 2009).Therefore, the bog ecosystem is very sensitive to the radioactive emissions in the environment and can concentrate the radionuclides in the peat (Karlsson & Bergstrom, 2000; Vanderploeg *et al.*, 2000; Schleich *et al.*, 2000; Shaw & Green, 2002). Mustonen *et al.* (1989) reported that the accident at the Chernobyl nuclear power plant in April 1986 caused an increase in concentrations of ^{137}Cs in composite peat samples from 30 up to 3600 Bq kg[-1] dry weight and in ash samples correspondingly from 600 to 68000 Bq

kg[-1]. It resulted in restrictions to the utilisation of peat ash for various purposes. Such economic and human health factors must be considered during war, terrorist acts and severe accidents with the pollution of the environment by radionuclides.

On the other hand, organic sorbents such as peat can be successfully used for the purification of radioactive waste waters due to economic and technical considerations (Razvorotneva *et al.*, 2009; Klavins *et al.*, 2012). The sorption of radionuclides on peat materials was investigated by Sanchez *et al.*, 1988; Helal *et al.*, 2006; and Abramenkovs *et al.*, 2012. Stevenson (1982) reported that humic substances are formed during the humification process of the peat. Humic substances can be divided into humic acids (HA), fulvic acids (FA) and humin. The authors (Sanchez *et al.*, 1988; Helal *et al.*, 2006) stressed that humic acids strongly affect a wide range of environmental processes, due to their ability to form organic chemical complexes, including combining with radionuclides. Humic acids participate in complex formation with metals ions and have an influence on the immobilisation of these pollutants by peat. It was shown (Wang *et al.*, 2006) that the presence of HA influence the sorption of Eu (III) on the alumina surface, depending on pH values. The sorption process is one of the methods for studying interactive behaviour between peat and radionuclides. Authors (Jain *et al.*, 2007; Nagao *et al.*, 2007 & 2009; Ibrahim & Omar, 2005) investigated the distribution of radionuclides in the environment and the influence of humic substances on the migration of radionuclides.

In this paper, the sorption of radionuclides ^{137}Cs, ^{55}Fe, ^{63}Ni and ^{60}Co on peat samples was studied for radioactive waste management purposes. Organic sorbents like peat can be successfully used for purification of radioactive wastewaters, and are favoured by economic and technical considerations (Klavins *et al.*, 2012).

Methodology

Peat samples were acquired from Dzelves, Svetupes and Viku bogs, using peat from different layers. The samples were oven dried over a period of 24 hours at 105 °C and were ground and sieved to obtain peat fractions with sizes: <0.25 mm, 0.25–0.5 mm, 0.5–2.0 mm and >2.0 mm. Analytical grade chemicals were used. Radionuclide solutions were prepared using deionised water and the appropriate radionuclide composition from the Salaspils' research reactor liquid radioactive wastewater. Solution pH and conductivity were measured using a universal Mettler Toledo pH meter/ conductivity meter.

Batch sorption studies were performed in isothermal conditions at different temperatures using a mechanical mixer and a 350 mL glass flask. A five-gramme peat sample was inserted into 250 mL of radioactive solution and mixed for the entire duration of the experiment. A two-millilitre aliquot of the solution was taken after a defined time interval and was centrifuged for ten minutes at 10000 rotations per minute.

Flow experiments were performed by using a sorption column loaded with 50g of peat. The radioactive solution was pumped through the column at the flow rate of 0.4 L/h. An Ortec gamma spectrometer with a high purity germanium probe was used for the measurement of γ-radionuclide concentrations in solutions and peat samples. Radioactivity of β radionuclides was measured using a HIDEX liquid scintillation counter.

Results and discussion

Experimental studies were performed to determine the gamma radionuclides in the peat samples. It was found, that the natural peat samples contained both natural and artificial gamma radionuclides (Table 1). The main natural radionuclides were ^{210}Pb, ^{40}K and ^{214}Bi.

The artificial radionuclides ^{152}Eu, ^{137}Cs and ^{60}Co were also found in the peat samples from Dzelves and Svetupes bog, while Viku bog contains ^{137}Cs and ^{60}Co radionuclides. Specific activity of ^{137}Cs varied from 8.0 Bq/kg up to 528.0 Bq/kg, which can be explained by the influence of the fallouts from the Chernobyl accident on contamination of the bogs. The presence of ^{152}Eu and ^{60}Co confirms this conclusion. Experimental results indicated that near surface peat samples have an increased radioactivity of ^{137}Cs radionuclide, but in the case of Viku bog, the radioactivity of the layer at 1.9

Table 1. Content of radionuclides in different layers of bogs

Nuclide	Dzelves bog, Bq/kg		Svetupes bog, Bq/kg		Viku bog, Bq/kg		
	20 cm	50 cm	0-100 cm	140-150 cm	0-100 cm	140-150 cm	190-200 cm
^{210}Pb	126.0	155.0	35.0	15.0	27.0	49.0	43.0
^{152}Eu	4.0	4.0	0.5	0.9	<MDA	<MDA	<MDA
^{137}Cs	8.0	53.0	448.0	28.0	96.0	58.0	528.0
^{40}K	76.0	49.0	39.0	15.0	146.0	174.0	258.0
^{60}Co	<MDA	0.06	0.06	<MDA	0.2	2.5	0.5
^{214}Bi	48.0	32.0	32.0	3.5	7.5	15.4	9.4

m–2.0 m depth had the highest value. These results also must be taken into account when giving the correct explanation of the radionuclide sorption's results.

Batch sorption mode studies indicated that during the 2.5 hours of the experiments, the initial radioactivity of the deionised water solution in the case of ^{63}Ni changed by a factor of 4 (Figure 1).

In the case of ^{55}Fe and ^{60}Co, the 96 % of radionuclides were immobilised by the peat after the peat and radionuclides solution mixing over a period of 2.5 hours. The peat's sorption capacity for radionuclide ^{137}Cs was 27% under the same conditions. Experimental results proved that peat samples could effectively remove the radionuclides from radioactive water solutions within the batch sorption conditions.

The flow experiments using the radionuclides ^{137}Cs also confirm the radionuclide sorption on the peat. It was found that the ^{137}Cs sorption ability of the peat samples decreased significantly during the first three hours of the experiment (Figure 2). Experimental data indicated that the pH of the solution also decreased from 9.0 to 3.8 in this time-period. The pH changes in the water solution occurred due to the acidic properties of the peat samples. The sorption efficiency stabilised around the pH interval from 4.0 up to 5.0, but the rise of pH more than 6.0 caused the sorption efficiency to decrease.

The results of both types of experiment are in a good agreement with the results of previous investigations (Jain *et al.*, 2007; Nagao *et al.*, 2007 & 2009; Ibrahim & Omar, 2005). The results obtained confirmed the authors' (Sanchez *et al.*, 1988; Helal *et al.*, 2006; Wang *et al.*, 2006) conclusions on the role of humic substances in the immobilization of radionuclides in the peat. These results together with the data on the radionuclides content in the peat samples point to a possible conclusion that during the emission of radionuclides in the environment (because of war, severe accidents and

Figure 1. The radionuclides sorption curves on peat from the batch sorption studies. The peat fraction was 0.5–2.0 mm. Deionised water temperature was 20±0.1ºC.

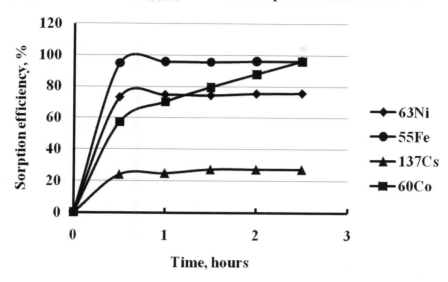

Figure 2. Sorption parameter changes during the flow experiments with the radionuclide ^{137}Cs: 1 – pH changes during experiment; 2 –sorption curve for ^{137}Cs; 3 – sorption efficiency ×10, %. Dzelves bog near surface peat samples, fraction 0.5–2.0 mm. Temperature 20 ±1 °C.

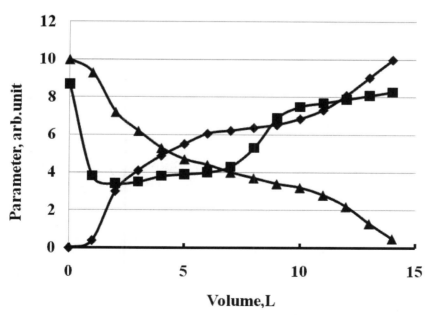

terrorist activities) a significant part of these radionuclides will be accumulated in the bogs. These phenomena could cause a serious impact on the peat industry since increased amounts of peat radioactivity can cause some restrictions on the utilisation of peat in the different branches of the industry (Mustonen *et al.*, 1989). On the other hand, the peat products can be utilised for the remediation activities of contaminated territories, especially for radioactive waste purification purposes. Peat filtration systems can be used both for decontamination of contaminated water sources (ponds, lakes, etc.), and purification of the secondary liquid radioactive waste streams. After incineration of the peat filters, ash can be easily cemented and disposed of in designated radioactive waste repositories. This is an important consideration for developing new purification systems for radioactive waste management purposes.

Conclusions

1. The radioactivity of peat from different bogs was studied. The artificial radionuclides ^{152}Eu, ^{137}Cs and ^{60}Co were found in the peat samples.

2. It was shown that the initial radioactivity of ^{63}Ni, ^{60}Co and ^{55}Fe radionuclides in solution in the case of the batch and flow sorption experiments decreased 4- 20 times.

3. Radionuclide sorption in the bogs must be taken into account for analysis of the radionuclides emission.

consequences in the environment during war, severe accidents and terroristic acts conditions.

4. Peat and peat products can be utilized for the radioactive waste management purposes.

Acknowledgements

The authors want to make acknowledgments to the European Regional Development Fund for the interest and support for the performed investigations according to the project No. 2010/0264/2DP /2.1.1.1.0/10/ APIA/VIAA/037.

Bibliography

Abramenkovs, A., Klavins, M., Rudzitis, J. & Popelis, A. (2012) Investigation of radionuclide sorption on peat. *Latvian Journal of Chemistry*, **4**, 342–346.

Convey, P., Hopkins, D.W., Roberts, S.J. & Tyler, A.N. (2011) Global southern limit of flowering plants and moss peat accumulation. *Polar Research*, **30**, 8929.

Gallagher, D., McGee, E.J. & Mitchell, P.I. (2001) A recent history of ^{14}C, ^{137}Cs, ^{210}Pb and ^{241}Am accumulation at two Irish peat bog sites: An east versus west coast comparison. *Radiocarbon*, **43**, (2b), 517–525.

Helal, A.A., Helal, Aly, A., Salim, N.Z. & Khalifa, S.M. (2006) Sorption of radionuclides on peat humin. *J. Radioanal. Nucl. Chem.*, **267** (2), 363–368.

Ibrahim, M.Z. and Omar M. (2005) Interactions between natural organic matter and radionuclides: An overview. *Journal of nuclear and related technologies*, **2** (1), 63-73.

Jain, A., Rawat, N., Kumar, S., Tomar, B.S., Manchanda, V.K. & Ramanathan S. (2007) Effect of humic acid on sorption of neptunium on hematite colloids. *Radiochim. Acta*, **95**, 501–506.

Jantulen, M., Reponen A., Kauranen, P. & Vartianen, M. (1991) Chernobyl Fallout in Southern and Central Finland. *Health Phys.*, **60** (3), 427-434.

Jungner, H., Sonninen, E., Possnert, G. & Tolonen, K. (1995) Use of bomb-produced ^{14}C to evaluate the amount of CO_2 emanating from two peat bogs in Finland. *Radiocarbon*, **37** (2), 567-573.

Karlsson, S. & Bergstrom, U. (2000) *Dose rate estimates for the Olkiluoto site using the biospheric models of SR 97*. Report Posiva 2000-20, Studsvik Eco & Safety AB, Sweden.

Klavins, M., Porshnov, D., Ansone, L., Robalds, A. & Dreijalte, L. (2012) *Peat as natural and industrial sorbent*. In: Proceedings of International Conference on Energy, Environment, Ecosystems and Sustainable Development (EEESD'12), University of Algarve, Faro, May 2-4, 146-151.

Le Roux, G. & Marshall, W.A. (2010/11) Constructing recent peat accumulation chronologies using atmospheric fall-out radionuclides. *Mires and Peat*, **7** (8), 1–14.

Lidman, F. (2009) *Radionuclide transport in peat lands*. Technical Report TR-06-37, Svensk Kärnbränslehantering AB, Stockholm, Sweden.

Lubyte, J. & Antanaitis, A. (2004) Migration of radionuclides in arable land of Lithuania. *J. Environ. Eng. Landsc. Manag.*, **12** (1), 22–29.

Mustonen, R.A., Reponen, A.R.and Jantunen M.J. (1989) Artificial radioactivity in fuel peat and peat ash in Finland after the Chernobyl accident. *Health Phys.*, **56** (4), 451-458.

Nagao, S., Sakamoto, Y., Tanaka, T. & Rao, R.R. (2007) Molecular size distribution of Pu in the presence of humic substances in river and groundwaters. *J. Radioanal. Nucl. Chem.*, **273**, 135–139.

Nagao, S., Sakamoto, Y., Rao, R.R. & Fujitake, N. (2009) Effects of Groundwater Humic Substances on Sorption of Np(V) on Sandy materials. *Humic Substances Research*, **5/6**, 9-17.

Nifontova, M.G., Makovskii, V.I. & Kulikov, N.V. (1987) Strontium-90 and caesium-137 in peat deposits of low-lying bog in the influence zone of the Beloyarsky atomic power station. *The Soviet Journal of Ecology*, **17** (3), 153-158.

Razvorotneva, L.I., Gilinskaya, L.G. & Markovich, T.I. (2009) Modified natural sorbents as radionuclides absorbers. *Vestnik Otdelenia nauk o Zemle RAN*, **1** (27), 1-3.

Ritchie J.C. & McHenry J.R. (1990) Application of Radioactive Fallout Cesium-137 for Measuring Soil Erosion and Sediment Accumulation Rates and Patterns. *A. Review J. Environ. Qual.*, **19**, 215-233.

Sanchez, A.L., Schell, W.R. & Thomas, E.D. (1988) Interactions of ^{57}Co, ^{85}Sr and ^{137}Cs with peat under acidic precipitation conditions. *Health Phys.*, **54** (3), 317–322.

Schleich N., Degering D. and Unterricker S. (2000) Natural and artificial radionuclides in forest and bog soils: Tracers for migration processes and soil development. *Radiochimica Acta*, **88** (9-11), 803-808.

Shaw, S. & Green, N. (2002) *The Availability of Soil-Associated Radionuclides for Uptake after Inadvertent Ingestion by Humans*. Report NRPB-W17, National Radiological Protection Board, Chilton, Didcot.

Stevenson, F.J. (1982) *Humus chemistry*. New York: John Wiley & Sons Inc.

Vanderploeg, H.A., Parzyck, D.C., Milcox, W.H., Kercher, J.R. & Kaye, S.V. (1975) *Bioaccumulation factors for radionuclides in freshwater biota*. Report ORNL-5002, Oak Ridge National Laboratory, Tennessee, USA.

Wang, X., Zhou, X., Du, J., Hu, W., Chen, C. & Chen, Y. (2006) Using of chelating resin to study the kinetic desorption of Eu(III) from humic acid–Al2O3 colloid surfaces. *Surf. Sci.*, **600**, 478–483.

War and forest
Pekka Virtanen
Helsinki, Finland

Abstract

Throughout the ages, forests have played a significant role in local disagreements and the great global wars alike as with the wars between Finland and the Soviet Union in the years 1939-1944. The forest may have protected from attacks but it could also conceal troops approaching the enemy. Moving and fighting in the forest required special skills and the Finns' experience in forestry and hunting came in handy. Strategies, tactics and weaponry were specially developed with the forested battlegrounds in mind. This short paper, which includes a small selection of photographs from the Finnish Wartime Photograph Archives ("SA-kuva-arkisto"), illustrates some of the ways that forests were used by the Finnish people in the 1940s.

Keywords: forest, war, Salpa Line, military history, museum

Introduction

The forests offered both light materials (branches and brash) for shelters and wood for strong and solid trenches, dugouts, barriers, bridges and roads. On both the war- and home- fronts, wood was also needed for building and heating; as fuel; and as industrial raw material for domestic demand as well as export products. Small-scale industry ranging from sawmills to tar burning sites was also set up at the front-line.

All the useful forest products, even resin and berries, were gathered by voluntary workers, both young and old. Parcels containing food, among other things, were sent from homes to the war-front, where the soldiers also used opportunities for hunting, fishing and picking berries.

Figure 1. Fuel wood being transported home

Figure 2. Harvesting Pine resin

Figure 3. Young and old harvesting berries

Figure 5. Hauling the timber in winter

Figure 4. Wood harvested and processed from the forests

Figure 6. Construction work using timber harvested from the forest

The war damaged both buildings and forests in many ways. In the worst cases heavy shooting turned forests into treeless memorials of the horrible power of war. As a result of the conflict, Finland had to cede one seventh of its forest territory and forest industry to the Soviet Union. Paying the heavy war indemnities had a long-lasting effect on the Finnish forest industry.

Making Good Use of Everything

In the war years and in the following period of shortage Finns tried to gather everything which was useful from the forests. Everybody from infants to the elderly helped in gathering the products of nature including, wood, resin, berries, nuts and fungi. This was done on a voluntary basis.

Food from the Forest

From the home front food was sent to the troops so that army-food was supplemented by these parcels from home. In addition to that, soldiers used every opportunity they found for hunting, fishing and picking berries.

War Demands Wood

Great amounts of wood were needed at both the war-front and home-front for many purposes: building, heating, fuel for cars, for the export industry and even for generating electricity. By-products of the paper industry included cellulose, fodder for horses and alcohol for people.

Trenches and Dugouts

Forest materials, especially wood, were used for making stables, bridges, carts and other structures and equipment. Great amounts of wood were also needed for stabilising trenches and dugouts.

Forest Concealment

Forests concealed soldiers and their equipment in different ways. It was easy to approach the enemy in the forest but in a threatening situation the forest also served as a hiding place. Forest also offered many kinds of materials for use as camouflage.

Figure 7. Camouflaged vehicles in the forest

Figure 8. Reviewing positions

Figure 9. Wooden walkway through the forest swamp

Figure 10. Transportimg a casualty

Figure 11. small-scale sawmill

Doctrines for Forest Battles

Forest Battles required special strategies and tactics. Fortifications as well as weaponry and other equipment were specially developed for forest conditions.

Moving through the Forests

The forest was a sheltered but difficult terrain, rough even for a horse. Wood was used for devices and structures that facilitated troop movement and transport.

Traces of War

Tens of thousands of houses and other buildings were destroyed in attacks. At its worst the heavy bombardments and shooting turned forest battle grounds into treeless wasteland.

Small-Scale Industry at the Warfront

Great amounts of timber, firewood and other raw materials were needed at the war-front. It was often impossible to transport these materials over long distances and therefore many kinds of small-scale industries ranging from sawmills to tar burning sites were set up at the front.

The National Salpa Centre

In Finland, there are many institutions that collect, study and display Finnish military history. For example the national Salpa Centre which consists of the Salpa Line Museum in Miehikkälä, the Virolahti Bunker Museum, the Salpa Trail in Miehikkälä and Virolahti and the Salpa Line Tradition Association. Its aim is to create an international centre

Figure 12. Building a bridge across the river

of fortification history combining local museums and the surrounding natural environment.

The Salpa Line is a massive line of defensive fortifications approximately 1200 km long that was built in 1940 – 41 and in 1944 in order to defend the Eastern border of Finland. The Salpa Line roughly follows this border and stretches from the Gulf of Finland to Savukoski, and then continues from there as a field fortified line all the way to the Arctic Ocean.

The Salpa Line has always been considered as one of the strongest fortified defence lines built during the Second World War. It has been compared, for instance, to the Maginot Line in France. It is possible to visit the

defence line at some of the two dozen renovated tourist sites, which are located near the Eastern border of Finland.

The selection of photographs in this paper is from the Finnish Wartime Photograph Archives ("SA-kuva-arkisto").

Figure 14. Making tar at the front-line

Figure 13. Part of the Salpa Line

Figure 15. Devastation caused by heavy bombardment

Sphagnum: the healing harvest

Thelma Griffiths, Ian D. Rotherham[1] & Christine Handley[2]

[1]Sheffield Hallam University, [2]BaLHRI / SYBRG.

Abstract

Sphagnum Moss or Bog Moss as it is sometimes known has been used for millennia for medical and sanitary purposes. This paper introduces the general uses and properties of *Sphagnum*. It then looks in more detail at the harvesting and processing of *Sphagnum* as part of the war effort during World War One. Finally, the timeline is brought into the twenty-first century with modern usage. Most of the work in the paper is based on research carried out by Thelma Griffiths whose interest in the subject came about through work at the Longshaw Estate, near Sheffield. The local connection with the *Sphagnum* 'industry' will also be explored.

Keywords: Sphagnum, World War One, Medicine

Introduction

Sphagnum moss species are major peat forming plants, which grow in wet, boggy places and often form large mounds or cushions over the surface. Over the years, if undisturbed these mosses are responsible for deep accumulations of partly decayed material, which slowly helps to form a peat layer. The moss is made up of minute tubes and spaces, giving it a structure similar to a sponge, enabling it to absorb large amounts of water.

However, one of the key characteristics is that water can be squeezed out of the moss without damaging its structure, the moss can be dried and when re-wetted is able to absorb fluid once again (Grieve, 1930). The virtues of its absorbent qualities have been known for centuries and in addition, it has healing qualities having mildly antiseptic and astringent properties. These absorbent and antiseptic qualities made it an ideal medium for wound dressings as well as other uses such as babies' napkins and sanitary products.

By the late nineteenth century, cotton dressings and cotton wool were used widely for wound dressings and other purposes. However, although cotton and cotton wool is quite effective it is many times less absorbent than *Sphagnum* and absorbs liquid in a different manner. *Sphagnum* can absorb 16-20 times its own weight in liquid compared with the four to six times of cotton. An experiment carried out at Edinburgh Royal Infirmary showed that 5lb of moss, after being pressed and slowly dried, weighed only 10oz, the other 4lb 6oz having been water (Cathcart, 1915). Instead of allowing the discharge of a wound to pass through the dressing directly above the wound as cotton wool does, *Sphagnum* moss absorbs the discharge laterally. This means the dressing is less likely to leak out onto surrounding clothes or sheets. In

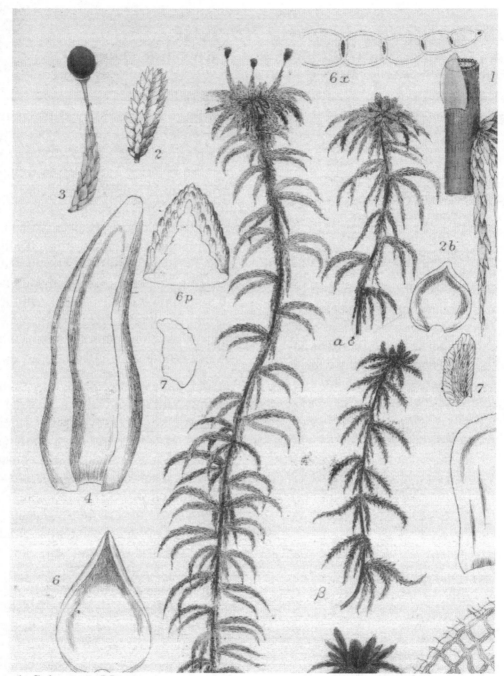

Figure 1. *Sphagnum* **Moss**

addition, the moss is not only cool and soothing but also has mild antiseptic properties, not possessed by cotton. However, the over-riding advantage is that wound dressings could be left in place for up to 2-3 days without the site of the wound deteriorating. All of these qualities coupled with the shortage of cotton because of the huge demand for surgical and other dressings in the

World War One conflict, meant that *sphagnum* was collected and processed on a vast scale. This harvest is now largely forgotten.

Historical and global uses

The medicinal use of *Sphagnum* moss has been known for millennia. 'Otzi the Iceman', the five thousand year old body found on a mountain glacier in 1991 showed signs of having used *Sphagnum* moss to dress a wound on his hand (Dickson, 2009). There is a Bronze Age burial in Fife where it was found on the chest of a body, possibly suggesting that it was put there to dress a wound (Dickson, 1978) and archaeologists excavating the site of a broch at Howe, near Stromness in Orkney in the early 1980s found the remains of *Sphagnum* moss, possibly *Sphagnum cuspidatum*. This was just one of seventy plant species identified at the site, fifty-four of which have known medicinal uses.

An early eleventh century Gaelic Chronicle refers to the aftermath of the Battle of Clontarf in Ireland, where the wounded soldiers insisted on taking part tied to wooden stakes for support with their wounds '*bound up with moss*'. (From Joyce's 'Child's History of Ireland' published in 1910, cited Cathcart, 1915). Grieve (1930) gives an example from the early sixteenth century after the Battle of Flodden where the Highlanders are reported to have '*staunched their bleeding wounds by filling them with bog moss and soft grass*'.

The use of *Sphagnum* on a military-scale for wound dressings appears to have declined in the nineteenth century until its accidental (re)discovery in Germany in the 1880s. A severe wound on a workman's arm was wrapped in fragments of 'peat' as there was no other suitable material to hand. After several days travelling to get medical attention, the original dressing was undisturbed and when it was removed the wound had started to heal rather than deteriorate. This prompted German scientists to investigate the properties of *Sphagnum* and its efficacy in treating wounds. The conclusions documented in several medical journals were that *Sphagnum* was an ideal material for surgical dressings. In 1895, the French War Department began using *Sphagnum* dressings. It was first employed on a large-scale in the Russian-Japanese War of 1904-05.

The First World War saw the greatest use of *sphagnum* for medical purposes but it was also collected on a smaller-scale in the UK during WW2. In December 1939, the Glasgow Herald reported that '*Sphagnum* moss picked on the moors of Scotland is being flown to Finland for use as hospital dressings'. In the early 1940s, *Sphagnum* was collected on the moors around Holme Moss and further north in England by volunteers. A request appeared in the Northern Rambler in June 1942 for walkers to collect *Sphagnum* moss, which elicited the response that the moors were 'out of bounds' for walkers so the request was advocating an illegal activity.

Laplanders and Canadian Indians laid dried *Sphagnum* in their children's cradles instead of a mattress, often covering it with the downy hairs of reindeer, 'and being changed night and morning, it keeps the infant remarkable clean, dry and warm' (Grieve, 1930). In both Lapland and Newfoundland, it has been used for dressing wounds. The Chippewa Indians, one of the largest groups of native American people, used *Sphagnum* moss as an absorbent, for pillows, mattresses, furniture stuffing, and as an insulator to keep milk either cool or warm. Eskimos traditionally used the dried moss to pad their sealskin boots instead of socks while in China, it has been used as a cure for haemorrhoids and eye conditions.

From the late nineteenth through the twentieth century and into the twenty-first, *Sphagnum* has been used for a variety of commercial products. Peat Products (Sphagnol) Limited, an English company was in operation from at least 1899 until January 1969. During the First World War, the company's products were endorsed by medical journals, and were advertised widely.

The products were made from a distillate of peat moss and included ointment, medical soap, suppositories and shaving soap. They claimed to be a remedy for a wide range of skin diseases and the suppositories were used in the treatment of haemorrhoids. Sphagnol preparations, according to one surgeon, were 'A valuable first aid dressing for wounds'. The company also produced veterinary preparations, and advertised in the Crufts Dog Show catalogue for a number of years in the 1930s.

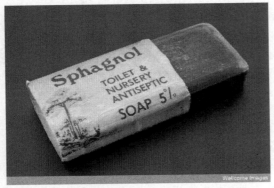

Figure 2. Sphagnol soap wrapper, dated by the Wellcome Institute 1945-1960

Sphagnol

Veterinary Preparations

Sphagnol Ointment and Soap embody the well-known healing properties of Peat and are rapid and safe in action. Eczema, Mange, Canker, Cuts, Bruises and poor condition of coat and skin quickly respond to Spagnol treatment.

Read this—

" Four weeks to-day a Bulldog was brought here to me, one of the worst cases of eczema I have ever seen ; the dog had been neglected and so the trouble had obtained a strong hold and extended from the back of the head to centre of spine and covered the shoulders. He was a mass of blood and matter. After cleaning the dog as well as the soreness would allow, I applied Sphagnol Ointment ; the result has astonished all who have seen him from the time of his entry here. The skin trouble has entirely cleared, and the skin, which was quite devoid of hair, is covered with a thick new coat."

And this—

" For the third show in succession my Chow Chow took all the firsts in his breed classes. All last year he was put down for lack of coat. I attribute his present condition to the constant using of the Sphagnol and have never found anything so magic for growing hair."

SPHAGNOL VETERINARY OINTMENT
1/- per tin.   Post free 1/2
5/9 per 1 lb. tin.   Post free 6/3

SPHAGNOL VETERINARY SOAP
10d. per tablet.   Post free 1/-
or obtainable from your Chemist.

FREE Samples on application from the Sole Proprietors:

Peat Products (Sphagnol) Ltd.

Department C.I.,

21 Bush Lane, London, E.C.4

Figure 3. 1938 Advertisement for Veterinary Products made by Sphagnol

A number of patents have been applied for since the mid 1990s for using *Sphagnum* moss for a variety of purposes. The following are some of the results produced by an internet search for 'US Patents *Sphagnum* Moss'

- Sanitary products including a sanitary napkin, diaper, incontinence pad, wound dressing.

- Dessicant for packaging materials.

- Water and oil absorbent medium.

- Mycorrhizal seed pellets.

- Medium for binding chlorine gas.

- Inhibition of biofilm formation and removal of biofilm.

Of the above, the final item appears to be the one that has had the greatest commercial success. Initially used for home pools and spas, in 2009 the application started to by used commercially in public swimming pools in the USA. Sterilized moss is placed in containers and the water is allowed to flow through it. By limiting the growth of bacteria, algae, mould and fungus it reduces the amount of chlorine and other chemicals that are required. It is also claimed that it removes heavy metals such as iron and helps stabilize the alkalinity of the water (Horizon Pool Supply, 2011). It is also being used by at least one hospital in Minnesota in its therapy pool, which claims the use of chemicals has been reduced by 30-50%, and has also cut the number of times the water needs cleaning by 50%, saving both water and staff time, and therefore money (Health Partners Press Release, 2011).

Sphagnum for Medical Purposes in the First World War

Need and Uses

As casualties mounted in the First World War, the need for enormous numbers of dressings became apparent very early on, and an address to the Medical Society of London in November 1914 referred to 'the great prevalence of sepsis' that was observed among the wounded. By 1915, when both sides were experiencing heavy casualties, *Sphagnum* was already being used alongside non-absorbent cotton and gauze dressings. However, the heavy casualties being suffered by British forces at that time were threatening to exhaust the available supply of cotton and gauze. Therefore, in the same year, 1915, *Sphagnum* dressings became an official part of medical supplies and the processing of *Sphagnum* began in earnest. In 1916, it was estimated that the minimum number of dressing required per man would be thirty, and that up to one hundred million dressings would be required in a six months period (Riegler, 1989). A further major advantage of *Sphagnum* dressings were their cheapness. When manufactured by the method used in Britain, the cleaned and dried moss was simply placed into muslin bags, which were then sterilised. Muslin was cheap and nearly all the labour was supplied by volunteers (Cathcart, 1915).

The three main medical uses for *Sphagnum* were surgical dressings, dysentery pads and rest pillows or pads. According to many sources, *Sphagnum papillosum* is the species, which makes the best surgical dressings. Lower grade species were used to make dysentery pads, and the waste moss was made into rest pillows (The Queenslander, 1917).

Surgical Dressings

The highest quality and the greatest quantity of *Sphagnum* were used for wound and surgical dressings. Its antiseptic and absorbent qualities meant that it could be used to dress a wound in a field hospital and the dressing could be kept in place until the casualty arrived at a main hospital perhaps two or three days later. Field (wound) dressings and surgical dressings were manufactured differently. This will be explained in more detail later. Cathcart (1915) also reported on the efficacy of peat moss, the semi-decayed *Sphagnum* moss that forms a layer between the fresh, growing moss, and the lower layers of actual peat. The peat moss nearest the surface, and therefore that, which is the least decayed, was found to be the best for surgical dressings.

Rest Pillows and Pads

These larger pillows and pads were made from lower-grade moss. The pads were used in hospitals for providing splint supports and the pillows for supporting the stumps of amputees. The quality of the moss meant the pillows were soft and flexible and had cooling or soothing properties.

Dysentry Pads

The use of 'second class' species of *Sphagnum* moss to make dysentery pads does not appear to be widely reported, and even when it is it is usually just a brief mention, as if it is of little consequence. However, due to the appalling (non-existent) sanitary conditions encountered, dysentry was rife amongst the troops. At Gallipoli, of seven battalions of Anzacs examined, 78% were found to be suffering from dysentery (Waugh, 2001) 'They were in a terrible state, all suffering from dysentery and enteric. Their insides had simply been turned to water, and all they had been able to do for them on shore was to tie their trousers tight round their legs with pieces of string. …'.

The circumstances which caused dysentery included 'the swarms of flies and the magnificent collection of dead Turks between the lines' ….. '…flies … simply billions of 'em everywhere. … All around in the open lay our own dead, whom no one could approach to bury by day or night, for to climb out of the trench even in the dark was to court disaster. … The stench was indescribable.' (Barrett, 2007).

The connection between physical health and mental health was beginning to be recognised. Dr A F Hurst, the officer in charge of a special neurological hospital reported that in Lemnos in 1915, 'Very few of them could hold their hands out without shaking, and they were all in a condition of profound neurasthenia. The vast majority of the men at that time were suffering from dysentery.' (Report on Shell-Shock, 1922). It would seem that, given the appalling physical effects of dysentery, together with the potential of mental breakdown, these pads are worthy of more than a single line because they were made from lower grade moss. If they played just a small part in making men feel more comfortable, and perhaps more importantly, enabled them to maintain just a little bit of dignity, then they fulfilled an equally important role as that of the surgical dressings.

Extent and Volume

It is impossible to come by an accurate total of dressings used, but a few statistics from a variety of sources give some idea of the scale of production and the amount of Sphagnum harvested:

- 22,000 dressings each month were produced in Aberdeen (Orcadian Features, 2005)

- In March 1916, the War Office requisitioned 5,000 dressings per month from Ireland, an increase of 50% of previous monthly output. Production was disrupted in April by the Easter Rising, but by May they had 'caught up' (Reilly, 2002).

- Between October 1917 and November 1918, Red Cross volunteers in Washington, Oregon and Maine made 595,540 dressings (Washington State History).

- When the war ended in November 1918 the American Red Cross had just completed an order for half a million dressings, and had just started on another order of one million. At the same time, the Canadian Red Cross was working on an order for 20 million dressings, and was producing between 200,000 and 300,000 per month (Riegler, 1989).

- It was estimated that an inexperienced woman could make five dressings per hour; an experienced one might make ten. It would therefore take a minimum of two million 'woman hours' to fulfil the Red Cross order of 20 million dressings (Riegler, 1989).

- Locally the Sheffield University Hospital Supply Depot produced a total of 85,000 Sphagnum moss dressings together with 117 moss pads (possibly dysentery pads or splint pads) (SUHSD, 1919). In addition, the depot agreed to supply 1,000 muslin bags per week for compressed Sphagnum moss dressings, which were being manufactured in Edinburgh. A total of 27,800 bags were produced (SUHSD, 1919).

- By the time the Armistice was signed in 1918 over a million bags of moss a month were being prepared and despatched to British military hospitals; the Germans used even more (Buckingham, 2013).

Gathering

The collection of *Sphagnum* moss appears to have been carried out across the UK wherever there were peat bogs, from Orkney to Dartmoor and Ireland during WW1. It was also collected in peat bog locations across the British Empire and, after it had entered the war, in the United States. The methods used in collecting and processing were sometimes different but in all cases the basic work was carried out largely by volunteers. They were co-ordinated through a series of local, regional and national depots and centres.

Collection of the moss could be done either by hand or by using a rake (Grieve, 1930). Gathering by hand must have been back breaking work but it cannot have been easy using either method. *Sphagnum* grows in boggy conditions and often in remote locations, which were not easily accessible unless you lived nearby and were used to working on the moors. A report from The Times in 1918 describes one of the collectors from Dartmoor, 'Often knee-deep in the great bogs and mires for miles around a man, who has devoted himself to the work, labours daily in the fair and foul weather. Nearly 5,000 sacks has this devoted worker collected since last spring.' (Buckingham, 2013). In Ireland, Mary Pakenham (a Voluntary Aid Detachment worker) wrote, 'Easily the most picturesque of our war activities was the gathering of Sphagnum moss from the bog. We had a special sort of two-ended sack which we hung round out necks like a stole and we went

barefoot over the bog fishing the clumps of moss out of the pools. There were three sorts, brown-and-thick, green-and-straggly and the commonest and much despised third class stuff which was red-and-measly.' (Reilly, 2002). As the *Sphagnum* was so full of water, advice was given that the moss should be squeezed out by hand as much as possible on the moor before putting it into the transport sacks. This would save on the volume and weight to be transported.

Figure 4. Irish notice regarding the collection of *Sphagnum* for dressings

In Dumfries and Galloway, the collection of *Sphagnum* moss was organised by the Reverend Adam Forman, manager of the family estate of Craigielands, near Beattock. '… he organised the collection and despatch of *sphagnum* moss for field dressings. … his organising powers were considerable and soon, with a battalion of Women's Army Corps workers at his back, he was organising *sphagnum* moss for the whole of Scotland.' (Forman, 1990)

*WACS (Women's Auxiliary Corps) pushing a trolley of sphagnum moss
on the wooden railway devised by my father.
His finest hour.*

Figure 5. Reverend Adam Forman's transport system of two wheeled trolley-like giant scooters used to push the sodden sacks of moss across the bog to the road

Figure 6. Kirkwall Moss Gatherers July 1917

Once at the edge of the moor, the sacks would be loaded and transported by a variety of means. On Orkney, local businesses provided lorries to both transport moss gatherers to the moors, and to take the moss back to Kirkwall (main town in Orkney).

In a memorandum written to assist the efficiency of other organisations, which gathered moss, Reverend Forman gave the following instructions:

- Camp the workers on or near the moor, with transport near at hand. Where this is impossible workers must be conveyed to and from the moors, and much valuable time and transport is expended on the journey.

- Workers should start in a line and keep in line.

- Workers should not bring their own food. It should be provided for all and be made as simple as possible. Meal times should be set, and the food made ready for the workers – a large kettle of fish is useful and beyond this, and cups, no utensils are necessary.

- All gatherers should understand that they are doing 'essential war work' and should undertake to carry out instructions. Where civilian and military workers are mixed, the civilians must obey orders on a par with military workers. (Fisk 1992)

In the UK there did not appear to have been any resistance on the part of private landowners to the gathering of *Sphagnum* moss. At this time and for most of the following century, much of the upland moors were closed to local people, used as shooting estates and patrolled by gamekeepers protecting the game-birds. However, collecting *Sphagnum*, irrespective of patriotic duty as part of the war effort, was seen in a positive light. Indeed according to *The Scotsman*, 'Proprietors and shooting tenants would hail with pleasure the total extirpation of this moss. It is within its simple, narrow leaves that the destructive heather beetle lays its clutch of eggs. … Owing to its perennial

dampness it is difficult or impossible to destroy *Sphagnum* by burning, and the picking of it by hand will operate potently to the benefit of game preserving' (Cathcart, 1915).

After the United States entered the war the University of Washington was heavily involved in the collection of *Sphagnum* moss and the manufacture of dressings. It required all of its female students to spend two hours per week on this work (Scherer, 1918). The Assistant Professor of Botany, J.W. Hotson, wrote extensively about the collection and processing of the moss, with detailed instructions regarding the making of dressings, their labelling and packing. Regarding collection, he gave the following instructions:

- Samples of moss should be taken to headquarters and approved before collection began. Until gatherers were experienced in the work, they should carry a sample with them to compare frequently with the moss they were gathering, to ensure they were collecting the correct species.

- Quality, rather than quantity, should be the aim, and care should be taken to ensure the moss was 'clean', and as free from other plants and debris as possible.

- The moss bed should be worked as deeply as possible, i.e. as far down as the moss remains intact, with the stem fairly well crowded with lateral branches.

- The moss should be gathered in double handfuls, and squeezed as dry as possible before putting into sacks.

- Moss should be picked methodically, taking as much as possible from one area before moving on to another.

Professor Hotson stressed the importance of careful gathering, as 'carelessness on the part of the collector may greatly reduce the efficiency of the sorter, frequently rendering otherwise useful moss absolutely worthless'. He did, however, go on to state 'with the difficulties confronting the collector, too much time cannot be spent on that end of the work as there are a hundred persons available for sorting where there is one for collecting. There is a happy mean to which we should strive in order to obtain the greatest result with the least labour' (Hotson, 1919).

Processing

Once the *Sphagnum* had been collected and taken to the local depot or collecting centre it underwent a series of processes before it was ready to be made into dressings or pads. Depending on the scale of operation the first stages could take place locally and then the partly processed *sphagnum* was transported to a regional centre for completion.

The first stage, which had begun on the moor, was to squeeze out as much water as possible to make it lighter to transport and as a preliminary to the drying process. Additional squeezing could then be carried out using a laundry mangle at the local depot. The moss had to separated out before further drying took place, carefully avoiding tearing it or breaking it into small pieces. If the moss was separated after drying it would easily become damaged (Grieve, 1930).

The drying and cleaning process varied depending partly on the weather conditions, the speed with which the *Sphagnum* was needed and the quantity being processed. Opinion seemed to be divided as to whether artificial heat should be used in drying the moss. Mrs Grieve recommended drying in the open air, but on Orkney, it was taken to the baker or the blacksmith to dry (*The Orcadian*, 1917). Hotson in America claimed that artificial drying made the moss more brittle, but also stated he saw 'no difference between moss dried in summer by placing it near a stove and that dried in trays in an ordinary Montreal workroom in winter'. He suggested that humidity of the circulating air was the controlling factor, rather than the time it took to dry the moss. He also stressed the importance of gentle handling of the dried moss (Hotson 1919). In Scotland, the methods seem to have been combined, at least to the extent of allowing the moss to be spread out to start the process and make it easier to get rid of any debris as Vickery (1995) describes, 'At Langholme, in Dumfriesshire, the Duke of Buccleuch's head keeper would take us out on the hill to pick *Sphagnum* moss as part of the war effort. We would collect it in sacks, and then lay it across the lawn on dust sheets to dry. Afterwards all the bits of heather and peat, dead frogs and other foreign bodies had to be picked out of it before it could be sent to the hospital.' Reverend Forman operated on a larger scale but also used the grounds of his estate, 'From far and wide lorries drove up to Craigielands laden with dripping sacks of moss which was spread to dry on frames on the tennis courts. Then, after a number of simple industrial processes, the moss was shredded, packed and despatched.' As Buckingham (2013) points out, many of the areas where collecting was taking place were also areas with the highest rainfall, 'After the moss had been gathered it had to be sorted and dried, usually by being left outside in wire trestles. Sometimes the drying period turned out to be long and frustrating when, Dartmoor weather

being what it is, it began to rain or a mist came down and made the moss wet again!'

After the *Sphagnum* had been dried and picked clean it was then ready to be made into dressings. This may have been done locally, especially if it was to be used in the local hospital, or transported to a processing centre.

Making the dressings

British method

The most basic dressings simply consisted of some moss being packed into a small muslin bag. It was packed loosely to allow for the moss to swell as it absorbed moisture. An amount of 2 oz of moss in a bag measuring 10 x 14 inches was recommended. These dressings were for use in home hospitals (Grieve, 1930).

Figure 7. Kirkwall (Orkney) ladies making dressings

For field hospitals abroad, the *Sphagnum* moss was compressed into cakes and then placed in muslin bags, very much larger than the size of the cake. These were much easier to pack to send overseas. In Scotland, there was a munitions factory where a hydraulic press was used to compress the moss into cakes. Thus, the machinery 'which one hour was moulding shell bases, was in the next devoting its energy to compressing the healing cakes of *Sphagnum* moss' (Grieve, 1930).

The dressings were then treated to eliminate any harmful bacteria. The early method of treating them was by sterilisation but this had the disadvantage of destroying some of the *Sphagnum*'s absorbent properties. Col Charles Cathcart F.R.C.S, a British pioneer in the use of *Sphagnum* dressings, recommended an improved method known as 'sublimation'. This consisted of dipping them in a mercurial solution followed by squeezing out any excess moisture and then drying them.

At the processing centre in Princetown on Dartmoor, they were hung in a drying chamber of at least 90° for 24 hours. When that stage had been completed they were ready for packing, first sealing the pillows into airtight hampers made by the inmates of Plymouth Blind Institution (Buckingham, 2013).

PLATE 47

The successive steps in the making of a sphagnum pad. (1) Frame on zorbik. (2) Moss in frame. (3) A thin film of non-absorbent cotton on moss. (4) Frame removed; zorbik folded from left. (5) Zorbik folded from right and the near end; spring clothes pins holding zorbik in place at the near end. (6) Far end of zorbik folded and held with spring clothes pins. (7) Zorbik envelope with moss side next the gauze. (8) Clothes pins removed. (9) Gauze folded in from left. (10) Gauge folded in from right. (11) Pad turned over. (12) Near end muffed. (13) Both ends muffed and patted even. (14) Ten pads tied for packing.

Figure 8. The USA method of making dressings

The British government also procured tons of garlic bulbs, the raw juice of which was diluted with water and added to the moss, which was then applied to wounds. Garlic is also noted for its antiseptic qualities. 'Where this treatment was adopted there were no specific complications, and thousands of lives were thus saved' (Grieve, 1930).

American Method

The Americans adopted an altogether more complicated approach as described by Hotson. He gave very detailed instructions of how they should be made which went through fourteen stages. American dressings comprised four elements; gauze, 'Zorbik' or 'Scot tissue', non-absorbent cotton, and *Sphagnum*. Zorbik was a thin sheet of wood pulp paper which was used to envelop the moss and prevent it sifting out. It was also used for gas mask filters. Labelling was also important, with information about the number of dressings and their size together with a note stamped on each bundle, 'N.B. The cotton side does **not** go next to the wound'. Finally, the best method of packing was described. In spite of his exacting instructions, Hotson also wrote 'do not become fussy about minute non-essential details'.

Volunteer effort

In the UK, much of the collecting and initial processing was undertaken by local volunteers either individuals or groups who already worked on the moors or lived in the local villages. Buckingham (2013) describes some of

the effort, which the people of Okehampton made to gather the *Sphagnum*. 'Typical of those engaged in collecting *Sphagnum* moss were members of the Okehampton Bible Class ... Other Okehampton volunteers included Mr T. Dick who gathered 200 sacksful in just two months and Mr John Durant who, by mid-1916, had collected a total of around 1000 lbs of moss, mainly around Yes Tor, using a specially made rake and walking 800 miles in the process.'

This effort was replicated across the country but even then more volunteers and groups were needed to keep up the effort. Youth organisations such as the Boy's Brigade, Scout Troops and Girl Guides were asked to take part, as were members of the Red Cross Voluntary Aid Detachments. Such was the importance of gathering Sphagnum moss for dressings that in 1920 the people of Widecombe-in-the-Moor were presented with a trophy in recognition of their work.

Local focus – Longshaw & Sheffield

The interest in *Sphagnum* moss was sparked for one of the authors by Doris Emma Elliott, who was a VAD (volunteer) nurse at Longshaw Lodge Convalescent Hospital for Wounded Soldiers during the First World War. Longshaw Lodge belonged to the Duke of Rutland at that time and had been requisitioned as part of the war effort. The Lodge had been built by the Duke to accommodate grouse shooting parties and was situated on the moors to the

The inscription reads:

'This 15" naval shell was presented by The Naval War Savings Committee in 1920 to the people of Widecombe in recognition of their efforts during the First World War gathering *Sphagnum* moss for use in the treatment of wounds.'

Figure 9. Commemorative Shell presented to the people of Widecombe-on-the-Moor in 1920

west of Sheffield in Northeast Derbyshire. The estate was sold in 1927 and the Lodge and part of the estate passed to the National Trust in 1931. Doris's granddaughter, Beverley Hardy, attended a talk about Longshaw during the First World War, and explained that her grandmother had told her about collecting *Sphagnum* moss for use in dressings during the war.

In many places, the collection of the moss was organised by the Red Cross Voluntary Aid Detachments, which had been established in 1909 to aid the Territorial Army medical services in time of war. Doris Elliott, who collected moss on Longshaw, was a 'VAD', and it is very probable that the moss that was gathered by her was sent to Sheffield to be processed and made into dressings by the Sheffield University Hospital Supply Depot (SUHSD). The depot was opened in November 1915, with accommodation, heating and lighting being provided by the University, and the labour being provided by volunteers.

In the summer of 1916, a *Sphagnum* moss department was started at the request of the Director General of

Voluntary Organisations, 'much of the moss being collected on the neighbouring moors'. (SUHSD Statement Undated). A total of 85,000 *Sphagnum* moss dressings were produced, together with 117 moss pads (possibly dysentery pads or splint pads) (SUHSD Final Report, 1919). One nursing sister wrote from France that 'all the surgeons have remarked that they have never used dressings so beautifully and practically made' (SUHSD Third Annual Report 1917-1918).

In addition, the depot was asked to produce a regular supply of muslin bags for compressed *Sphagnum* moss dressings, which were being manufactured in Edinburgh. It was agreed that they could supply 1,000 bags per week if the muslin was provided, and the Director General of Voluntary Organisations furnished them with 7,200 yards of the material

Figure 11. Cyril Newbury just after joining up

Figure 10. Doris Elliott (in uniform) at Longshaw

(SUHSD Third Annual Report, 1917-1918). In total 27,800 bags were produced (SUHSD Final Report 1919).

One of the patients at Longshaw Lodge Hospital was Cyril Newbury, from Dunedin in New Zealand. He spent several months there in 1915. He had taken part in the Gallipoli campaign and had landed at Anzac Cove on 22 June 1915. Within three weeks, he was in hospital in Malta suffering from dysentery. He was then diagnosed with neurasthenia ('nerve trouble', commonly known as 'shell shock'). He arrived at the base hospital in Sheffield on 17th September, and from there he was sent to Longshaw for convalescence. He died on 8th July 1916 near Armentieres.

Canada and USA

In Canada and the United States, a number of universities were engaged in the processing of *Sphagnum* moss and making dressings. The University of Toronto Women's Club volunteered to process moss in February 1915 (Riegler,

1989), and The University of Washington claimed that it was furnishing 60% of the supply in the United States (Yearbook, 1918), a claim which may well have been true, given the industrial scale on which they appeared to operate, as shown in Figure 12.

Conclusion

This short chapter outlines the use of *Sphagnum* and *Sphagnum* products for a variety of purposes in different countries at different times. The use appears to have culminated in the effort, which took place during the First World War to supply medical dressings on a vast scale. The effort described here only highlights a few examples from within the UK and in the USA and Canada. Similar harvesting and production was also being carried out in Germany and elsewhere. Added together the amount of *Sphagnum*, which was used over a period of a few years, is colossal. In the Sheffield area alone, 85,600 dressings were produced.

Figure 12. Drying racks at the University of Washington in Seattle

At a conservative estimate of 2oz of dried moss per dressing this equates to approximately 5 tons of dried or 75-100 tons of wet *Sphagnum* harvested locally. The impact of this harvest on the lives of those who gathered it and whose lives were saved or made more comfortable by being treated with it is part of the human story touched on here. There is much more detail available which can develop these stories. We understand little of the impact on the landscape or on the ecology of the moors and bogs.

Bibliography

Anon. (1916) Sphagnum moss dressings in Ireland. *British Medical Journal*, August 12th 1916.

Barrett, M. (2007) *Casualty Figures, How five men survived the First World War*. Verso.

Buckingham, J. (2013) A War Industry in Princetown. *Dartmoor Magazine*, Summer 2013, pp.22-23.

Cathcart, C.W. (1915) Cheap Absorbent Dressings for the Wounded. *British Medical Journal*, July 24 1915.

Dickson, J.H. (1978) Bronze age mead. *Antiquity*, **LII**, 108-113.

Dweck, A.C. (2012) *Natural Products – satisfying the consumer dream* http://www.dweckdata.com/

Fisk, R.J. (1992) Collecting Sphagnum for surgical dressings. *Bulletin of the British Bryological Society*, **59**, 32-33.

Forman, D. (1990) *Son of Adam*. Andre Deutsch Ltd, London.

Grieve, M. (1931) *A Modern Herbal*. Society of Herbalists, London.

Hotson, J.W. (1919) Sphagnum from bog to bandage. *Puget Sound Biological Station*, **2**, 1918-1920.

Hurst, A.F. (1922) *Report of the War Office Committee of Enquiry into 'Shell-shock. 1922*, Imperial War Museum reprint 2004, London.

MacDonald, L. (1980) *The Roses of No Man's Land*. Penguin, London.

Orcadian Features (2005) *How a five year old played his part in the Great War effort*. www.orcadian.co.uk/features/articles/sphagnummoss.htm

O'Reilly, J., O'Reilly, C. & Tratt, R. (2012) *Field guide to Sphagnum mosses in bogs*. Field Studies Council, Shrewsbury.

Reilly, E. (2000) *Women and Voluntary War Work*. In: Gregory, A. & Paseta, S. (eds) *Ireland in the Great War*. Manchester University Press, Manchester.

Riegler, N.N. (1989) Sphagnum moss in World War I: The Making of Surgical Dressings by Volunteers in Toronto, Canada, 1917-1918. *Canadian Bulletin of Medical History*, **6** (1), 27-43.

Scherer, J.A.B. (1918) *The Nation at War*. George H. Doran Company, New York.

Vickery, R. (1995) *Dictionary of Plant-Lore*. Oxford University Press, Oxford.

Waugh, S. (2001) *Essential Modern World History*. Nelson Thornes Ltd, Cheltenham.

Websites

Creative Water Solutions http://www.cwsnaturally.com/blog/water-chemistry/moss-how-did-this-get-started/

Health Partners Press Release 25 July 2012 http://www.healthpartners.com/public/newsroom/newsroom-article-list/7-25-12.html

HistoryLink.org – the Free Online Encyclopaedia of Washington State History http://www.historylink.org/index.cfm?DisplayPage=output.cfm&file_id=9837

Horizon Pool Supply 14 September 2011 Hail! Sphagnum Moss http://www.cwsnaturally.com/blog/water-chemistry/moss-how-did-this-get-started/

Scottish Natural Heritage, All about Sphagnum Moss http://www.snh.org.uk/pdfs/education/sphagnum%20moss.pdf

Sheffield University Hospital Supply Depot, *Third Annual Report 1917-1918 with the Final Report to May 9th 1919*. Women War and Society 1914-1918, Imperial War Museum http://www.tlemea.com/waw.asp?view=norm&cmd=nav&imageCount=17&number=635&xpage=/SANdata/Women@Work/xml/reel70/355/l-r-355-052.xml&DocId=17014&HitCount=2&hits=e2c+e2d+&bhcp=1

Sheffield University Hospital Supply Depot Statement, undated, Women War and Society 1914-1918, Imperial War Museum http://www.tlemea.com/waw.asp?view=norm&cmd=nav&imageCount=6&number=636&xpage=/SANdata/Women@Work/xml/reel70/355/l-r-355-054.xml&DocId=17016&HitCount=2&hits=b75+b76+&bhcp=1

The Queenslander, 13 October 1917, Notes from Ireland http://trove.nla.gov.au/ndp/del/printArticlePdf/22343299/3?print=n

The Times Newspaper, 3 September 1918 cited in www.legendarydartmoor.coluk/moss-gatherers.htm

University of Washington Yearbook 1918 http://content.lib.washington.edu/cdm4/document.php?CISOROOT=/uwdocs&CISOPTR=27658&REC=1

Washington State History http://www.historylink.org/index.cfm?DisplayPage=output.cfm&file_id=9837

Ways with Weeds http://www.howe.scapaflow.co/

Below: Floral moss on drying screens—St. Marc

Centre left: Floral moss drying on ground—St. Marc.

Left: Vegetation on peat bog—St. André

Right: Unloading floral moss at baling shed—Bagotville.

Harvesting floral moss in Canada, 1945 © Ian D. Rotherham

Impacts of conflict and war on peatland landscapes

Paul A. Ardron
BaLHRI

Abstract

This chapter explores the initial and knock-on effects of conflict and war on peatland landscapes. These impacts are considerable, diverse but in most instances remain largely un-recognised.

In peatland environments, the natural processes of ground 'healing' often quickly disguise any destructive human activities. In some instances, the signs may be apparent to the specialist but, generally, because of the extreme physical processes at play, these environments appear natural. Peatlands are generally quite open environments and are thus more readily influenced by the weather. This situation is especially the case in the uplands. The typically stronger winds in upland areas will easily mobilise any disturbed soils as will the proportionally heavier rainfall. The rainfall will also, in areas with low levels of atmospheric pollution, positively affect levels of "vegetation healing". In particular, the pollution sensitive *Sphagnum* mosses will rapidly colonise and disguise areas of disturbance in 'clean' upland areas. However, where these mosses are scarce the mobility of any bare soils will usually have the same effect! Thus, the average person will likely walk onto a heath or moor and perceive it to be a wild place, little impacted by humans;

rather than a completely modified anthropogenic landscape covered by a multitude of man-made scars stitched over by nature.

Indeed, the moors and heaths we see today have been totally shaped by centuries of "asset-stripping" and general disturbance: peat and turf-cutting on a vast scale; mining; quarrying and piecemeal stone-getting; continual harvesting of heather, bracken, rushes, *sphagnum*, gorse, birch and other vegetation for subsistence and industry; grazing activities; game management; and of course, military activity, conflict and war. As well as the actual areas of disturbance connected with these activities, the related infrastructure is even more widespread and fundamental to the development of the landscape we see today.

Archaeology on peatlands which relates to military training and logistics, set battles and other types of conflict will be discussed, along with the impacts of these activities on the pre-existing historical landscapes and environment: in particular, the effects on biodiversity and ecological succession. Although major land uses such as peat cutting, quarrying, and military action often have generic impacts on peatlands, sometimes they may prompt more specific ecological change.

Case studies from the Peak District are cited to demonstrate the range and significance of human activity on peatland landscapes. The two main case studies have quite different histories: one site bears the scars of military training, the other significant evidence of conflicts in land ownership and utilisation.

Introduction

Extensive anomalies in the vegetation and topography testify to the massive impact human activity has had on our peatlands. Longstone Moor in the White Peak of Derbyshire, a relict area of limestone heath is just one example. Its very name implies an association with the nearby long standing settlements of Great and Little Longstone. For

centuries and until about one hundred years ago, the inhabitants of these two villages and probably others in the vicinity, will have continuously relied upon and utilized its natural resources: peat, heather, rushes, gorse, minerals, stone etc. Although the underlying geology is limestone, this area was covered by windblown acid loess during the immediate post-glacial period, which allowed peat to form. Taking into account the altitudinal and slope characteristics of the moor it would more than likely have developed a relatively shallow but non-the-less extensive cover of blanket mire. However, this has largely been stripped away for fuel, probably even before late medieval times when peat resources in the White Peak were all but exhausted (Ardron, 1999; Ardron, 2014). The infrastructure connected with the peat cutting and other forms of exploitation are everywhere on the moor and include

Figure 1. Longstone Moor looking east towards Betney Cob (visible in the distance)

myriad faint tracks indicated by vegetation change. On some parts of the moor drainage is impeded and beds of soft rush (*Juncus effusus*) abound. The latter species along with mat grass (*Nardus stricta*) often mark out areas of mineral soil exposure and disturbance. However, the dominant vegetation is heather or ling (*Calluna vulgaris*) a dwarf shrub which flourishes on the South Pennine moors in general where pollution during the industrial period, extensive drainage and, management for grouse favoured its expansion. Longstone Moor itself was an outlying grouse moor, and it still supports a small relict population of this British endemic. The moor is also riddled with rakes: lines of humps and bumps, the pits and spoil heaps left after the extraction of lead and other mineral resources. These features support a number of rare and significant species: notably lichens and lead tolerant plants.

There are a number of small water bodies on Longstone Moor, including several dew ponds, inhabited by newts and other significant species; all are the result of human activity of one sort or another. Open water is rare in the White Peak but, is also scarce on the South Pennine moorlands generally. When it does occur, it is more-or-less always the result of human intervention. Some of these pools have been created by military activity and may be the result of explosions, the movements of heavy vehicles, trench works and the like. Anthropogenic water bodies increase diversity and sustain a significant variety of local and rare species. The image in Figure 2 shows the larva of a great diving beetle (*Dytiscus marginalis*) feeding on the remains of a recently emerged southern hawker dragonfly (*Aeshna cyanea*) in a flooded peat pit on blanket mire above Stanage Edge in the Peak District. Both of these species rely on open water to breed, so would only occur casually in peatlands devoid of open water bodies. Although the Stanage Edge site resulted from peat cutting, others caused by wartime activity do occur on peatlands in the Peak District and elsewhere. For instance, on the high moors NW of Sheffield, a large circular pool in the peat blanket is thought to be the result of the explosion of a German, Second World War V1 bomb (Collier, 1990).

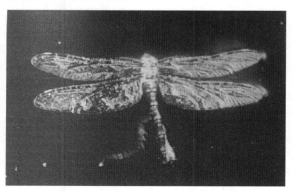

Figure 2. Larva of a great diving beetle (*Dytiscus marginalis*) feeding on the remains of a recently emerged southern hawker dragonfly (*Aeshna cyanea*) (from Ardron, 1999)

The military history of Longstone Moor, and for that matter most upland areas, is something of a grey area; many minor incidents are forgotten, others occurred too far back in time. Furthermore, the military are not inclined to advertise their activities. However, conflict takes many forms and Longstone Moor, along with many other areas of the higher White Peak, is likely to have been affected by "turf wars" during medieval times, when the vital peat resource dwindled. Some of these events are documented in surviving Court Rolls but the nature of any associated violence is unstated. However, there would no doubt have been many clandestine incursions aimed at the peat resource itself, but how stiff a defence the locals put up is debatable. What is more certain is that the area was used in the Second World War by the army, for training purposes and, Betney Cob, a hill to the east was occupied by the Home Guard. Parachute training and the movement of Bren gun carriers on the moor necessitated the demolition of dry stone walls and, Scots Pines, which appear to have been quite extensive on the drier southern half, were felled for use as pit props (P. W. Wood pers. comm.). The army were still in place in 1944 and apparently, as late as the 1950s, the area was littered with the remains of mortar bombs. The extent of the military activity suggests the surface of the moor must have been extensively disturbed during the second world war period. However, the actual number of Scots Pines felled on the moor, their origin and the long-term impact of their removal and the other wartime disturbance remains uncertain.

Ecological Change

Some of the impacts of human activity on our peatlands have been introduced above using one case study as an example. As we have seen, a number of these activities have had significant effects on the vegetation and landform. These changes stand as visible archaeology in the peatland landscape and although a palimpsest, the individual causes may sometimes still be determinable. The fauna and flora which has developed on these altered landscapes is not necessarily associated with any particular anthropogenic feature but instead has responded to changes in micro topography, aspect, drainage, mineral soil exposure etc. For instance, mat grass (*Nardus*) has become widespread as the dominant species where cotton grass (*Eriophorum*) formerly was abundant, because of any human actions, which removed the peat cover and exposed the underlying mineral soil. This vegetation change has produced a very considerable knock-on effect, facilitating the arrival of new animal and plant communities. For instance in the Upper Derwent Valley of the Derbyshire Peak District, distinctive spider and beetle communities occupy the mat grass of ancient peat cuttings, while equally characteristic assemblages of species are found on the adjacent uncut cotton grass mire and on the botanically diverse transition zone between. This situation could be 'reversed' and the *Eriophorum* return if further human actions lead to waterlogging.

Looking at military activity, at one extreme, the effect of a large scale modern battle on the landscape and resulting ecological succession will obviously be great: an area of prime peatland vegetation could in the short term be turned into an almost bare quagmire by multiple explosions, trampling of soldiers and scouring by heavy vehicles. With time, vegetation would return but, no doubt, much altered from what was there before. In the main, the colonizing vegetation would be that which favoured a very disturbed land surface, perhaps with pools and raised humps and bumps. The underlying mineral soil and base rock strata could have been disturbed: thereby radically altering the soil chemistry. Previously the vegetation could have been species rich but of one extensive community; because of the radical disturbance it would most likely develop into a mosaic. Obviously, any particularly destructive non-military activity such as mining could have a similar effect. Returning to those more singular impacts of human activity touched on above, military activity, particularly battles, not only causes widespread disturbance but also leads to contamination of the site by all manner of bits and pieces of equipment, both large and small. There will of course also be the remains of the casualties of the conflict: men and animals, combatants and those that got in the way. All of these will stimulate or sometimes inhibit certain fauna and flora; some from the original environment, others from elsewhere. However, the likely increased diversity may contain some very peculiar bedfellows, some of which will be inconspicuous and as a result could be very ephemeral. There are for instance bryophytes and lichens, which are extremely niche specific and some that actively colonize metal contaminated sites and substrates. There are also species of plant and animal that grow specifically on animal remains; these species will always flourish for a time in the aftermath of a savage battle. The moss *Tetraplodon mnioides* is a very good example: it is specifically associated with decaying animal matter found in the uplands; while fungi of the genus *Onygena* colonize hooves and hair.

As suggested above, ground contamination can inhibit colonization. Some sites poisoned through military activity may lay bare for years before they recover. For example, the Wellington bomber Z8980 that crashed on the edge of Ringinglow Bog, close to Sheffield on the 17th July 1942 (Collier, 1990) left a patch of oil and metal contaminated, blackened ground that is still visible today. However, although these sites may look barren, it is very unlikely that they will be totally devoid of life. Inconspicuous "niche species", such as ephemeral lichens, algae and microorganisms may colonize the most inhospitable environments, even fragments of metal and other 'foreign' bodies.

Figure 3. *Tetraplodon mnioides* **on the carcass of a mountain hare (from Ardron, 1999)**

Figure 4. *Onygena equina* **fruiting on the horn of a dead sheep**

Figure 5. Contaminated patch of ground at the crash site of Wellington Z8980

Conflict Archaeology

Relicts of peacetime military activity and conflict can be found almost anywhere we choose to look and many are well known and monumental in scale. However, peatland archaeology in general is more than likely ill-defined, sometimes ephemeral and often over looked; even by trained archaeologists. The peat itself can hide any artefacts or casualties, which sink below its surface. In healthy peatland landscapes, away from sources of pollution, the process of *"sphagnum* healing" may quickly disguise any signs of disturbance and, the re-growth of coarse dwarf shrubs and hummocky moorland vegetation will readily aid the process. Paradoxically, even on peatlands affected by erosion, any disturbed surfaces or peat made features will soon degrade confusingly. Therefore, on moors particularly badly affected by erosion, many manmade anomalies in the peat surface have been interpreted as part of that process. Sometimes extensive areas of archaeology are misinterpreted in this way, for instance, in the South Pennines, huge areas of peat loss as the result of historical peat cutting. Past disturbances of the peat surface caused by military activity and battle are just as likely to remain unseen or miss-identified if no related artefacts are found or, if there is no historical record to indicate their presence or, records are missing or unclear.

Actually, the most 'durable' form of archaeology on the peat may actually be the vegetation itself, which, as we have seen above, can be a very good marker of change. Unfortunately, this 'tool' of landscape interpretation falls well outside of mainstream archaeology; few formally trained archaeologists recognize the resource and fewer still fully appreciate its significance. While historical and veteran trees are recognized as part of the archaeological resource, though again not adequately understood by the profession, most "Botanical Archaeology" remains outside the remit and very much remains the preserve of just a few landscape specialists. However, the potential when interpreting historical landscapes is great and particularly so when working in peatland contexts.

Black Dike located on the moors to the west of Howden Reservoir in the Upper Derwent Valley, of the Peak District is a particularly dramatic example of an anthropogenic peatland feature highlighted and marked by distinct forms of vegetation change. This complex linear feature stretches for two and half kilometres along a ridge, cutting through *Eriophorum vaginatum* dominated blanket mire. In places it is 50 metres wide and in general about 2 metres deep, where it cuts through the covering peat down to the underlying mineral soil. It has been interpreted in many ways but is clearly part of an extensive boundary system. Along the entire length of the feature can be seen the remains of a degraded bank which probably originally separated two parallel ditch works. Such double ditches occur elsewhere on the surrounding moors and have been interpreted as Dark Age boundaries. Whatever the exact origins of this type of feature were, they clearly were very significant and Black Dike is by far and away the most prominent of these features in the landscape and contains considerable evidence of conflict: at least conflict of interest and ownership! Any double ditch is likely to signify a battle of wills between two landowners proclaiming their equal strength. However, over the years Black Dike has clearly been party to many a minor and perhaps, not so minor battle. At the eastern end of the feature, the blanket mire has been almost totally stripped away for peat fuel by two long standing farming settlements. The remains of these now abandoned farms lie in the valleys either side of the ridge. The two settlements obviously considered the double ditch the boundary of their grazing land and turbary because, each worked the peat back at right angles to the boundary feature but, the one to the north side significantly further than the other. These two adjacent areas of over-cutting, down to the mineral soil, subsequently re-vegetated and at least the northernmost appears to have been used for summer grazing, evidenced by its place name: "Cow Hey". The majority of the peat cutting appears to have taken place prior to the seventeenth century since "Cow Hey" is shown more-or-less at its present day extent on William Senior's survey plan of the area produced in 1628 (Chatsworth Archive; Fowkes and Potter 1988). At the same time, or perhaps afterwards, the two farmers seem to have been using Black Dike as a 'route' across the moor, presumably each keeping to their own side of the central ditch. However, they also cut into the peat along the dike apparently in a haphazard piece-meal manner; so much so that the extent of cutting either

Figure 6. Black Dike looking east (from Ardron, 1999)

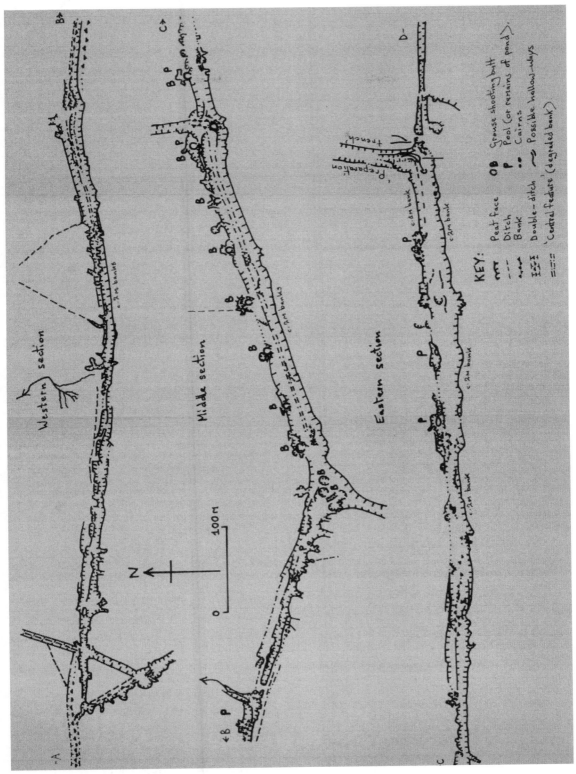

Figure 7. Sectioned plan of Black Dike (from Ardron, 1999)

side of the dividing feature varies considerably. Whether or not there was any conflict involved in this process is unclear but there is no doubt the "bounds were set"!

The overcut "Heys" are today dominated by *Nardus* grassland. *Nardus* has also colonised much of the length of the Black Dike, again indicating where the peat has been removed down to mineral soil. However, along some parts of the feature, *Nardus* is limited and *Eriophorum vaginatum* is still the dominant type of vegetation. The degraded central bank of relatively desiccated peat has been reduced to a somewhat intermittent and hummocky feature, marked by growths of dwarf shrubs, notably crowberry (*Empetrum nigrum*). In a few places where there are natural depressions, pooling has occurred and here common cotton grass (*Eriophorum angustifolium*) and *sphagnum* are the dominant forms of vegetation. The types of vegetation described above form a patchy 'mosaic' along the feature; the differing patches marking the position of the piece-meal peat cutting and the depth of the cutting.

Figure 6 shows the middle and eastern section of Black Dike running down towards the two Heys. The degraded central bank, colonised by dwarf shrubs, is clearly discernable while, *Nardus* traces the right hand side of the dike as a pale strip. On the left side, the cutting has been shallower and *Eriophorum* still dominates. The right hand edge of the dike has eroded because of the deeper cutting and because it faces northwards and is

therefore more prone to the effects of weathering. Figure 7 is a plan of Black Dike drawn in three sections to show the complexity of the feature (Ardron, 1999; Ardron 2014). The majority of the features shown on the plan are visible from the air, clearly defined as vegetation anomalies and/or change.

Scars of War

So, to the more specific traces and impacts of violent conflict in all its forms, from the clash between two warriors lost in the mists of time to the massed training activity and staged battles of modern warfare. Documentation and oral history will generally testify to the latter and more than likely evidence will still be found on the ground: perhaps the tracks left by heavy military vehicles, pits in the ground the result of explosions, trenchworks of various kinds, isolated rocks and, on the moors, even ancient marker posts and the like extensively scarred by bullets and mortar blasts. As we have seen above, military activity can induce more-or-less the same environmental changes as other major land uses such as peat cutting and quarrying, particularly if the peat has been removed down to the mineral soil. However, there are some broad differences. When there has been quarrying or mining, the peat will usually have been removed first as "over-burden". Therefore, the areas of extraction usually remain clearly defined; in the case of peat cutting, there may have been total removal of the peat down to the mineral soil, in which case vegetation change will usually mark out the extent and form of the allotment or, if the cutting has been more piece-meal and incomplete a patterned mosaic of vegetation is likely to result. By contrast, military activity generally results in significant disturbance so, on peatlands the sub soil and underlying rock strata will more than likely have been exposed and scattered over the peat randomly, resulting in a somewhat amorphous mosaic of vegetation. There are of course exceptions, such as First World War mock trenchworks. These may occur as elaborate patterns visible on aerial photographs and are found on both upland moors and lowland heaths, where ever training occured.

Now to the minor skirmishes mentioned above, unrecorded by history and, very unlikely to have had any lasting impact on the land surface. Some of these engagements may, non-the-less, have been very potent and have left their mark. Almost any contact between combatants will produce some artefact evidence. In acid environments, metal items and bones may deteriorate rapidly and only leave trace evidence, but in waterlogged anaerobic peatlands, organic matter may remain well preserved indefinitely. Stone tools and pottery will survive in either environment. As a result, flint arrowheads and other Mesolithic to Bronze Age projectiles, perhaps from conflict, may occur at the peat-mineral soil interface; while later artefacts of similar purpose lie preserved in the overlying peat mass. Modern warfare and battles produce abundant artefact evidence but, the associated disturbance often destroys, damages, or mixes this and the earlier resource, as well as other hidden archaeology: one final, unfortunate major impact!

Acknowledgements

Thanks to all those involved with my peat research over the years, particularly Dr Oliver Gilbert and Professor Ian Rotherham. Thanks also to my brother-in-law Mr P.W. Wood, a hill farmer and the source of many an insight and some valuable pieces of information. In addition, the Dukes of Devonshire and their archivists Mr M. Pierpoint, and Mr P. Dey for allowing access to the Chatsworth archive.

Bibliography

Ardron, P. A. (1999) *Peat cutting in upland Britain, with special reference to the Peak District - its impact on landscape, archaeology, and ecology.* Unpublished PhD thesis, University of Sheffield, Sheffield.

Ardron, P. A. (2014) *Peat cutting in upland Britain: its impact on landscape, archaeology, and ecology.* In press, Wildtrack Publishing, Sheffield.

Collier, R. (1990) *Dark Peak Aircraft Wrecks 1.* New Edition. Wharncliffe Publishing Limited, England.

Fowkes, D.V. & Potter, G.R. (1988) William Senior's survey of the estates of the first and second earls of Devonshire c. 1600-28. *Derbyshire Record Society*, **Volume XIII**. Derbyshire Record Society, Chesterfield.

The difficulties of warfare in a bog. © Ian D. Rotherham

Burbage and Houndkirk in the Second World War: defending Sheffield and training the liberators

Bill Bevan

*in*Heritage

Defending Sheffield's Steelworks

Sheffield was the first city in Britain whose World War 2 defences were augmented by the construction of bomber decoys. These were designed to lure German bombers away from their intended urban and industrial targets using fires and lights (Dobinson, 2000; Payne, 2006). Sheffield was the first city chosen to be defended this way because of the strategic importance of the city's steelworks. The first decoy was built somewhere to the west of the city in August 1940. This was followed by a system of six decoys known as Special Fire (SF) sites, later known as Civil Starfish. The first SF site was built at Curbar Gap by late 1940. Others followed by the end of the year, located at Thorpe Salvin near Worksop, Norton, Bramley, Ulley and Houndkirk. These ringed the city and were originally intended to be operational for up to 18 months (Payne, 2006). Houndkirk is one of only two surviving sites, the other being the one at Curbar Gap (Payne, 2006).

Houndkirk decoy was decommissioned in December 1945 (Payne, 2006). It comprised a system of ditches laid out to represent the city's railway marshalling yard and streets based on a plan drawn by an artist who had been flown over Sheffield at night. There was also a control bunker, which was later converted to an experimental radar station, an access track loop and access control point to the south. The decoy used controlled fires and lights to replicate the fires of Sheffield's steel furnaces when opened to cool the molten metal, the railway marshalling yard and the sparks made by tram power conductors on the electric cables. An account written in 2000 by Oliver Murphy, a member of the Royal Artillery's Searchlight Regiment during World War 2 describes the laying out of the ditches. Theatre lights were used to duplicate the cooling furnaces. Different sets of fires were also lit to simulate the effects of enemy bombs hitting a city, including basket fires to recreate incendiary devices and other fires erected on scaffolding. Most of these structures have left no archaeological trace, though a cruciform arrangement of ditches and banks may be the foundation remains of a device known as a grid fire (Payne, 2006). Soldiers billeted in Dore and who camped on site overnight operated the decoy (Ron Priestley pers. comm.).

In 1945, the control bunker was used to test a radar station, Air Ministry Experimental Station 149 (anon., 1992). The station comprised a mobile signal van, fuel store, generators, wooden storage and workshop huts, antenna, telegraph pole with wires to the operators' van and a van used as a rest room. The operators were mostly Royal Canadian Air Force, billeted in Dore.

Apart from the now lost evidence for bomb craters near to the access control point, there is no record of the decoy or surrounding area having been bombed. How successful the decoys were may be gauged by Sheffield having not been significantly bombed after the '*Sheffield Blitz*' in December 1940.

Training the Liberators

Burbage Valley was used for military training during World War 2 by a number of units between at least 1941 and 1944. Ron Priestley, whose family grazed sheep on the moorland, recalls the moors being regularly closed to the public while training was undertaken.

The evidence for military training stretches across a large area of the Burbage Valley. It comprises numerous earthfast boulders scarred with bullet holes, mortar shell scars and at least four filled-in foxholes. Some of the boulders give the appearance of concrete pillboxes. The majority of boulders are usually hit only on one side. To the south-east of Carl Wark and below the southern part of Burbage Edge there are groups of shot boulders

Figure 1. World War 2 bullet scars used by climbers for bouldering © Philippa Davey

that appear to show areas where troops advanced in one direction as if assaulting a series of positions. Where these trails of bullet-ridden rocks stretch for hundreds of metres, the direction of assault is always uphill. There are also at least four foxholes (square pits with earthen embankments dug as defensive positions), including three in an approximate line at SK267815 that face north-east towards part of Burbage Edge where boulders are covered in a dense pattern of bullet and mortar scars. An outcrop just south of Upper Burbage Bridge was also the scene of a ferocious assault.

Military training was undertaken on Burbage from at least 1941 until 1945 (Ron Priestley and Mr K. Rackham pers. comm). Specific events that we know of comprise the following. The British 2nd Batallion Rifle Brigade fired mortars west from Burbage Edge towards an area south of Carl Wark in 1941 (Mr K. Rackham pers. comm.), though this appears not to be responsible for any of the visible evidence. Troops who were not British, possibly US or Canadian, fired heavy guns north from Toad's Mouth in 1943 (Mr E Drabble pers. comm.). Troops advanced west from Burbage Edge to Surprise View a number of times in 1943/44 (Mr Labul pers. comm.). The witness was not close enough to see who they were but collected spent .303 cartridges afterwards, which were British army issue also used by the Canadian army but not the US. Mr Labul thinks they may have been British and Canadian paratroopers who he remembers were based at Totley at

the time, having encountered French-speaking airborne troops there in early 1944.

The motor mechanic who had a garage at Fox House in the 1940s and 1950s told a group of archaeologists who visited in the 1950s that American airborne troops had practiced in Burbage valley during the Second World War. However, a search of histories of American airborne units based in Britain prior to D-Day suggests that they were all stationed in south-west England and Leicestershire. Some Americans were based at High Green, Sheffield, but these were a transport unit (Steven Acaster pers. comm.). An American unit was stationed at Blackshaw Moor, Staffordshire (a few miles north-east of Leek) in 1944 prior to D-Day (Tony Lack pers. comm.), but this is probably too far for them to have trained on Burbage. An American unit reputedly camped near Baslow (Joe White pers. comm), but little else is known about when or who they were. It is possible that Canadian troops were mistakenly identified as American. The Home Guard also trained in the area, but this appears to have all been further east near to Houndkirk quarry (Steven Acaster pers. comm).

Some of the troops who trained on Burbage may have been deployed in the Normandy landings or subsequent action during the liberation of Europe. Canadian forces were responsible for landing at "*Juno*" beach on D-Day on June 6th 1944, including paratroopers who dropped on the eastern flank of the bridgehead. British paratroopers were dropped at *"Gold"* and *"Sword"*. The following year, British airborne troops landed at Arnhem on September 17th 1944 in an attempt to capture a bridge across the Rhine. On March 23rd 1945, Canadian paratroopers dropped east of the river near the town of Wesel. Any of these units may have been the soldiers who trained on Burbage prior to combat action.

Bibliography

Anon. (1992) *Burbage Moor GH*. [Field Notes].

Dobinson, C. (2000) *Fields of Deception*. Methuen, London.

Payne, A. (2006) *Houndkirk Decoy: a survey and interpretation*. Scaramouch, Sheffield.

Big Moor shadow woodland surveys World War Two field finds

Andy Alder

Nottingham Trent University

Abstract

This paper stems from a poster presented at the War and Peat conference in Sheffield, September 2013. It profiles some Second World War artefacts discovered in the area of Big Moor, Peak District National Park, Derbyshire during *Shadow and Ghost Woodland* surveys during the summers of 2011 to 2013.

Introduction

During the period of 2011 to 2013 shadow woodland survey work was undertaken by Nottingham Trent University students and volunteers from the shadow woodland project. The surveys were undertaken in the Big Moor area of the Peak District National Park's Eastern Moors.

Fieldwork overview

Four 1-day surveys were undertaken with the aims of recording veteran trees and ancient woodland indicator species in the area of Big Moor Plantation, Barbrook, Ramsley Moor and also to go in search of Deadshaw - the long lost woodland - looking for evidence of shadow woodland.

Whilst undertaking these surveys several Second World War artefacts were found, purely by chance.

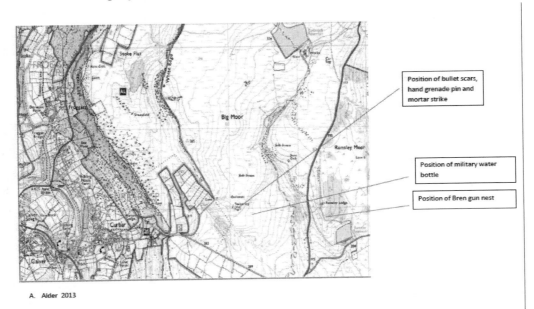

Position of bullet scars, hand grenade pin and mortar strike

Position of military water bottle

Position of Bren gun nest

A. Alder 2013

Figure 1. Map extract of Big Moor study area showing location of WW2 finds

Big Moor and the surrounding areas were used extensively during the Second World War as a training area, as Barnett and Smith (2004) state "The eastern moors were used for military training and are littered with slit trenches and gun platforms, as well as unexploded munitions buried in the peat" They go on to say "Rock out-crops, prehistoric cairns and packhorse guidestones are peppered with bullet and mortar scars"

The area was used by both the American Airborne Division and the Home Guard for training and Bill Bevan in his book *Sheffield's Golden Frame* references many anecdotes from this period in the local area.

Portable Finds found during the survey

A Second World War military water bottle found below Swine Sty. The cork was still contained within the bottle.

Figure 2. Military water bottle © Andy Alder (2013)

Hand grenade pin mechanism and bullet cap found at Swine Sty.

Figure 3. Hand grenade pin mechanism and bullet cap © Andy Alder (2013)

Bullet holes and remnant bullets were found at Swine Sty. These appear to have been from a variety of ammunition, but commonly are Lee Enfield 303 rounds.

Figure 4. Bullet holes at Swine Sty © Andy Alder (2013)

Mortar strike on rocks at the Swine Sty "Target", and example of 1940's "Rock Art". This mortar strike has been much recorded in the past and is illustrated by Barnett and Smith (2004) in *The Peak District (Landscapes through time)*.

Figure 5. Mortar strike © Andy Alder (2013)

Figure 6a &b. Possible Bren gun nest © Andy Alder (2013)

A possible Bren gun nest was found on Ramsley Moor containing over three hundred 303 cartridges and live ammunition. Figure 6a (top photograph) shows the position overlooking the A621 Ramsley Moor and Big Moor Estate entrances. This is an ideal position to guard the route across the moors.

Conclusion

The Eastern moors of the Peak District National Park are still littered with artefacts from World War Two. Many books have been written about this and have recorded aircraft crashes from the period, but there is still much to find and record. As Bevan (2007) says "It may be difficult to picture this now when walking over the quiet moorlands, but Burbage and Houndskirk were in the frontline during World War 2, They were part of the defence of Britain and a training ground in advance of the allied invasion of Europe".

Acknowledgements

I would like to thank my survey teams who worked so hard during the surveys in often unpleasant conditions. With special thanks to Simon Taylor, Rowan Alder, Tony Smith and Jacqui Parker (my unofficial PA).

References

Barnett, J. and Smith, K. (2004) *The Peak District (Landscapes through time)*. Windgather Press, Macclesfield.

Bevan, B. (2007) *Sheffield's Golden Frame (The Moorland Heritage of Burbage, Houndskirk and Longshaw)*. Sigma Leisure, Wilmslow, Cheshire.

Figure 7. The Survey Team

Langsett and Midhope at war 1939-1945

Mike G. Kirby

Langsett and Midhope at War 'All Our Stories' community history project team

Introduction

This project evolved from many years of walking and exploring in the northern Peak District of England. In doing so, the eye of the historian was inevitably drawn to the idiosyncratic features that occur on an otherwise featureless moorland landscape. In particular, concrete tracks appear to lead to nowhere, brick-lined trenches are to be found in the midst of peat bogs, and almost every winter, the remains of artillery shells are squeezed to the surface by the harsh frosts. This dangerous legacy even today provides a challenge for the local Mountain Rescue Team and National Park Rangers. For the historian, superficial conversations with local people provided few hard facts; nevertheless, elderly residents did provide a tantalising glimpse of the very important role of this area as a tank and artillery range during the Second World War. Thereafter, work with local history societies coupled with an appeal for information made though local media, has produced a skeletal picture of the workings of a major military training area which played host to a wide spectrum of soldiery who, as can be expected, interacted with the local population in a variety of ways. Early in 1939, local construction firms participated in the development of the facilities leading to widespread speculation as to the purpose of the buildings. When tanks appeared at nearby Penistone railway station Local Home Guard platoons were deployed to secure their passage to the Langsett training area confirming to the locals that this was indeed to be a shooting range for the army. What no local resident could have foreseen though was the arrival of large numbers of foreign soldiers both from the British Empire and the New World. Stranger still, displaced Polish troops encamped in the area and due to the political situation during and after the war, many were resettled across the region.

Keywords: Peak District National Park, Second World War, Military Training Areas.

The Project

The project team has been provided with an opportunity to research and compile a study of the people whose lives were affected by the use of the Langsett training area. Overall, this work is a wartime history, written from the viewpoint of ordinary people and there are four distinct themes to this study. These are:

1. Local Army Personnel;

2. Local Non-combatants;

3. Foreign Army Personnel; and

4. Post-war Resettlement.

Figure 1. Remains of Moving Target North at Langsett

Local Army Personnel

Local people served in the armed forces and used the facilities at Langsett. Their experiences are being examined within the context of well-documented national studies, however there has been very little written, from the soldier's viewpoint, on the effectiveness of their training. It is to be hoped that some understanding of this training will provide a clear picture of the workings of the facility, as it is against this background that important social issues are to be assessed.

Local Non-combatants

Local people also played a non-combatant role in the defence of the area, notably the conscientious objectors who manned the static defences on the adjacent dams. Uniquely, the region around the dams itself provided the government with a workforce with which to crew these defences. For many years, there had been a significant number of local people attending meetinghouses of the Quaker faith. Indeed, Midhope Hall played host to regular gatherings, as did nearby Sheephouse, Judd Field and Lumbroyd (Bower & Knight, 1987). Using the powers of the National Service (Armed Forces) Act 1939, these men were recruited and trained to maintain the static and catenary defences, and to provide services for the uniformed soldiers. In the event of further air raids, they were to activate a number of smoke pots placed around the edge of the dams in order to obscure them from German bombers (WO32/15272, 1941). Temporary Nissen huts were erected in the surrounding fields and a community, of sorts, began to form (Hallam, 1990). The local Quakers were soon joined by men sent out from the Local Tribunals.

These had been set up by the government to assess the validity of registered conscientious objectors. They were a disparate and complex mix of Jehovah's Witnesses, Christians, Socialists, Pacifists, and Trade Unionists. Whatever their personal reasons for objection, they were put to defence work; this activity being made compulsory and specifically classified within the Act as '*passive air defence duties*' (Barker, 1982). Local reaction to the '*conshies*' varied; but even now there is precious little debate about their role in the war. Nationally, objectors were sent away to work in other areas, leaving their communities to make often grossly misleading assumptions as to their safe havens and easy-going living conditions (Rose, 2003). Andrew Marr (2009), writing in his populist history gives a somewhat enlightened view of this subject and offers an alternative, if only brief look at the objector's war. Angus Calder (1969) goes further and cites the heroism of many objectors who took on dangerous work such as bomb disposal and front-line medical duties. It is hoped that access to private archival material, principally from Quaker sources, and testimonies from local oral history gathering, will indeed add much to this discussion.

Foreign Army Personnel

The influx of foreign soldiers brought with it problems of race, class and culture. The American army arrived en-masse in 1943 and with them came substantial numbers of black, or 'coloured' soldiers with them, albeit in a purely support role. The issue of segregation was experienced by the local population for the first time, and for some, this left a lasting impression. Popular histories of the war make much of the affluence of the average GI, their popularity with the British women and their strange use of the English language. Nationally, Cooksley (2007) observes that any initial curiosity soon wore off and gave way to the oft quoted 'over-paid, over-sexed and over here' attitude, made worse with the realisation that the GI's good manners did not extend to their dark-skinned colleagues. Generally speaking, the Americans were typical of many of the foreign soldiers who found themselves stationed in Britain; to many locals in comparison with the war-weary British, they seemed 'ebullient' (Sokoloff, 1999).

A completely new experience for the local population, both urban and rural, was the appearance of the first black soldiers who arrived in Penistone to support the fighting white troops. This was not atypical of the national picture where the influx of more than 130,000 black soldiers into Britain with its mere 8,000 black inhabitants created great interest to a public generally ignorant of the US policy of segregation and 'Jim Crow' laws (Calder, 1969). Outwardly, the British Government refused to allow the US to 'import' any of its 'colour bar' regulations into the British Isles. However, within parliament, there was much political anxiety and several peers, notably the Duke of Buccleuch, wrote angrily that 'much intercourse is allowed... I personally dislike this mixture of colour ... [our] ... unsophisticated country girls should be

Figure 2: Local resident, Alice Badger (nee Milne) with an example of the Cleared Ordnance

discouraged from marrying these black men' (Rose, 2003). This attitude compares, albeit distastefully, with the local squire in the Langsett area, the Earl of Wharncliffe writing to the War Office with his complaints of 'a big black face grinning at him through his [breakfast room] window' (Smith, 1988). According to Mass Observation surveys in 1943, there was widespread public disapproval of the segregation policy within the US forces stationed here. For his part, General Eisenhower introduced a special arrangement for the black troops in Britain, which was described at the time as 'separate but equal' (Smith, 1988). Laudable as these efforts were, conflicts between white and black Americans, and occasionally their British hosts, did occur and this is evident in local history gathering. There are also stories of black GI's singing in local church choirs and helping local farmers. Both nationally and locally, newspapers picked up on these human interest stories and in the main they convey a positive picture of the black American soldier in Britain. Nevertheless, there are other instances where the subject of segregation in the US armed forces was experienced in detail, particularly by local women in Sheffield, Barnsley and Huddersfield. Considering the crucial role of the black soldiers in munitions handling at Langsett, this petty racism only serves to highlight the ultimate stupidity of a segregated military (Norton *et al.*, 2007). It is indeed this most dangerous work, still classified by the US military as 'menial duties' that the contingent of black soldiers performed here (Norton *et al.*, 2007).

Post-war Resettlement

After VE day in 1945, nearby Cawthorne village became a resettlement camp for Polish soldiers who had fought alongside British troops in the Western Desert, Italy and in the

North-West Europe campaign. Whilst in the camp they were tasked with the dangerous job of clearing unexploded ordnance from the Langsett training area. The winter of 1945-46 proved to be particularly harsh and in the event, little was done to clear the range; card games under a smoke-filled tarpaulin being the preferred pastime. Faced with the prospect of returning to a homeland now under Soviet rule, and under strong pressure from the British Government to do so, many Polish soldiers questioned their future. In the event, almost all the 'Cawthorne Poles' accepted that assimilation into the local community was the only viable option and arrangements were made to re-educate and re-settle them. It is their story that will bring the project to its logical end.

Conclusion

In conclusion, therefore, although there are a plethora of secondary works available on the subject of the battles of the Second World War and the use of tanks in them, almost nothing has been published on the subject of training. Similarly, the wartime experience of local people has attracted sparse attention until now. Thanks to this project, much work has been done to document real peoples' experiences of war and, almost at the eleventh hour, some of their recollections have been recorded for posterity. Much use will be made of these efforts; however, there are areas of study still somewhat clouded in obscurity, which beg investigaton. There are indeed sensitive subjects that promise to deliver some stimulating findings of direct relevance to local communities. It is hoped, that gaps in our knowledge may be filled. The successful completion of the project should provide the team with an opportunity to research in areas historically subjected to secrecy, controversy and indeed taboo. Undoubtedly, the project will provide important new material about the roles of Langsett and Midhope, and the experiences of its people during the war. This is not only the experience of life on the home front but significantly, the development of awareness and attitudes brought upon the inhabitants by the necessities of war and the influx of military materials, both men and machines. In the final analysis, local experiences of conflict will be compared and contrasted with the wider national view. In doing so, it is hoped that a realistic view of how ordinary people from diverse backgrounds coped with extra-ordinary circumstances during almost six years of global war.

Bibliography

Barker, R. (1982) *Conscience, Government and War: Conscientious objection in Great Britain 1939-45*. Routledge & Kegan Paul (London and Boston), London, p.80.

Bower, J. & Knight, J. (1987) *Plain Country Friends: The Quakers of Wooldale, High Flatts and Midhope*. Wooldale Meeting of the Religious Society of Friends, Yorkshire, p.6.

Calder, A. (1969) *The People's War: Britain 1939-1945*. Jonathan Cape, London, p.496.

Cooksley, P.G. (2007) *The Home Front: Civilian Life in World War Two*. The History Press, Stroud, pp 99-100.

Hallam, V. (1990) *Silent Valley at War - Life in the Derwent Valley, 1939-45*. Sheaf Publishing Ltd., Sheffield, p11.

Marr, A. (2009) *The Making of Modern Britain. From Queen Victoria to V.E. Day*. Macmillan, London, pp408-409.

Norton, M.B., Sheriff, C., Katzman, D.M. & Blight, D. (2007) *A People and a Nation: A History of the United States*. Eighth Edition, Wadsworth Publishing, Boston, p762.

Rose, S. (2003) *Which People's War? National Identity and Citizenship in Britain 1939-1945*. OUP, Oxford, p 173.

Smith, G. (1988) *When Jim Crow Met John Bull: Black American Soldiers in WW2 Britain*. I.B.Tauris, London, p 99.

Sokoloff, S. (1999) How are they at home?: community, state and servicemen's wives in England, 1939-45. *Women's History Review*, **8**(1), p.39.

WO32/15272 (1941) *Conscientious Objectors: right to non-combatant service 1941, Section 7*. HMSO, London.

Local memories of military impacts on the Peak District: air crashes, defences and training areas.

Christine Handley
SYBRG

Abstract

This short chapter arose out of discussions at the War & Peat conference that highlighted some of the local memories and knowledge of the military impacts around the Peak District. Contributions were invited from members of the audience and together with material gathered through the *Moors for the Future's Moor Memories Oral History Project* form the basis of the chapter. The focus is on people's memories of the aeroplanes which crashed on the moor, the legacy of the moors being used as training grounds and the protection put in place on local reservoirs after the 'Dambusters' raids. They complement the chapters by Dr Bill Bevan, Mike Kirby and Terry Howard elsewhere in this volume.

Introduction

Local memories of the air crashes span the period from the early 1940s (during WW2) into the 1960s; the photographs illustrate what remains and the memorials, which have been erected near crash-sites. The recollections about the defensive protection on the reservoirs span a similar period, from when they were built to when they were dismantled. Memories of the impacts of military training date from the 1970s, they look at the longer-term legacy for the moors which still continue today. The focus for this chapter arose through discussions amongst delegates at the conference and the written and oral reminiscences set out below reflect them. Whilst they also complement other contributions, which cover the Peak District, in this volume, they only represent a small fraction of the material, which relates to military activity and the impact of war on the local landscape. The personal reminiscences are left to stand alone to reflect the themes of 'War and Peat'.

Air crashes

During WW2, there were several plane crashes across the high moorland plateaux around Kinder, Bleaklow and Black Hill. These three excerpts from interviews carried out as part of the *Moors for the Future: Moor Memories Oral History Project* give first hand accounts of local experiences of crashes and their aftermaths.

Arthur Huddleston: New Mills – plane crash and Home Guard

"... planes that came down on Kinder. Well we did [have] because during the war my father was in the Home Guard

& me brothers were till they got called up, …. my youngest brother & I, were in the Scouts. And they used the Scouts as runners between various places & the thing I do remember is one particular night I was on duty, was the Home Guard in Hayfield [had] gone to New Mills … and there was just a caretaker there and the phone rang and it was from Upper House ... And they rang up to say they wanted some assistance because a plane had just come down and I said well it's difficult because they're in New Mills. So we contacted them … and it turned out it was, I can't remember the plane, what it was, but the crew were all Canadians, six of them and they laid them out here in these garages, here at the Royal Hotel, that's where they kept them, and they brought them down the next day. No [none survived]. There was quite a lot of planes came down on Kinder and we used to go looking for them. We used to get bits, pieces of Perspex and things like that. Something we could make something of. So that's kind of what happened."

Holme Village Workshop October 2010: Oxford crash

"You see that Oxford the first one that crashed in the war just up road here [from Holme]. Another one crashed over … during war and it were bombed up 'n all. Up Cliff Lane. … Over Bob Gill's, Haigh Howard's' bungalow. And Jack Gill, you know, … was living up Peacock [Farm] on his own. Jack jumps out of bed, gets his britches on and comes running down into Holme banging on doors "They're here!

They're here! They're here!" Well it were an Oxford, an Oxford plane that had crashed. … They took every scrap away. They exploded a bomb you know. … What they did, they had tractors & they made sleds, sledges with corrugated sheeting, roof sheeting, & they fetched every bit of it."

Derek Bailey: Salvage and 're-cycling'

"During the war everything in the plane which was reusable was, what would be called now, recycled. … It would be the RAF Regiment who used to turn up and take everything, e.g. the engine and what have you, if it could be salvaged from the wreck. But the bits and pieces that were left lying around these kids were sent around to pick up anything that was useful to the engineers and model makers. Now this is made out of crashed parts on an aircraft except for that and that which I think is a hardwood of some kind. But we used to get the Perspex from the windscreen, all the broken bits, and take them out down and give them to the people who were interested in them. …

Everybody who was anywhere near used to do things like that, you know. So recycling is not new it's been going on an awful long time."

There have been other crashes on the moors since the end of WW2 involving military aircraft and as the example from Geoff Kay shows too, how smaller private aircraft got into difficulties. The moorland terrain, poor weather conditions as well as problems with the aircraft itself have all been contributory factors in the crashes. The first two quotes describe the same incident from different perspectives.

Peter Wolstenholme – from War and Peat conference: Air crash at Higher Shelf Stones

"A Boeing Superfortress RB-29A. 44-61999, from the 16th Photo. Reconnaissance Squadron, 91st Recc. Group, 311th Air Div. SAC. USAF was on a flight from Scampton, Lincolnshire to Burtonwood, Lancashire on November 3rd 1948. Low cloud covered most of the country so the aircraft was flying on instruments, the crew thought flight time elapsed should have been sufficient to clear the hills so they descended just short of clearing the high ground and crashed at Higher Shelf Stones. The aircraft caught fire and all 13 on board perished. The bodies were recovered the following day, the wreckage remains on site to this day, probably because the deep peat would make heavy recovery impossible at the time.

Photographs (Figures) 1 and 2 were given to me by the late Bert Riggs, who I worked with at Osborn Mushet Tools

Figures 1 and 2. Photographs taken shortly after the Boeing Superfortress crashed on Higher Shelf Stones © Bert Riggs

Figures 3, 4 and 5. Photographs taken in the 1970s of the Boeing Superfortress that crashed on Higher Shelf Stones © Peter Wolstenholme

in the 1960s. Bert hiked the Peak District most weekends and took these two photos shortly after the accident. Photographs (Figures) 3, 4 and 5 were taken by me in the 1970s."

Holme Village Workshop October 2010: Liberator and Flying Fortress

"Like all these aircraft, I mean, go to the Liberator, you can go to that one, er not so much on Sliddens Moor but you can go to top of Shelf Stones, Higher Shelf Stones to the Flying Fortress there, they just missed the top of, just missed getting over the top.

Aye they did, they missed. But that were spewing black smoke. It were on fire I think."

Meteor Plane Crash 1950s.

"We differ, me and David, about this aircraft. I thought it crashed on Black Hill.

No it didn't. Derek says not. I'll stand corrected then. That Meteor crashed 54 years ago. It wasn't on the Black Hill, it

Figure 6. Remains of the Superfortress aeroplane in 2012 © Herbert Beardsell

Figure 7. Looking towards Black Hill and the moorland around Holme village © Christine Handley

was just this side, straight up from [the] Fleece [Inn, in Holme village]. Yes, a Meteor plane. I know my wife was hanging clothes out when we were newly married. We lived at Brown Hill and it came over spewing black smoke out and straight into the… hillside."

Geoff Kay, Midhope - Moor Memories

"There is still ammunition there from the Army days – shells, small bombs, bits of aircraft [on Midhope Moor]." Geoff recalled two incidents from his childhood, which took place next to the family's farmhouse … about 50 years ago when a small aircraft landed in the field because it had run out of petrol (fuel?), his father helped to fetch some and they were able to take off again. On another occasion, probably in the mid/ late 1960s, it was on a Sunday, a glider crash-landed, hit their garden wall and the chap (pilot) died. He had come from Doncaster. … the pilot appeared to be trying to avoid the houses and there were plenty of other places he could have tried it was just unfortunate that he couldn't avoid the wall."

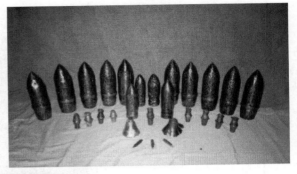

Figure 8. WW2 ordnance collected from Midhope Moor in a single day © Dave Burgess

Figure 9. Remains of tank targets on Midhope Moor © Dave Burgess

Training areas

Peter Wolstenholme – from War & Peat conference: Bullet holes at Doctors Gate Culvert

"In the 1970s, I hiked from Doctors Gate Culvert over to Higher Shelf Stones to see the site of the Flying Fortress aircraft. On the way, I found spent 303 bullets in an eroding peat bank indicating that this had been used as a 'back-stop' for military rifle training targets."

John Littlewood – Moor Memories

John Littlewood was a gamekeeper working on the moors around Midhope in the 1970s and early 1980s. As part of the moorland management for grouse, strips of heather moor are burnt on rotation to keep the heather short and new shoots growing. He describes some of the difficulties encountered whilst burning the heather due to the military use of the moors.

"It's got some good roads on it [Midhope Moor] but it can be a very bad moor to burn. There's parts on it, as you know, where I don't know if you know during the war when it got burnt out a lot of peat haggs got took up, same as Pike Low, that was a bad place. … I think it was, from what I've been told it was started off by Americans based there [Midhope] and it was a flare that set it off [moorland fire]. … it set all Pike Low on fire and it were burning for weeks upon weeks and on Pike Low especially where its all stony it took all the peat out. So therefore you've got edges of peat up on Pike Low and that so and yes it were a bit difficult places to burn."

"… [big moorland fire – out of control], I think it must have been about '82 but I'll have to check on that … I was working at Fitzwilliams when this big one went up. There were 2 bombs went off in that, because up Duke's Road there were a lot of bombs from war, because they used to use it in war on a like Sheffield, with all lighting systems and that so Germans 'd drop all the bombs on there. 'Cos I don't know if you know but up on Strines Moor there's a stone shed, like a shed in moor, that used to be the battery house where they kept the batteries for lighting it all up… what they did, they used to call it the battery house, they had all these big batteries and what they did, they simulated Sheffield. Put lights everywhere as if it were the city and then when t'Germans came along they dropped their bombs on there instead of the city and that moor was absolutely plastered in live bombs from the war."

"Up to John Warhurst retiring, they used to have one day a year or one week a year where they [all the local gamekeepers] used to go up and collect all these live bombs up and they used to put them in heaps. Used to put 'em in heaps yes. [Just leave them?] Yes, well they used to do it and local policemen would come and deal with it and army whatever and they used to, but they stopped doing that some time ago."

"But I mean that fire at Fitzwilliams all the keepers from the area came, you know Roger France and everybody come to help wi' that, that were a big fire, yes. …. No, nobody was injured, we were lucky it was one morning that happened, on a Sunday. We were going back to the fire and there were two explosions and somebody, I don't know who it was, somebody rang bomb disposal and they came…"

John Ownsworth - Moor Memories and from War and Peat Conference

"But when I first started going on Low Moor [in the 1970s] there were so many shells on the ground you couldn't avoid standing on them near the moving targets. Mainly 75mm semi-armour piercing ones but occasionally I found high explosive ones, which were painted red. There were also a lot of 6 pounders, 37mm & sometimes 0.5 and then lots of small arms fire like 0•300 American rounds, 0•303's. I only found one or two 20mms but there must have been a few more than that.

Then David Green, who's now dead unfortunately, … was a nice chap, and he let me go on his part of the moor and he also told me where the camp was where some of the permanent staff were billeted and he let me go on that piece of land with my metal detector and I found all sorts of things in there. Like tops off potbelly stoves, cutlery and a 37mm round, a complete round. "

"Also at Langsett(s) there the reservoirs on the west of Sheffield were protected by 40mm Bofors anti-aircraft

Figure 10. Concrete plinth for catenary defence pylon at Midhope © Christine Handley (2012)

guns. They all had at least two Bofors guns at the dam head to protect against low flying German aircraft. They also put booms of drums fastened together by chains across the reservoirs to stop torpedoes being directed at the bank. A local chap [Mr Mosley] ... took these photographs. He was an official in the Waterworks ... I've got photographs of them letting off the smoke defence, which they put around all the local reservoirs, and it looked just like fog. It was completely blotted out..."

The final set of recollections comes from Ben Cherry who grew up at Midhope. He was a boy during WW2 and remembers the defensive structures which were put in place across the local reservoirs after the RAF carried out the 'Dambusters' raids to protect against similar attempts by the Germans. He was working at the farm when some of the defences were taken down and this forms part of his story. As with many others, he is able to describe the sites of military training on the moor and where to find the remains. When interviewed,

he declined to be recorded, so the extract below is based on notes, taken at the time.

Ben Cherry – Moor Memories: Defensive protection for the local reservoirs.

"Almost at the far end (from Coit field entrance) of this stretch of path there are the remains of the footings for one of the searchlights which were built as part of the [Midhope] reservoir defences which Ben showed us. Looking across from the reservoir bank, Ben pointed out where the tank training ground was on the moorland hillside opposite (just below Pike Low). It is possible to make out some of the training platforms and the line of the railed trackway that the targets were pulled along powered by a 'donkey' engine."

"He remembers the dam protection pylons etc being built in the early 1940s ('42 or '43). The cables which were strung between the pylons were about 6" in diameter; they were made by Callender Cables and came on big drums. The pylons were built on the hillsides above the reservoirs on concrete plinths that were sunk up to 15' into the ground. They were anchored by 4 'guy' ropes also on plinths arranged in a diamond shape around the central pylon. A pylon was erected in one of the fields above Midhope Hall farm; the footings of which are still visible – the field has been renamed the 'Pylon field'. The 'guy' ropes were attached at 100', 200' and 300' up the main pylon to give it stability although the pylon had a 'ball-shaped' footing which allowed the pylon to move in the wind. A cable was strung between the pylons on either side of the valley looped over the top and through the fastenings. It was likely that the cable was ferried across the reservoir by boat and then hauled up the other side (of the valley), winched up the pylon and attached at the top."

"The pylon at Midhope was dismantled in November 1953 and Ben was one of the farm workers who helped the men from 'Tommy Wards' to do so. The pylon structure and cables were cut in lengths in the field and then loaded onto a tractor trailer and taken down to the lane to be loaded onto the lorries provided by TW Wards (TWW). The lorries were only 3-ton ones so it took several days to take all the sections away and they were piled up along the lane as Ben and the farm team were able to work faster than the TWW crew as they only had a couple of lorries to cart the scrap away. It was tricky work taking the sections down by tractor as the sections were very heavy and there was a danger that the trailer would push the tractor and run away with them.

(The pylon field is on a slope as is the field below so they were manoeuvring down an incline.) At the end of the week, the TWW foreman asked the farmer if he could pay the farm workers a bonus for helping them as it would have taken them far longer without their help with the tractors. The farmer agreed and they each got paid £5 which was a lot of money as they were getting £5 for an 80hour week working on the farm at the time."

"He can also remember seeing the pilots practising low-level flying being almost on eye level as they flew down the [Midhope] valley – possibly training to take part in the 'Dambusters' raid. They didn't stay long in the valley but soon moved over to the Derwent valley to continue their training."

Conclusions

The paper reflects some of the breadth of local knowledge around military activity on the Peak District moorlands close to Sheffield. However, the quotes and stories in this chapter are only a small fraction of what is available, taken mostly from one project archive. Further work, using this archive, could usefully be developed.

The impacts and legacy of military activity continue to engage and interest a range of people, communities and organisations. This book, from the 'War and Peat' conference, is one example. The centenary of the outbreak of World War 1 and the ageing population of survivors of World War 2 have provided new foci of interest. More oral history projects are developing to record memories both locally, in the Peak District, and elsewhere in the country. The range of information in this chapter shows how the collection of memories through oral history can add to this historical record.

Acknowledgements

The transcripts and recordings from the *Moor Memories Oral History Project* are available at the Derbyshire Archives Library in Matlock and at the Holmfirth Library in West Yorkshire. Copies of the booklets and podcasts which were compiled as part of the project can be found on the Moors for the Future's website http://www.moorsforthefuture. org.uk/moor-memories. The author would like to thank all those who took part and shared their memories.

Bibliography

Handley, C. and Rotherham, I. D. (2011) *Hills, Dykes and Dams: Moor Memories in the Bradfield, Midhope and Langsett Areas*. Wildtrack Publishing, Sheffield.

Handley, C. and Rotherham, I. D. (2011) *Mosses and Cloughs: Moor Memories in the Home Valley Area*. Wildtrack Publishing, Sheffield.

Handley, C. and Rotherham, I. D. (2012) *Moor Memories from Across the Peak District*. Wildtrack Publishing, Sheffield.

The moorland access campaigns – (with some military interludes)

Terence Howard
The Ramblers Association

Abstract

The campaign to gain, or regain, public access to what is considered *our* moorland heritage did not start with the Kinder Trespass of 1932 as some may believe. The many myths that have grown up around this *iconic* event has obscured its real contribution to this long running campaign, perhaps one of the longest in our history. A *Time Line* of the access campaign will be used to build the picture of the campaigns' developments from its first major stirrings with the Crookesmoor Enclosure riots of 1791 to the "Right to Roam" Act in 2000 (Countryside and Rights of Way Act 2000). Throughout this time-line there were military "interludes" some directly affecting access and access campaigning, from direct intervention of the military to such as training and target practice. During wartime years, 1914-18 and 1939-45, ramblers generally supported or tolerated this intervention but what caused consternation were how the moors were being abused and vandalised and the duplicity of some landowners.

Keywords: Access; Moorland Campaigns; 'Right to Roam'

Introduction

The campaign to gain, or regain, public access to what is considered *our* moorland heritage did not start with the Kinder Trespass of 1932 as some may believe. The many myths that have grown up around this *iconic* event has obscured its real contribution to this long running campaign, perhaps one of the longest in our history.

The many newspaper headlines from this time right up to the passing in Parliament of the *Countryside and Rights of Way Act, 2000* reads as though it was a military campaign as the following examples show:

- RAMBLERS BATTLE WITH KEEPERS

- SIX ARRESTS AFTER MASS INVASION

- RAMBLERS WIELD THE WEAPON OF TRESPASS

- THE COUNTRYSIDE AT WAR

- RAMBLERS MARCH IN BATTLE FOR MOORS

- RAMBLERS ON WARPATHS

- WALKERS SET FOR BATTLE ON ACCESS

- WALKERS FIGHT FOR MOORLAND ACCESS

- RAMBLERS LOCKED IN OLD LAND BATTLES

- THE MOORS FIGHT IS NOT OVER

- RAMBLERS FIGHT ON

- RAMBLERS WIN 50 YEAR BATTLE

- HEATHER AND PEAT HEROES

- FREEDOM AND RESPONSIBILITY

A *Time Line* of the access campaign can be considered appropriate to build the picture of its development from its first major stirrings around the Crookesmoor Enclosure riots of 1791 to the "Right to Roam" Act in 2000 (Countryside and Rights of Way Act 2000). Along the way, various attempts had been made to introduce Access Bills in Parliament but, not surprisingly, they failed. Although access campaigning often went alongside the need to protect the Peak District from development in the early twentieth century, trespassing on the enclosed moorlands was commonplace to those who "dared". In fact to some trespassers it was a game trying to avoid the gamekeepers, some even followed a code "The fine art of trespassing" or how to avoid being caught and what to say if you were.

Throughout this time-line there were military "interludes" some directly affecting access and access campaigning, from direct intervention of the military to such as training and target practice. During wartime years, 1914-18 and 1939-45, ramblers generally supported or tolerated this intervention but what caused consternation were how the moors were being abused and vandalised and the duplicity of some landowners.

The Roots of the Campaign

The roots of the campaign are evident within the Sheffield Enclosure Act of 1791 when **six thousand acres** of common land were taken out of public access with resulting riots. The absent Duke of Norfolk, as Lord of the Manor of Sheffield along with Freeholders and Gentry benefited from this enclosure, which was supposed to improve the commons and wastes for agriculture. When the Commissioners who were appointed to carry out the enclosure of the common land met at the Rising Sun at Bents Green there was also a number of "individuals" probably there to disrupt the meeting. The meeting was abandoned. When the Commissioners met again, they were accompanied by a troop of Light Dragoons.

On Crookesmoor local people gathered to stop the Commissioners from enclosing the land. They drove them from the commons and burned and destroyed the property of freeholders and landowners who supported and benefited from the enclosures. Fearful of the riotous behaviour the militia, Dragoons from Nottingham, were called in to quell the riots and to allow the enclosures to proceed. It seems one man was found guilty of arson, condemned to death and executed. Because of the rioting, troops were billeted in the town on a permanent basis. Their barracks were built in the White House area (now around Whitehouse Lane at Walkley, a suburb of Sheffield).

A quote from Carolus Paulus from his book written in 1907 – *"Forgotten Facts in the History of Sheffield"* illustrates the point. *"By the Inclosure quite a number of village greens were taken from the poor inhabitants and appropriated to the use of the landed classes, Brookhouse Green, Heeley Green, Newfield Green, Owlerton Green, Rivelin Green being amongst the number. Perhaps the two acres granted to the poor were intended as full compensation"*. The moors to the west of Sheffield suffered the same fate where they were "preserved" for Grouse rearing and shooting and the public were denied access even for simple bilberry gathering. Carolus Paulus goes on to say, *"It may be imagined that before these Acts were passed the freedom to roam over the moors would be well nigh unlimited, and that the same were used for various beneficial purposes by the inhabitants at large, without fear of trespass"*. He continues, from *"The Old English Village"* – 1912, *"May the time not be too far distant when the wide moorlands shall once more be appropriated for common use, that instead of ministering solely to the pleasures of the rich, they may become the treasure house of the poor and the barren but picturesque remnants as the breathing spaces for many"*.

Ebenezer Elliot (1781 – 1849), the Sheffield Corn Law Rhymer and Chartist, from a verse in his poem *Footpaths* gives a contemporary account of how the Enclosures affected ordinary people.

Wolves with the hearts of devils!

They steal our footpaths too!

The poor man's walk they take away,

Where now, unseen, the flowers are blowing,

And all unheard, the stream is flowing:

What worse could devils do?

Our "Time Line" begins.

In 1876, the Hayfield and Kinder Ancient Footpaths Society was formed. This is considered to be the *birth* of the *"Right to Roam"* campaign.

During the 1880s and 1890s, a real interest in rambling was beginning to develop, although mainly from the middle classes. In 1884, the first attempt to introduce an Access Bill in Parliament by James Bryce failed, not surprisingly. Eighteen-ninety four saw the Hope Valley Railway open. This gave a great opportunity for working class people to get out into the hills, such as Kinder Scout. It provided the *great escape* to get away from the filth and pollution of Sheffield and Manchester offering fresh air and exercise. However, the situation led to greater conflict with landowners and their gamekeepers who wanted the moors preserved for grouse and shooting.

Perhaps the real organised campaign for the *Right to Roam* started here in Sheffield in 1900, with the formation of the *Clarion Ramblers* by G.H.B.Ward. This followed an organised walk around Kinder Scout. He later became dubbed as the Prince (if not the King) of Ramblers. From the start, he researched the history of our local moorlands, along with their *political* history and started on the path of access campaigning at a local and national level. He exposed the inequalities of the Enclosure Awards in and around Sheffield. These are listed below in chronological order:

- Bolsterstone Award (1782) – 2,041 acres enclosed;

- Sheffield (Ecclesall) Award (1788) – 806 acres enclosed;

- Sheffield Award (1805) - 6,000 acres enclosed;

- Bradfield Award (1826) – 18,128 acres enclosed; and

- Hathersage Award (1830) – 10,000 acres enclosed.

G.H.B. Ward identified many paths over the *forbidden* moorlands, which he claimed were rights of way that had been *stolen*. Such routes included Doctors Gate between the Snake Pass road and Glossop, and the Duke of Norfolk's Road over the Bradfield Moors to Abbey Brook. His research and lifetime's work on access and our countryside is best recorded in the unparalleled and unrivalled little gems of the *Sheffield Clarion Handbooks*. He edited and wrote these handbooks from the early 1900s up to his death in 1957. (Later editions were not the same).

In 1908, another attempt was made to introduce an Access to Mountains and Moorlands Bill in Parliament, again it failed.

In 1909, the Clarion Ramblers organised a *raid* (a trespass) over Doctors Gate, in successive years they were joined by Manchester Ramblers. Eventually they were successful and the landowner conceded to the path (but with some restrictions).

Nineteen fourteen saw the start of the First World War. Many young men clamoured to take part because of the *hype* it generated. Some nine hundred young *professional* men volunteered to join the Sheffield "Pals" Battalion of the 12th York and Lancasters. Initially, they were based at Redmires where a camp was set up, a bleak outpost for many. They practiced trench digging around Lord's Seat overlooking Redmires and on Roper Hill above the camp. There were route marches over all the surrounding moors, including the Burbage Valley as well as *nights out* or bivouacs on the moors in all weather conditions. There was no live firing practice on the moors at this time that we know of. In 1915, the 'Pals' went to Cannock Chase for live firing practice then onto Egypt before arriving in France on the Somme in 1916. On the first day of the offensive, 1st July 1916, two thirds of the nine hundred were killed or wounded. The moorlands around Lord's Seat, Redmires, would be one of the last places in Sheffield most of these young men would ever see. Lord's Seat or Quarry Hill, later dubbed Hill 60 after a similar looking hill at Ypres another WW1 battlefield, was used for training by other battalions from around the country. (It was used again in the Second World War for Homeguard Training).

G.H.B. Ward, or Bert as he was known to his fellow walkers, was an inveterate trespasser, particularly on Kinder Scout. In 1923, he was served an Injunction by a Kinder landowner. It was to prevent him from trespassing on Kinder and not to incite others to trespass on Kinder. Although he appeared to act within the terms of the Injunction, he was caught on a *friendly* camera trespassing on Kinder with other ramblers in 1924.

Also in 1923, a notorious reward notice appeared in the Manchester Evening Chronicle offering a £5 reward

to identify two ramblers trespassing on Kinder. It provoked an outcry at the time and was never used again. The footnote to this was the two trespassers were never identified because they were both from Sheffield. Ann Beedham in her book *Days of Sunshine and Rain* identified one of them as Willis Marshall.

In 1925, The Law of Property Act gives the public the right of access "for air and exercise" to all commons in urban areas in England and Wales. This was too late for Sheffield, as they had already gone.

1926. The Access to Mountains and Moorland Bill fails yet again.

1927 and successive years saw mass gatherings of ramblers and cyclists in the Winnats Pass, Castleton on a Sunday in June, to campaign for access to mountain and moorland and the protection of the Peak District. These

Figure 1. The forbidden moorland © Terence Howard

gatherings were also to form the basis of the campaign for National Parks. Bert Ward was involved in setting up these mass rallies and was one of the main speakers. A first class orator, who asked for and demanded the *"Right to Roam"* He also expected *"Every rambler to be at the Access to Mountains Annual Demonstration in the Winnats Pass at 3pm"*.

Marching towards access

In 1927, the Duke of Rutland sold part of his Longshaw grouse shooting estate in Burbage and the surrounding moors to Sheffield Council for £21,000. This was for water supplies, and to build a reservoir under Carl Wark. Sheffield Ramblers Federation tried with some success to gain limited access to the former private moors but it was mainly via concession paths.

The sale of the Longshaw Estate was completed in 1931 paid for through public contributions as well as by the City Council. It was then handed to the National Trust to manage for public benefit. The acquisition of Blacka moor followed in 1933 when J.G Graves, a public benefactor and a member of the Ramblers Federation, was influenced to purchase the land and give it to the City. This he did for the health, recreation and well-being of the citizens of Sheffield.

In 1929, a party of young people was trespassing on Stanage and while there, they agreed to set up a *Woodcraft Folk* group in Sheffield as they had heard of similar groups in London. It was a cooperative outdoor organisation and

one of its first leaders was Albert Richardson (later to become Lord Mayor of Sheffield in 1975). They had camps and rambles. It was on one of the trespass rambles that a gamekeeper stopped them and demanded to know what they were doing as they were trespassing. Albert simply replied that they were out to get some fresh air and exercise so they pushed past the keeper and went on. On other rambles, they were treated in a similar way; being threatened by guns and the threat of having dogs set on them. Albert said, *"I've taken children out of the city to see a bit of grass, some had never seen a cow. It was their opportunity to see a bit of sunshine on Stanage, you couldn't see it in the city"*. Another young rambler said, *"The Sunday ramble offered the opportunity for quietness, education, exercise and to meet other young people who had nothing else to do on a Sunday – it was a mass escape which offered excitement and freedom"*. One of Albert's favourite tales was when they were crossing a moor and were stopped by a keeper. They asked the keeper whose moor it was. He replied it belonged to the Duke. They then asked, *"Where did he get it?"* The keeper replied, *"His ancestors"*. And then they asked, *"Where did they get it?"* He replied, *"They fought for it"*. The response was, *"Well, fetch the Duke and we'll fight **him** for it"*.

If anything epitomises the campaign for access to our mountains and moorland it has to be the Kinder Mass Trespass of 1932. Various books, newspapers, media accounts and papers have given wide-ranging views of this trespass ranging from a single *one-off* event that achieved nothing, to helping create our National Parks and giving access to our mountains and moorlands. Neither is correct. Mass trespasses were nothing new but this trespass had a different dimension, which did not become apparent until fifty years later. The true or truer story of the Kinder Trespass continues to develop, perhaps the latest and best account comes from Keith Warrender in his book "*Battle for Kinder Scout*" which builds on Benny Rothman's original account. Benny Rothman was the leader of the Kinder Trespass in 1932.

The story goes:

A group of young people from the British Workers' Sports Federation were having an Easter camp at Rowarth, near New Mills. The host group from Manchester wanted to take their London counterparts onto Bleaklow so they could see and experience the wilderness and peat groughs. They were stopped at Yellowslacks by keepers and turned back. It was a huge disappointment and on their return, they realised that if there had been more of them they could not have been stopped. So the idea of a mass trespass developed.

It was decided to hold a mass trespass on Kinder Scout on the 24th April. The trespass was well planned and publicised and it was to start at Hayfield.

We have always been lead to believe it was a *Manchester trespass*, when in fact there were young people from far and wide that attended. No less than two contingents, maybe three, came from Sheffield. One of the groups had twenty to thirty ramblers who walked up Jacob's Ladder, over the Kinder summit, to join the mainly Manchester Group and others at the prearranged site at Ashop Head where victory speeches were to be made.

Benny Rothman once told me (the author) he was the reluctant hero of the day, as the main speaker did not arrive, and being the smallest he was the easiest to lift onto the rock platform in Bowden Bridge quarry where he could deliver a speech. Although only nineteen, he was an accomplished speaker. The group then set off, past the Kinder Reservoir, for William Clough.

Although the story is well told by Keith Warrender there is still some doubt as to where the trespass took place and to what extent it was a major trespass.

The most likely place was below Sandy Hey. This would be on the bank just above the Public Right of Way in William Clough. After the confrontation with the keepers who had rounded on them, they pushed ahead up the bank. Some said they rejoined the Public Right of Way further up William Clough to join the Sheffield contingent at Ashop Head for victory speeches. If that was the case, it was only a minor trespass but it was the intent that really mattered. However, the real trespassers on the day were the Sheffield group who had a full day of trespassing over Kinder.

Back in Hayfield five walkers including Benny Rothman, were charged with *Riotous Assembly* and arrested by the police. One young man had been arrested earlier in the day during the confrontation and charged with assaulting one of the keepers. Apparently, what happened was that this young man had nothing to do with the trespass, but saw the keeper go down and he went across to help him. For his trouble, he was given a six-month prison sentence and a criminal record for something he did not do.

At the trial of the six at Derby Assizes, four were found guilty of Riotous Assembly, one of Grievous Bodily Harm and one acquitted. The jury comprised of two Brigadier Generals, three Colonels, two Majors, three Captains and two Aldermen. Some would say the jury was loaded against them but Benny did not criticise them as he said they were only responding to

the trumped up charges made against them by the police. After the trespass and imprisonment, each then went their own way and nothing more happened. It seemed that it was a *one-off* event; but was it?

Getting there

The Kinder Trespass was not welcomed by the established rambling organisations. In fact it was openly condemned by the Manchester Ramblers Federation but less so in Sheffield as the Sheffield ramblers were considered more radical in their views. However, Bert Ward kept rather quiet about it. Although he held strong socialist ideals, he did not like political extremism. Steve Morton who was a very active member of the Sheffield Federation and involved in all access matters said of the trespass, *"This is going to hold us back as we have just received intimation from the landowners*

Figure 2. Trespass over the moors © Terence Howard

they were prepared to open up some land for access". They did not, not surprisingly. In June of that year, 10,000 ramblers gathered at the annual Winnats Pass rally to demonstrate against the imprisonment of the five Kinder trespassers.

At a meeting arranged at the Victoria Hall in Sheffield by the Sheffield Ramblers Federation to demonstrate against the prison sentences of the Kinder *martyrs* they agreed to hold another mass trespass. This time it was to be along the disputed Duke of Norfolk's Road above Bradfield to Abbey Brook. Bert Ward identified this as a *stolen* footpath. Twelve rambling clubs took part with over 200 walkers including a large contingent from the Woodcraft Folk. They walked from Malin Bridge, through Wisewood, over Loxley Common, Kirk Edge and to Bar Dyke. There are contemporary accounts of what happened on the day by Albert Richardson and a young teenager from the Woodcraft Folk. Albert recalls, " *After the Kinder dispute, they'd decided that they were going to hold a meeting in Sheffield to organise a protest at the activities of the police and the keepers over the Kinder ramble. There was a meeting organised in the Victoria Hall by the Ramblers' Federation, and they'd notified all the rambling clubs that this was going to happen. There was about twelve rambling clubs represented at this meeting, and we decided that we would make a mass trespass from Malin Bridge through the valley there, right over to Broomhead Moors and then to Abbey Brook.*

When we met at Malin Bridge, the press didn't know anything about it, and we didn't know whether the police of the gamekeepers did, so we walked up the Loxley Valley and over to Abbey Brook. When we got towards the shooting butts we saw the police on top of the hill - ...- and as we approached the butts they all came down the hillside. I should say there was about thirty policemen at the time and about forty gamekeepers, and the gamekeepers had got pit shafts and the police had got dogs, and they approached us and told us we'd got to go back.

And a colleague called Hardy, of Shipton Street Settlement, was in charge of the ramble, and he said, "If you want to stop a trespass you must escort people onto the nearest major road. That's the ruling and the law." And the police wouldn't listen to it. They said, "No, you've got to go back." They said – they were persistent – that we must go back. And he said "Well, sit down a minute and let's talk this out." So we all sat down again. He says, "Now, are you hungry?" So we all shouted "YES!!!", so he said, "Well then, get your rucksacks off, get your flasks out, and get your grub out, and get down, and we're stopping here while we've eaten it. We're not in any hurry."

And we followed what he said and all started eating, and the gamekeepers were getting annoyed, and they'd all got pit shafts, and they were getting very annoyed with it all, and the police were a bit upset, and one or two of the gamekeepers started doing a bit of pushing on one or two of the lads. Well, the police stopped them and they told them they weren't having any of that. It got to be – you know – he was in charge, the police officer, and he said he'd got to see that everything's in order and "We don't want that."

But one of the trespassers DID push one of the I.L.P lads, and straightaway he hit back at the gamekeeper, and hit him hard, and the police immediately grabbed them both and told them that they had got to stop.

So, ultimately, we decided that we were walking back then. We'd go back, but we'd go at our own time and own pace and own way, and we made it as long as we could, and the policemen kept saying, "You know, you could cut a bit and be reasonable." And we said, "This is what we intend doing and we're going to do it." "

A group of youngsters from the Woodcraft Folk, a co-operative youth group, were also on the Trespass. One of them, a girl of sixteen, kept a diary of events at the Abbey Brook Trespass in 1932. This is her account: "*Pleasant to see so many Woodcraft Folk ready for the Mass Trespass on Sunday. I think there were more Woodcrafters than anybody. We managed to get off pretty well to time, and went through the Wisewood Estate, over Wadsley Common, over Kirk Edge, and so on to the top side of Bradfied for dinner. Of course we got plenty of stares as we marched along singing Woodcraft and Bolshie songs. After dinner, we all set off for Smallfields, where the Mass*

Trespass was to start from. We were all told to keep together, and no names were to be mentioned.

When we arrived at the beginning of the moors, two gamekeepers were there, with a man on a bike. A gamekeeper advised us to go back, and as we went straight on, he sent the cyclist with a message, we presume, to get assistance. The next part of the journey was about five miles of rough moorland, up and down tufts of grass and falling in bogs. When we got to Peter's Rock, which is a point overlooking Abbey Brook, we met with opposition in the form of about forty gamekeepers, among who were a few policemen.

Someone said that we ought to make our way down to the shooting butts, but others said we ought to carry on over the edge to Foulstone Delf. A gamekeeper was in the vicinity, and after a meeting of the Executive Committee, which all took time, we agreed to carry on, but in the meantime the gamekeepers who we had seen in the bottom, they of course rounded up on us and stopped us, but only by the use of big pit props. Two lads got it worse than any of us, as one refused to give his name and address. After much discussion and argument, we set off back across the way we had come, accompanied this time by the police and the gamekeepers, who kept urging us on. But they swallowed the remarks very well which we all could not resist from making, and I am sure they must have enjoyed their five mile walk on a Sunday afternoon. We shall make them into ramblers yet! There was a full day of excitement, although we had to turn back, but numbers make a difference. Next time we want a thousand, not two hundred."

In 1939 after fifty years, the *Access to Mountains Act* finally succeeded. However, as it worked its way through the Parliamentary stages it was not welcomed by the Ramblers as they saw it as a *Landowners Protection Bill*. Some Ramblers wanted to oppose it while others said although it was bad they should work with it and expose it for what it was worth.

War is declared

During World War 2, many of the moors were used for military training, firing practice and the training of the Home Guard. A young rambler remembers going to Burbage and seeing white plaster heads with German Helmets on hidden in the rocks and used for live firing practice. The same rambler also remembers a young lad being killed by picking up a live grenade near Toad's Mouth on the road from Sheffield to Hathersage.

The war also saw a frantic rush for iron railings to be melted down for armaments. However, for whatever reason the three miles of iron railings erected alongside the Long Causeway at Stanage and around this grouse moor were given an exemption. This caused outrage in Sheffield as ordinary people were giving their railings for the war effort but this particular landowner got away with it. At the same time, many ancient stone guideposts were removed, taken down and buried or the directions

chiselled out "*In case German Paratroopers land*". Whether or not there was a need for this was strongly disputed as the Germans were known to have many tens of thousands of maps and should they arrive would know where they were. One joke of the time said, "*What's the point of removing Blackpool from the signs but leaving Blackpool Tower standing*". Perhaps the most poignant incident was when John Bunting, a rambler and Home Guard volunteer was training on Midhope Moors. In his words, he was regarded as a hero during the war for protecting his country. After the war, he went rambling on Midhope Moor again but this time he was turned off by a keeper. He was now the enemy.

After the war, the City Council started to open up more of the moorland tracks and paths around the Burbage area because of pressure from the Ramblers groups. It took a few more years before all the paths were accessible but the freedom to roam was still illusive. In 1948, the military cleared Burbage of its unexploded missiles and left, leaving behind peppered and split rocks, a slightly damaged Carl Wark Hill Fort, and a damaged packhorse bridge. On White Edge, Big Moor, similar damage was experienced. It seems the cleared unexploded bombs and shells were destroyed in the Upper Burbage Valley and on Leash Fen. However, *lost* unexploded ammunition can still be found from Derwent Edge to Midhope and Langsett.

1949. The Labour Government passes the *National Parks and Access to the Countryside Act*.

1951. The establishment of the Peak District National Park and protracted negotiations start for Access Agreements to allow people to walk freely on previously forbidden moorland.

1953. Access Agreements for the southern part of Kinder Scout signed.

1955. Access Agreement for the whole of Kinder Scout signed.

1961. Access Agreement for Langsett Moor.

1962. Access Agreement for Stanage.

By 1962, less than fifty percent of land was accessible to the public. Most, that was accessible, belonged to public bodies such as Sheffield City Council, the Peak District National Park, and the National Trust. The pace of agreements appeared to be stalling. The Ramblers Association kept pushing the Peak District to make more agreements and even some of the moorland belonging to Local Authority Waterworks. Although here there was no sign of allowing the public onto the Waterworks moorland. The remaining fifty four percent of *forbidden moorland* seemed as far away as ever; but was it?

On the horizon

Growing up in the 1950s and 1960s the tales of the Kinder and Abbey Brook trespasses were exciting and real folklore to those of us in the Woodcraft Folk. Camping and rambling every weekend in the countryside was our real education.

In October 1981, it was heralded that the fiftieth anniversary of the Kinder Trespass would be taking place in Hayfield. A day of walks and celebration would be held at Bowden Bridge quarry, now a car park and a bronze plaque would be unveiled to celebrate the event. One of the main speakers was John Beadle, Chairman of the Peak Park Planning Board along with Benny Rothman, leader of the Kinder trespass of 1932.

A Sheffield Rambler wrote to the [*Sheffield*] *Morning Telegraph* reminding people that we still did not have the right to roam over much of our moorland. Most the moors to the west of Sheffield were still *no go* areas for ramblers and that the public must be reminded of the fact. Two young Sheffield men picked up on this fact and, knowing that the Kinder Celebration at Hayfield was only a few months away, were both keen to *get something going* in Sheffield. Early in 1982, a public meeting was called with thirty plus people attending, including several veteran ramblers, some of whom took part in the original trespasses of 1932. Although the meeting agreed to support and join the Kinder Celebration at Hayfield, they also agreed to hold a trespass on a local moor before the celebration. On 28th March, a mass trespass took place, the first in fifty years, over Bamford Moor with around three hundred people taking part. On 24th April, Sheffield ramblers walked from Edale over Jacobs Ladder to join the Kinder celebrations at Hayfield as they had done fifty years earlier. It was here that the real influence and inspiration of the original Kinder trespass was felt.

The Sheffield ramblers were so inspired by Benny that on return to Sheffield they agreed to set up a campaigning group for public access to moorlands. It became known as the *Sheffield Campaign for Access to Moorland* also known by the acronym SCAM. In 1982 SCAM was born. Steve Morton, who condemned the original Kinder trespass and now a supporter of SCAM, acknowledged that he was wrong in 1932. He said that now the group must keep the pressure on to maintain the momentum from where it had left off in 1932. Benny Rothman reflecting on the original trespass also maintained that he and others in 1932 should have carried on and worked with the Ramblers Federations and not

stopped after the 'Kinder' trespass. Albert Richardson said, *"It will never be finished until we run this country"*. In the same year that SCAM was formed, 1982, the land at Kinder Scout was bought by the National Trust. They declared it open access in perpetuity.

SCAM organised a regular programme of trespass rambles over all the *forbidden moorlands* attracting large numbers of people. The walks were to be more than just *political statements* but to show people what they had been deprived of for so long. The *forbidden moorlands* were: Snailsden, Thurlstone, Midhope, Broomhead, Bradfield, Derwent, Hallam, Bamford, Eyam, Offerton, Abney, Big Moor, Ramsley, Leash Fen and the Chatsworth Moors. There was always a strong educational content to the walks. Some of the places explored and *rediscovered* included the New Cross with its sword, the *murdered* Old Woman Stone (a prehistoric Standing Stone felled by keepers in

Figure 3. 50th Anniversary of the Kinder Trespass at Bowden Bridge © Terence Howard

1932), the vandalised base of the Moscar Cross, Second World War targets, numerous burial mounds, circles and crosses, ancient trackways, and the search and rescue of an old guide stone. And there was much more besides.

Although landowners knew of the trespasses, they kept away when one was organised on their land, probably believing if nothing was said or done the walkers would *go away*. This time the *tactics* were different and there was a determination to keep trespassing and not to give up. The trespasses were held on a reasonably frequent basis on all the forbidden moorlands. Landowners or their agents were always informed of the walks along with the Peak District National Park Authority, who were responsible for making access agreements. Therefore, they were continually reminded and made aware of the demand for public access to the moors. Occasionally landowners were

invited to join these walks of *discovery* on the moors. They declined the invitation. The police were always informed of the trespasses but never took any action. It was all very 'polite'. We [SCAM] were talking directly to landowners and their agents on what can be considered a friendly basis. Each knowing and understanding the others view although not necessarily agreeing.

As a small action group, SCAM did not have the same political clout as the Ramblers' Association who was embarrassed into being more proactive by SCAM. This they then did with vigour, SCAM being the *foot-soldiers* on all the access demonstrations.

In the late 1990s, several Labour politicians supported and proposed an Access Bill. It passed its three readings in Parliament. In 1999, the Queens Speech to Parliament outlined proposals for "Right to Roam" legislation. The *Countryside and Rights of Way Act* was

Figure 4. SCAM members at Bradfield © Terence Howard

passed by the Labour Government in 2000. It gives the public the legal right to walk over and enjoy all our mountains and moorland, unhindered. In the same year, SCAM gave Sheffield City Council a bronze plaque commemorating all the campaigners who have worked for access and for our National Parks. It is placed at the entrance of the Town Hall in Sheffield. A full City of Sheffield Council meeting unanimously thanked and congratulated SCAM for their contribution to the campaign for the *Countryside and Rights of Way Act.*

In September 2004, the legal right to wander freely was first introduced in the Peak District. This should not be surprising because this was where all the vigorous campaigning had taken place. I remember on the first day of access going through the brand new access gate leading onto Bamford Moor,

looking round and feeling free at last and not being watched by keepers. It was a strange feeling and I could not help thinking of all those generations of access campaigners who worked so hard and never saw this day, Bert Ward, Benny Rothman, Steve Morton, Albert Richardson and many, many more.

We owe our love of the moors to all the access campaigners of the past and more recently for giving us the opportunity to return to our moorlands.

Bibliography

Elliot, E. (1831) *The Corn Law Rhymes.* Sheffield

Paulus, C. (1907) *Some Forgotten Facts in the History of Sheffield and District; Being an Account of the Attercliffe cum Darnal Inclosure Act.* Kessinger Legacy Reprints

Figure 5. Legal access to open land © Terence Howard

Paulus, C. (1912) *Old English village: noted on the ancient acre strips and common lands and their present-day survival at Laxton, Notts*. St. Catherine's Press, London.

Rothman, B., Smith, R. & Waghorn, T. (2012) *The Battle for Kinder Scout: Including the Mass Trespass of 1932*. Willow Publishing,Timperley.

Sissons, D. (ed.) (2002) *The Best of the Sheffield Clarion Ramblers' Handbooks, Ward's Piece*. Halsgrove, Tiverton.

Peat, politics and patrimonialism: back to the future on Thorne Moors

Kieran Sheehan
JBA Consulting

Internal Drainage Boards

The history of Internal Drainage Boards (IDBs) is shrouded in the mists of time but there is a general consensus that they were set up in the form of Commissioners of Sewers in the reign of Edward 1 (1272-1307). Although *Wikipedia* (2013) states an earlier date of 1252 but in all likelihood there is confusion with the creation of a Commission for draining Romney Marsh by Henry III (Venables *et. al.*, no date). It would be fair to say, however, that the forerunners of today's IDBs were set up in the thirteenth century.

Up until the sixteenth century, these bodies worked in an *ad hoc* way throughout England with their charters being renewed periodically. It was during the reign of Henry VIII that the situation became more formalised when, in 1531, they were made permanent bodies (Witham Fourth District Internal Drainage Board, no date). However, these bodies were still managed *ad hoc* under separate Acts of Parliament (sometimes many) and the powers they possessed differed from one board to the next.

In 1930, this situation was rectified when the Land Drainage Act (LDA) set up Internal Drainage Boards as we know them today with defined catchment boundaries. This situation was brought up to date under the Land Drainage Act 1991 (LDA 1991) which was a consolidating act setting out the powers and responsibilities of IDBs and Local Authorities with regard to land drainage.

Legislation

The LDA 1991 was amended in 1994 (LDA 1994) to include duties, to which an IDB must adhere, with respect to the environment and recreation. This says: *It shall be the duty of an internal drainage board.....so far as may be consistent .....so to exercise any power conferred...to further the conservation and enhancement of natural beauty and the conservation of flora, fauna and geological or physiographical features of special interest....and to take into account any effect which the proposals would have on the beauty or amenity of any rural or urban area or on any such flora, fauna, features, buildings, sites or objects* (LDA 1991 s61A). However, these duties do not apply in the case of an emergency.

Section 40 of the Natural Environment and Rural Communities (NERC) Act 2006 says *Every public authority must in exercising its functions have regard... to the purpose of conserving biodiversity*. However, in reality this is more process than outcome driven.

Under the Conservation of Habitats and Species Regulations 2010 Internal Drainage Boards are defined as 'competent authorities' meaning they have to comply with these Regulations.

Elections

Internal Drainage Boards are public bodies whose members are elected and appointed for a three-year period beginning on the 1st of November of that year. Elected members must, on the relevant date, be:

- both the owner and occupier of not less than 4 hectares of drainage rateable land, or:

- an occupier of not less than eight hectares of land, or:

- the occupier of land which has an assessable value of £30 or upwards, or:

- the appointed representative of someone who meets the above criteria.

The voting system used in elections is a little peculiar and is not a simple one man one vote election. Instead, the number of votes a member has is related to the assessable value of the land they hold within the Drainage District. In essence, this gives more votes to the larger landowners.

In certain Drainage Districts, where a 'Special Levy' is applied by the Drainage Board on the Local Authority, the Local Authority (under the Local Government Finance Act 1988) has the power to appoint Drainage Board members. However, they can only do so up to a level equal to the other members of the board plus one, or shall be roughly equal to the proportion of the Drainage Board's expenses that are raised by special levies on the Local Authority. Special levies are raised on those properties that are deemed to derive a benefit from the activities of a drainage board if they are not 'agricultural land and buildings'. This includes dwelling houses, factories, offices etc.

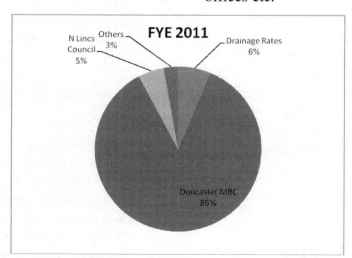

Figure 1. Breakdown of Tween Bridge Internal Drainage Board by income sector in 2011

In the LDA 1991, a special levy is provided for to raise money to cover the shortfall between the annual expenses of the IDB and the amount of income derived from the ratepayers, i.e. those with agricultural land and buildings. In many boards this is a substantial amount (see Figures 1 and 2).

Despite the mantra of 'he who pays the piper, calls the tune', many boards give the impression that they are being run by their elected members, rather than the council tax payers that fund them. Barrett (2012, p. 12) in his report into the governance of the Caldicot and Wentlooge Levels Internal Drainage Board considered this in his deliberations and concluded that this impression was true. Indeed JBA (2006, p. 84) say: *that while rate payers are taking up their full allocation of seats, contested elections are very rare and tend to only occur when there is a contentious local issue.* They follow this up by saying: *Some Boards adopt an unwritten policy of matching*

nominations to places to ensure a spread of interests and to avoid the cost of a contested election. We made efforts to speak directly to a few rate payers at random to seek their views - and found little awareness but also no dissatisfaction with this practice. All were of the opinion that the mechanism existed for them to express their views or to stand for election if the need arose. However, in terms of a demonstration of democracy it leaves something to be desired (JBA, 2006, p.54). In addition, many IDBs themselves, whilst happy with their existing elected membership, were unhappy with the lack of representation across the spectrum of beneficiaries (stakeholders) within the drainage district (Rhead *et al.*, no date).

This potential lack of democracy is not entirely the fault of the Internal Drainage Boards themselves. The Local Authorities which pay special levies to the IDBs have, to a certain extent been complicit in this as they have not taken

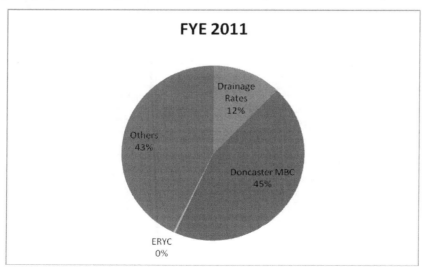

Figure 2. Breakdown of Black Drain Internal Drainage Board by income sector in 2011

up the places allocated to them as Drainage Board members. Barrett (2012) recognised this in the case of Caldicot and Wentlooge only last year. Similarly, the Ouse and Humber IDB had difficulty in getting local authority representation on their board from the East Riding of Yorkshire Council in 2011 (Rhead *et al.*, no date). Specifically they say *26 IDBs highlighted difficulties in Special Levy Paying Local Authorities appointing members, in some cases this was because the Councillors of the Special Levy Paying Local Authority had not elected a representative.* JBA (2006, p.57) reported that the average attendance by Local Authority representatives at IDB meetings was 47%, somewhat less than the 68% of elected members. They also report that whilst Local Authority representation on boards is intended under the LDA 1991 to be proportional to the amount of financial contribution the Local Authorities make to the IDB, under-representation on IDBs is more common than over-representation (JBA, 2006, p.57).

IDBs also have the ability to co-opt members onto their boards to address the lack of representation of stakeholders, however, this is very uncommon: only six IDBs in England and Wales had co-opted members and only one of these had more than one, Strine IDB had two (Rhead *et al.*, no date).

Conservation

It seems clear, therefore that there is a democratic deficit within IDBs, however, it is unclear what this means for conservation. Hickling in 1983 (p.216) said that, *IDBs have...little regard for nature conservation.* However, a trawl through the World Wide Web would lead to a different conclusion with a proliferation of policies (Black Sluice IDB no date) and projects being undertaken by IDBs in partnership with conservation and statutory bodies (Defra, 2011). It is interesting to note in the latter press release from Defra that £100,000 is being spent to help farmers and rural communities to reduce the risk of flooding, maintain farmland and create new wildlife habitats when the money went to the local Internal Drainage Board. JBA (2006 p.84) stated, *There are a number of IDBs which do not fully recognise their environmental duties and do not accept their purpose is no longer one solely of providing efficient land drainage.* However, they do caveat this by saying that this is not true for all boards and they should be treated individually. Some Wildlife Trusts felt that, *'the local IDB was only paying lip service to environmental considerations and that dominance by farmers meant there was a reluctance to sanction expenditure or to consider different methods of operation if it impacted on field drainage '* (JBA 2006 p.32). And, the RSPB did not believe there had been any fundamental change in the sector overall although some boards did deliver significant environmental enhancements (JBA 2006 p.32).

Interestingly the Wildlife Trusts also reported that their level of satisfaction increased with an increase in IDB size and income.

Therefore, in terms of implementing conservation projects, there are likely to be different levels of support for these throughout the different boards within the county. One can postulate that those boards with the greatest number of elected members, some who may have been on the board for many years: over thirty in many cases (JBA 2006 p.54), are more typically the smaller, more rural boards and that these are the most wedded to the idea that their sole focus should be on land drainage.

Thorne Moors

The Thorne Moors Water Level Management Plan was granted funding of £3m in February 2011 by the Environment Agency and was to run over five years. The bid and

supplementary information (Jones and Sheehan, 2010) was put together by an informal group of Internal Drainage Boards who made an initial contribution to the production of a plan for the moors in 2004 (Figure 3). The six IDBs in the project are:

- Black Drain Drainage Board
- Dempster Drainage Board
- Goole Fields District Drainage Board
- Reedness and Swinefleet Drainage Board
- Thorntree Internal Drainage Board
- Doncaster East Internal Drainage Board

The lead IDB for the project is Doncaster East IDB that has a Local Authority majority in its membership. It is the successor board to a number of

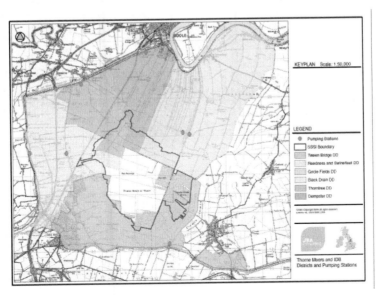

Figure 3. Thorne Moors SSSI and IDB WLMP Partnership

others in the Doncaster Area, specifically Tween Bridge Internal Drainage Board in the case of Thorne Moors. This majority stems from the fact that the IDB includes the town of Thorne within its area and, as a result, the Special Levy on the council accounts for a large proportion of its funding (see Figure 4).

It is clear from the Minutes of the WLMP Steering Group that the plan would not have proceeded without the Local Authority appointed members supporting it (Doncaster East IDB, 2012), due to the opposition to the plan from the elected members representing the other boards in the partnership. At previous meetings, the elected members had not managed to agree any Terms of Reference for the Steering Group and had then questioned its legitimacy to make decisions. Many members had not even provided their contact details in spite of numerous requests to do so. Why was there this inherent opposition to the implementation of the WLMP for Thorne Moors?

The main reasons given at the meetings for the opposition of the elected members to the plan can be summarised as follows:

1. Drainage Boards are concerned with land drainage, not conservation;

2. The plan is a waste of money;

3. The works will raise water levels on the moors and therefore flood the surrounding land;

4. The works will increase the future flood risk on the surrounding land.

During the Steering Group meetings and at numerous IDB meetings prior to the securing of the funding for the plan, many of these objections were addressed. The responses to these are set out in summary.

Point 1 has been shown to be inaccurate as IDBs have a duty to *further the conservation and enhancement of natural beauty and the conservation of flora* [and], *fauna* under the LDA 1991 (as amended);

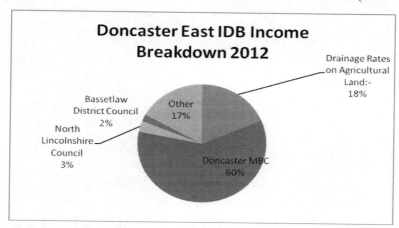

Figure 4. Doncaster East IDB Income Sources 2012

Point 2 is difficult to argue with as it is a value judgement but the plan is an expression of Government policy and has been fully-funded by the Environment Agency so no residual cost will fall on the ratepayers of the IDB district;

Point 3 is more subtle but, if you assume that when the Moors were being used for peat extraction by Scotts, they installed a series of trapezoidal drains to remove water falling onto the moors as quickly as possible to allow machinery on site and to drain the moors. Since the land surrounding the moors is at a lower level (generally) than the remaining peat mass (Figure 5) and is a pumped drainage catchment, the water will then pool here unless pumped away, i.e. on the agricultural land. Intuitively then, if we retain the water on the moors, it will discharge water more slowly or it will evapo-transpirate into the atmosphere

reducing the flood risk to surrounding catchments and reduce their pumping requirements;

Point 4 is based on the assumption that the water that falls on the moors will be held on the moors by the dams etc. and this will increase in depth until it flows over the top onto the surrounding land. This patently absurd, however, at the Steering Group Meeting of the 7th December 2012, a request was made that the IDB provide a guarantee that the land around the moors would never flood: this is something that would never be asked of the Environment Agency or an IDB in normal circumstances. It is impossible to give such a guarantee.

Perception

Those wishing to oppose the plan are still promulgating the four main reasons behind the objections to the WLMP

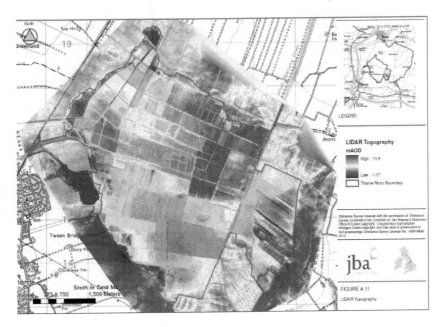

Figure 5. Topograpy of Thorne Moors SSSI

within the local area. This is even though they do not hold water (sic). This has led to a negative public perception of the WLMP in the locality and the conflation of the WLMP with any flooding in the surrounding area. Off-hand comments in the street, such as *you are going to flood Thorne*, even though patently absurd, have been said to the author.

The situation in the town of Crowle is especially interesting, as this town has suffered from surface-water flood events in recent years. Crowle is situated on raised ground to the east of the SSSI shown in Figure 5. A cursory glance at the LiDAR map for the area between where restoration works are taking place on Crowle Moors and Crowle town shows clearly that peat bunding and damming is taking place at a much lower level (60cm AOD) than where the flooding has being occurring in Crowle (4m AOD), see Figure 6.

In order for the water from the works, which are designed to hold water on the moors, rather than discharge it into the surrounding catchment, to reach Crowle it would need to flow 3.5m uphill as well as cross three drains whose beds are below sea level. However, the perception, possibly fuelled by misinformation, has reached such a level that the WLMP is now being connected to the shooting of deer on Thorne Moors and a number of boisterous public meetings have taken place and libellous leaflets put through letterboxes in Crowle (Figure 7).

Why is there such animosity and hostility, especially when the arguments promulgated by those opposed to the implementation of the plan are untrue?

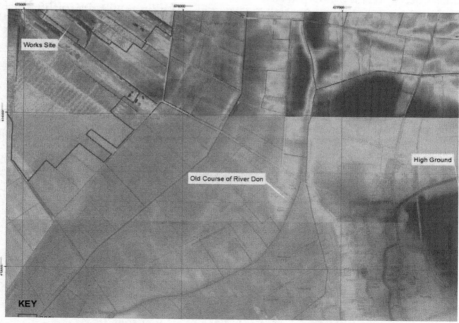

Figure 6. LiDAR Map of Crowle Area (Contains Ordnance Survey data © Crown copyright and database right 2013)

Could there be another reason for the opposition to the WLMP coming from board ratepayers surrounding the moor that is much more subtle?

Patrimonialism

This term was originally coined by Max Weber (1947) and was originally meant to signify a government characterised by a bureaucracy that dispensed patronage in return for reward, typically payments in kind or favours. This is a very common form of government in much of the developing world and under feudal regimes, such as formerly existed in Western Europe. In view of the fact that IDBs are anachronistic hangovers from feudal times, is it possible that these public institutions are the last vestiges of a patrimonial governmental system that existed in the UK prior to the introduction of Universal Suffrage in 1928. According

to Brinkerhoff and Goldsmith (2002), a pure patrimonial system is one *where a government office is treated as a type of income-generating property, even if the sovereign can reclaim this property at will. Authority is thus decentralized, with incumbents typically free to decide exactly how to carry out their administrative responsibilities*. To a certain extent the latter sentence does describe the way that individual IDBs behave in practice but it does little to explain why many boards, especially the smaller ones, still believe that they are there purely to carry out drainage activities and only pay lip service to conservation.

Many IDBs are run by a small clique of elected landowners based on the amount of land that they own. Since many boards avoid contested elections and adopt unwritten policies of matching nominations to places, it is

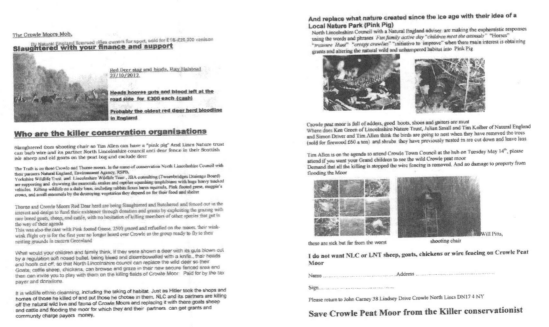

Figure 7. Anonymous Leaflet delivered to letterboxes in Crowle

evident that elected positions on IDBs can be for life and are, therefore, effectively heritable property. This places the holders of these positions in a very powerful position in a local context, which may allow patrimonial practices to creep in. Brinkerhoff and Goldsmith (2002) set out a comparison table showing the idealised distinctions between patrimonial and rational-legal governmental systems and this has been reproduced in part in Table 1.

In an inheritable, patrimonial system, the temptation to rent-seek (in the economic sense) is very great. In this sense economic rents are simply windfall gains that would be absent in open markets. In essence, this activity is the use of market distortions to divide and consume the economic pie, effectively a zero-sum game. It is a means of taking revenue from one group and giving it to another, for example rate payers and council-tax payers (JBA 2006, p.57). This activity is not overt and it is unlikely that those that engage in it are aware they are doing it. However, it is instructive to note that according to Venables *et al.* (no date), many IDB board members felt frustration over disempowerment due to the actions of the Environment Agency. This may be because of the drive in Government policies to amalgamate IDBs, increase the number of stakeholder members (co-option), the imposition of new rules on conservation and procurement and the reduction of Grant-in-Aid for new infrastructure projects.

Conclusion

In summary then it may well be the case that the present battles over the future of Thorne Moors have less to do with drainage and rather more to do with a perceived threat to the power of the elected members of the Internal Drainage Boards surrounding the moors. In this regard, they are right to feel threatened: amalgamations will dilute their individual influence within their local board and they may be forced to pay more in future for the drainage of their land. The increase in stakeholder members called for by the

Table 1. Idealised distinctions between patrimonial and rational-legal governmental systems, some of which may be applicable to certain Internal Drainage Boards (after Brinkerhoff and Goldsmith 2002)

Patrimonial	Rational-legal Bureaucratic
Important orders may be given orally	Important orders are put in writing
The public and private realms are blurred	The public and private realms are kept separate
System is decentralized allowing wide discretion on the job	System is decentralized allowing little room for discretion on the job
Internal controls are lax	Internal controls are strict
Documentation is spotty with sensitive matters left off the books	Thorough records are maintained and regularly audited

Environment Minister in July 2012 (River Stour IDB, 2012) will dilute their influence still further and the imposition of new rules will increase their fixed costs as will the lower grant rates available under the new Outcome Measures (EA, 2011).

In view of the above has, in fact, the WLMP become a new front where disgruntled drainage board members can air their frustrations in their fight with Defra and the Environment Agency? This is rather than the traditional battleground it has been between conservationists, landowners and industry? If this is so, it will mark a major change in Thorne Moors' role as a cause célèbre for conservationists, where it holds a special place in many a naturalist's heart.

References

Barrett, A. (2012) *Audit of Accounts 2010-11 Caldicot and Wentlooge Levels Internal Drainage Board Report in the Public Interest*. [online] Available at: < http://www.wao.gov.uk/assets/Local_ Reports/397A2012_Caldicot_ Wentlooge_Levels_IDB_Audit_of_ Accounts_2010-11_Final.pdf> [Accessed 3 September 2013].

Black Sluice IDB (Internal Drainage Board) (no date) *Conservation Policy*. [online] Available at: < http://www. blacksluiceidb.gov.uk/information-for- you/conservation-policy.html> [Accessed 4 September 2013].

Brinkerhoff, D. W. and Goldsmith, A. A. (2002) *Clientelism, Patrimonialism and Democratic Governance: An Overview and Framework for Assessment and Programming*. Bethesda, MA: US Agency for International Development.

Defra (2011) *£100,000 fund to help farmers protect wildlife and manage flood risk*. [online] Available at: < https://www.gov.uk/government/ news/100-000-fund-to-help-farmers- protect-wildlife-and-manage-flood-risk> [Accessed 3 September 2013].

Doncaster East IDB (2012) *Minutes of the Meeting Held 7th December 2012*. [online] Available at: < http://www. thornepeatland.org.uk/media/761/ minutes_of_the_meeting_held_7_ december_2012.pdf> [Accessed 4 September 2013].

Environment Agency (2011) *Flood and coastal risk management outcome measures*. [online] Available at: <http:// www.environment-agency.gov.uk/ research/planning/122070.aspx? [Accessed 4 September 2013].

Hickling, R. (1983) *Enjoying Ornithology*. Poyser, London.

JBA (JBA Consulting) (2006) *Internal Drainage Board Review Final Report February 2006* [online] Available at: < http://archive.defra.gov.uk/environment/ flooding/documents/who/idb/jbareport. pdfk> [Accessed 3 September 2013].

Jones, A. J. and Sheehan, K. A. (2010) *Thorne, Crowle and Goole Moors Water Level Management Plan Final Report*. [online] Available at: < http://www. thornepeatland.org.uk/

media/515/2008s3746_thorne_wlmp_ hydrogeology_report_20final_figs.pdf> [Accessed 4 September 2013].

Rhead, B., Vickers, T. and Moodie, S. (no date) *Internal Drainage Board Membership And Representation Survey Analysis*. [online] Available at: http:// www.ada.org.uk/downloads/other/ downloads_page/IDB_Membership_ and_Representation_Survey_Analysis. pdf [Accessed 3 September 2013].

River Stour IDB (2012) *Minutes of the Meeting of the Board held on Thursday 26 July 2012*. [online] Available at: <http://www.riverstouridb.org.uk/ documents/minutes260712.pdf> [Accessed 4 September 2013].

Sunderland, D. (1999) 'A monument to defective administration?' The London Commissions of Sewers in the early 19th Century. *Urban History*, **26** (3), 349 – 372.

Venables, J., Moodie, I. and Edwards, S. (no date) *An introduction to Internal Drainage Boards (IDBs)*. [online] Available at: < http://www.ada.org.uk/ downloads/publications/IDBs%20 An%20Introduction.pdf> [Accessed 3 September 2013].

Weber, M. (1947). *The Theory of Social and Economic Organization* (trans. A. M. Henderson and Talcott Parsons) Free Press, New York.

Wikipedia (2013) *Internal Drainage Board Responsibilities*. [online] Available at: < http://en.wikipedia.org/ wiki/Internal_drainage_board> [Accessed 3 September 2013].

Witham Fourth Internal Drainage Board (no date) History. [online] Available at: < http://www.w4idb.co.uk/ history.htm> [Accessed 3 September 2013].

This volume of papers was published as part of a major event 'War & Peat' conference organised by Professor Ian D. Rotherham and colleagues held in September 2013 in Sheffield.

War and Peat

The military heritage of moors, heaths, bogs and fens.

The Biodioversity and
Landscape History Research Institute

British Ecological Society

International Peat Society | IMTG MTO

Wildtrack Publishing, Venture House, 103 Arundel Street, Sheffield S1 2NT

Visit our website: www.ukeconet.org for further information
The South Yorkshire EcoNet